UNDERSTANDING
MEDICAL
TESTING

UNDERSTANDING MEDICAL TESTING

KATHLEEN DESKA PAGANA, R.N., B.S.N., M.S.N.

Department of Nursing,
Lycoming College,
Williamsport, Pennsylvania

TIMOTHY JAMES PAGANA, M.D.

Surgical Oncologist,
Williamsport, Pennsylvania

A PLUME BOOK
NEW AMERICAN LIBRARY

MOSBY

TIMES MIRROR
NEW YORK AND SCARBOROUGH, ONTARIO

Publisher: Thomas A. Manning
Editor: Nancy L. Mullins
Editing supervisor: Lin Dempsey
Manuscript editor: Diane L. Ackermann

MOSBY MEDICAL LIBRARY

NAL books are available at quantity discounts
when used to promote products or services. For information
please write to Premium Marketing Division,
The New American Library, Inc.,
1633 Broadway, New York, New York 10019.

PLUME TRADEMARK REG. U.S. PAT. OFF. AND FOREIGN COUNTRIES
REGISTERED TRADEMARK—MARCA REGISTRADA
HECHO EN FORGE VILLAGE, MASS., U.S.A.

SIGNET, SIGNET CLASSICS, MENTOR, PLUME, MERIDIAN and
NAL BOOKS are published by The New American Library, Inc.,
1633 Broadway, New York, New York 10019, in Canada, by
The New American Library of Canada, Limited,
81 Mack Avenue, Scarborough, Ontario M1L 1M8.

Library of Congress Cataloging in Publication Data

Pagana, Kathleen Deska, 1952-
Understanding medical testing.
"A Plume book."
Includes index.
1. Diagnosis. 2. Consumer education. I. Pagana,
Timothy James, 1949-   . II. Title.
RC71.3.P33   1983   616.07´5   82-19102
ISBN 0-8016-3778-3 (Mosby)

F/D/D 9 8 7 6 5 4 3 2 1   01/A/075

Printed in the United States of America

We lovingly dedicate this book to our parents

Margaret and Edward Deska
Mary and the late Charles Pagana

for the confidence, education, love, and
support they have given us

Preface

Gone are the days when patients were passive participants in their medical care. Today patients want and often demand to be actively involved in their care. From working with patients and their families we have identified a specific area of stress to all patients: medical testing. Why did the doctor order the test? What will it show? Will it hurt? How long will it take? Can I eat before the test? How much does it cost?

As a concerned nurse and doctor, we believe the patient has a right to know the answers to these questions about medical or diagnostic testing. Hence the purpose of this book is to decipher the maze of medical testing in an interesting, informative, and enjoyable manner.

A major feature of this book is the consistent format used throughout. Chapters are arranged according to body systems (such as heart, lung, kidney, and reproduction). The advantage of this feature is that tests relating to a certain problem (such as EKG, stress testing, and cardiac catheterization) are all discussed in the same chapter.

Each chapter begins with a brief discussion of anatomy, physiology, and common problems relating to that particular body system. This should facilitate a better understanding of the related medical procedures. The diagnostic studies for each chapter are divided into several categories:

1. X-rays and nuclear scans (studies of a body area after the ingestion or injection of radioactive material)
2. Endoscopy (direct observation of a body organ or cavity through a lighted flexible instrument)
3. Blood tests
4. Stool (feces) tests
5. Special procedures

Normal values, purpose, procedure, and pertinent facts are discussed for each test. The *normal values* include the expected outcome, measurement, or range for the test results of a healthy person. The *purpose* for a particular test includes the reason for performing the study, the information provided by the test, the specific anatomy and physiology involved in the study, the complications associated with the test, and the contraindications for that study. The *procedure* describes the actual method of performing the study and includes patient care before, during, and after the test; where the study is performed; the patient's position during the test; and the need for anesthesia or sedation.

The *pertinent facts* contain information of special interest to the patients, such as what the patient feels during the test; the duration of the test; special care before, during and after the test; and the customary cost of the study.

It is important to stress that the procedure for each study may vary somewhat in different hospitals and in different areas of the country. For example, the preparation for the intravenous pyelogram (IVP) commonly includes giving bisacodyl laxative tablets to cleanse the bowel. However, enemas may be given to achieve the same goal of an empty bowel.

One area in which one will certainly see variance is the customary cost of each study. The approximate prices are described mainly because of consumer interest and also to give some estimate of the complexity of certain procedures and of the expertise required to perform and interpret these studies.

A unique feature of this book is the inclusion of case reports in each chapter. Case reports include the presentation of a commonly seen patient problem, the results (and normal values) of the medical tests performed, and a discussion explaining interpretation of the studies. Patient treatment based on test results is mentioned. The purpose of the case study reports are to stimulate the reader's interest by providing an actual common patient problem (such as diabetes, heart attack, or lung cancer) and logically assessing and treating the problem based on accurate medical and diagnostic testing.

Over 50 illustrations and photographs are included to enhance the reader's understanding of medical testing. Examples include anatomy, methods of test performance, and test results.

The detailed table of contents can assist the reader in locating information easily within the test. Appendix 1 provides a complete list of commonly used abbreviations and symbols. Appendixes 2 and 3 list the normal values for blood and urine studies. These normal values may vary from laboratory to laboratory because of different units of measurement or different laboratory methods.

Most important, the information included in this book is not limited to one specific type of diagnostic testing. All types such as blood tests, urine tests, x-ray and nuclear studies, ultrasound, endoscopy, noninvasive vascular techniques, computerized tomography, amniocentesis, and many others are included—more than 250 tests.

In summary, this book provides the information needed to ensure complete patient understanding of medical testing so that studies can be performed accurately and safely. Knowledge of this information should make the patient a truly informed and involved participant in his or her medical care. Most of all it is our hope that this book will help allay some of the fears and anxieties related to medical testing. One final word of caution; this book is not meant to be used for self-diagnosis. All studies must be carefully interpreted by a physician in light of a complete review of the patient's history and complaints.

   We would like to sincerely thank Roberta Giese Perini of Garden State Professional Services and Sally Schriver Lenig of Montoursville, Pennsylvania, for the meticulous typing of this manuscript. We certainly appreciate the outstanding effort they made to help us meet our publishing deadline. We would also like to especially thank Julie Courtney for her excellent illustrations.

Kathleen Deska Pagana
Timothy James Pagana

Contents

4 Diagnostic studies used to evaluate the liver, gallbladder, bile ducts, and pancreas, 49

8 Diagnostic studies used to evaluate the kidneys, ureters, and bladder, 125

9 Diagnostic studies used to evaluate the thyroid and parathyroid glands, 150

10 Diagnostic studies used to evaluate the adrenal glands, 161

11 Diagnostic studies used to evaluate diabetes mellitus, 174

UNDERSTANDING MEDICAL TESTING

1

Diagnostic studies used to evaluate the heart

ANATOMY, PHYSIOLOGY, AND DISEASES AFFECTING THE HEART

The heart is located in the mediastinum, which is the midline cavity between the lungs. The heart is divided by a septum into a right and a left side. The right side contains unoxygenated (venous) blood. The left side contains oxygenated blood. Each side is composed of an atrium (auricle) and a ventricle (Fig. 1-1). The unoxygenated venous (prelung) blood enters the right atrium from the large veins (venae cavae) within the chest. The blood then flows from the atrium into the right ventricle, which pumps the blood forward into the pulmonary artery. This artery leads to the lungs where the blood mixes with the air and becomes "oxygenated." The oxygenated blood then returns to the left atrium via the pulmonary veins. The left atrium empties its blood into the left ventricle. The left ventricle pumps the blood into the aorta and through the arteries of the body. It is the pumping force of the left ventricle that pushes the blood through the arterial system of the body.

The flow of blood must be constantly forward. Valves exist between the atria and the ventricles of the heart to prevent any backward flow of blood. The tricuspid valve is located between the right atrium and right ventricle. The mitral valve is located between the left atrium and the left ventricle. During contraction of the ventricle (systole), the backward flow of blood from the ventricle into the atrium is prevented by the tricuspid and mitral valves. The pulmonary valve is located between the pulmonary artery and right ventricle. The aortic valve is located between the aorta and left ventricle. These latter valves prevent potentially harmful backflow of blood from the pulmonary artery and aorta, respectively, into the ventricles during relaxation (diastole) of the heart. The valves of the heart are very commonly affected by disease. Rheumatic fever, bacterial infections, infestations, and endocrine disorders (such as thyroid disease) can destroy these valves and thereby interrupt their function. It is also not uncommon to have malformed valves present at and existing since birth (congenital). Occasionally these malformed valves function appropriately; however, usually their function is inadequate and they must be surgically repaired or replaced.

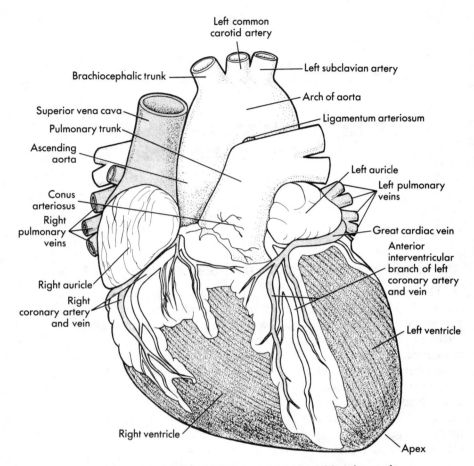

Left common carotid artery

Left subclavian artery

Brachiocephalic trunk

Arch of aorta

Ligamentum arteriosum

Superior vena cava

Pulmonary trunk

Ascending aorta

Left auricle

Left pulmonary veins

Conus arteriosus

Right pulmonary veins

Great cardiac vein

Anterior interventricular branch of left coronary artery and vein

Right auricle

Right coronary artery and vein

Left ventricle

Right ventricle

Apex

Fig. 1-1. Front view of the heart and great blood vessels.

Diseases affecting these valves do so in such a way as to cause either narrowing (stenosis) of the valve, which obstructs the forward flow of blood through the valve, or insufficiency, which results in an abnormal backward flow of blood. As a result, any one valve can be affected by stenosis or insufficiency (for example, mitral stenosis or mitral insufficiency). Mitral stenosis would obstruct the flow of blood from the left atrium into the left ventricle. Mitral insufficiency would allow backward flow of blood from the left ventricle into the left atrium. This abnormal blood flow usually results in an audible swish sound (murmur). This can be easily detected by the physician or nurse with the use of a stethoscope.

The heart wall is made up of three distinct tissue layers. The bulk of the wall is called the myocardium. The inner lining surface, which comes in contact with the blood, is called the endocardium. The outer lining of the heart wall is called the epicardium. The heart itself exists within a saclike tissue called the pericardium. The space between the epicardium and the pericardium is called the pericardial space. The myocardium contains the muscle cells of the heart, which contract to

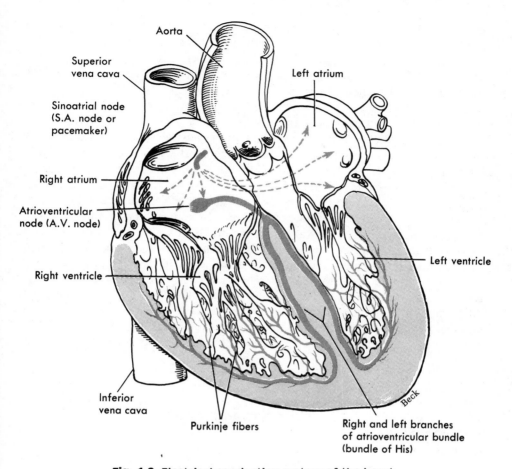

Aorta

Superior
vena cava

Left atrium

Sinoatrial node
(S.A. node or
pacemaker)

Right atrium

Atrioventricular
node (A.V. node)

Left ventricle

Right ventricle

Inferior
vena cava

Beck

Purkinje fibers

Right and left branches
of atrioventricular bundle
(bundle of His)

Fig. 1-2. Electrical conduction system of the heart.

From Anthony, C.P., and Thibodeau, G.A.: Textbook of anatomy and physiology, St. Louis, The C.V. Mosby Co.

provide the pumping action of the heart. The cells within the myocardium receive their blood supply from the right and left coronary arteries. These arteries arise from the aorta near its origin (Fig. 1-1). When there is obstruction of one of these coronary arteries, death of the myocardial cells usually occurs. This is called a myocardial infarction (heart attack). Occasionally collateral (or secondary circulation) will occur around this obstruction, precluding a heart attack. If there is a chronic decrease in the blood flow to the myocardial cells, such as that caused by obstruction, the patient may experience pain (angina) when the heart cells are asked to function at a level higher than the resting state (for example, during exercise).

There are specialized cells located in the upper portion of the right atrium that are called the sinoatrial (SA) node (Fig. 1-2). It is here that the electrical impulse that normally stimulates contraction of the heart begins. The SA node usually generates an impulse about 60 to 100 times a minute in the resting state. These impulses are then carried through the atrium and to a second group of specialized cells called the atrioventricular (AV) node, which is located in the lower part of the right atrium. The AV node (Fig. 1-2) relays the electrical impulse from the SA node to a third group of specialized nerve fibers called the bundle of His. This bundle is located in the septum between the right and left ventricles. The ends of these nerve bundles are called Purkinje fibers. These fibers carry the impulses throughout the ventricular wall and stimulate the myocardium to contract (Fig. 1-2). Inflammation of the heart or coronary artery disease (lack of blood supply) can affect this specialized nerve system of the heart. As a result, the patient's heart may not beat as fast as is required by the body. Under these circumstances, often the patient will require an artificial pacing device (pacemaker). This pacing device takes over the function of the SA node and stimulates the heart to contract.

Any portion of the heart can be malformed by congenital abnormalities. The result of these malformations vary from essentially insignificant minor problems to very severe interruptions in blood flow that inevitably are fatal. The scope of this text does not permit a description of these many intriguing abnormalities.

The pericardium also can be affected by disease. The most common disease affecting the pericardium is inflammation (pericarditis). There are many causes of inflammation including bacterial infection, tumor, viral infections, and auto-immune diseases. Fluid can build up between the pericardium and epicardium. This is called a pericardial effusion and can be a result of pericarditis, trauma, or tumor.

X-RAYS AND NUCLEAR SCANS
Cardiac catheterization (cardiac angiography, angiocardiography)
Normal values

Normal heart, blood vessels, pressures, and volumes.

Purpose

Cardiac catheterization is a procedure that allows one to study the heart and the major blood vessels surrounding it. During this study, a catheter is placed through a vein or artery and into the heart and surrounding vessels. Through this catheter the inside of the heart can be viewed, pressures can be recorded, and radiopaque dye can be injected. Measurements for cardiac function are determined. Cardiac catheterization can be performed for any of the following reasons:

1. To identify, document, and locate blockage within the coronary arteries (Fig. 1-3)
2. To identify, document, and estimate the severity of cardiac valve disease, ventricular or atrial septal defects (holes connecting the right side to the left side of the heart), and abnormalities of the great vessels
3. To evaluate the success of previous heart surgery
4. To evaluate the pumping function of the heart muscle
5. To identify a ventricular aneurysm (weakened outpouching of the heart wall), which may follow a heart attack

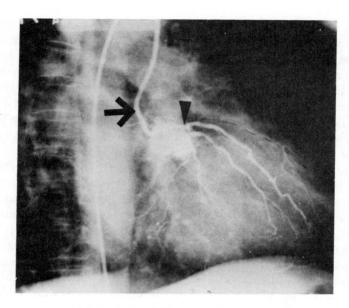

Fig. 1-3. Coronary angiogram, lateral view. Black arrows indicate angiocatheter; black pointer indicates narrowing of the left coronary artery. Dotted line indicates what would have been the normal course of the anterior descending coronary artery had proximal narrowing not occurred. Dye-filled vessels represent collateralization (new blood vessel formation).

Possible complications of cardiac catheterization include the following:
1. Abnormal heart rhythm that may lead to ventricular failure, or cessation of the heart beat
2. Perforation (making a hole) in the heart by the catheter
3. Stroke or heart attack caused by the dislodgement of a fatty clot
4. Arterial complications (such as clotting, embolism, or bleeding)
5. Allergic reaction to the dye, which may range in severity from hives to shock
6. Infection at the skin puncture site

As with any procedure, the incidence of these complications is greatly reduced when the procedure is performed by competent and experienced personnel in a well-equipped cardiac catheterization lab.

Procedure

The patient is kept fasting from solid foods for 6 to 8 hours before catheterization. Fluids are often permitted until 3 hours before this study. The patient is usually sedated with diazepam (Valium) and either meperidine (Demerol) or morphine 30 to 60 minutes before the study. Young children require general anesthesia for this study. Patients who have valvular abnormalities will also receive a penicillin injection to prevent bacterial growth on the valves of the heart. Skin testing for iodine allergies may be done before the study because iodine will be injected during the course of the study.

Cardiac catheterization is performed under strict sterile conditions. The catheter insertion site (usually the groin) is prepared and anesthetized (numbed) with a local anesthetic such as lidocaine. Electrocardiogram (EKG) leads are placed on the four extremities and the EKG (also discussed in this chapter) will be monitored during the study. An intravenous (IV) needle is inserted to allow quick access to the bloodstream in the event that cardiac drugs may be needed.

To study the right side of the heart, a sterile radiopaque (that is, can be seen on x-ray) catheter is inserted into the vein of the arm or leg and then passed up into the superior vena cava. The catheter is advanced through the right atrium and ventricle and then into the pulmonary artery (Fig. 1-1). The course of the catheter is followed by x-ray. X-ray dye is injected and films are taken at any time. The heart is constantly monitored during the procedure. Some heart beat disturbances may occur as the catheter is passed into the ventricle. Blood pressures are recorded at regular intervals throughout the procedure. As the catheter is passed through the heart, the pressures within the superior vena cava, the right atrium, the right ventricle, and the pulmonary artery are recorded. Blood samples are drawn from the heart for analysis of oxygen content. Catheterization of the right side of the heart is usually performed in a cardiac catheterization laboratory. It may also, however, be performed at the bedside.

For left-sided heart catheterization, the catheter is usually passed backward from an artery in the arm or leg into the aorta and then into the left ventricle. The EKG and blood pressure readings are monitored closely during the procedure. Once the catheter is correctly positioned by fluoroscopy (moving x-ray pictures), pressure readings are measured and blood samples are drawn for oxygen content. X-ray dye is injected into the left ventricle and movie-type x-ray films are taken (cineventriculography). If the coronary arteries are to be injected with dye, the patient may be given nitroglycerine sublingually (under the tongue) because of its dilating effect. During the injection of the dye into the coronary arteries, the table is moved from side to side. The patient may feel as if he or she is falling. Left-sided catheterization is performed in the cardiac catheterization laboratory.

After the study of either side of the heart, the cardiac catheter is removed. If access to the artery or vein required making a small incision (a cutdown), this area is then sutured closed and covered with a dry, sterile pressure dressing. The catheter insertion site is then immobilized for several hours. Pressure is applied to the site. Vital signs (temperature, pulse, respiration, and blood pressure) are monitored frequently over the next 4 to 6 hours. The puncture site is assessed for signs of bleeding, and the pulses, color, and temperature of the extremity used for access are carefully monitored.

For most patients, cardiac catheterization is an anxiety-producing experience. The patient must lie still on a hard x-ray table that may rotate in several positions. The room is usually darkened to allow for visualization of the fluoroscopic screen. The patient's arm may feel as though it has gone to sleep if the arm artery was used for access. As the catheter passes through the heart and touches the ventricles, the patient may feel palpitations (that is, the heart skipping a beat). When the radiopaque dye is injected, the patient may feel a warm flush. This feeling of warmth frequently is so strong that it simulates being thrown into a fire. Although transient (4 to 10 seconds), it is very uncomfortable. Some patients have a tendency to cough as the catheter is passed into the pulmonary artery of the lungs. Cardiac catheterization is performed by a cardiologist or radiologist.

Pertinent facts

- Usually the physician who will perform this test obtains written permission for this study from the patient.
- Most patients will describe this test as being very uncomfortable (see Procedure).
- Food or fluids should not be eaten or drunk for at least 6 to 8 hours before the procedure to prevent the patient from vomiting and aspirating the vomitus into the lungs.
- Most patients are very tired after this procedure. The physician often orders bed rest for several hours to allow complete sealing of the arterial puncture. If the arterial site should bleed, much blood can be lost in a short amount of time.
- An ice bag may be applied to the insertion site. The physician may order a sandbag to be placed over the insertion site for pressure.
- The patient's vital signs are monitored very carefully after this test to detect any abnormalities.
- After this test the patient's pulses and skin temperatures are carefully assessed. The patient should immediately report any signs of numbness, tingling, pain, and inability to move an extremity to the nurse.
- The duration of cardiac catheterization is approximately 1 to 3 hours.
- The customary cost of this study is approximately $1500.

Cardiac radionuclear scanning (myocardial scan, cardiac scan, myocardial scintiphotography, radioisotope scanning)
Normal values

Normal myocardial cells.

Purpose

Cardiac radionuclear scanning is a noninvasive and safe method of recognizing cardiac disease. Many different radioisotopes (radiocompound materials) can be used for this study. These compounds are injected intravenously (into the vein). With the use of a radiation detector placed over the heart, an image of the heart can be recorded and photographed.

Basically, cardiac scanning is used to evaluate blood flow to the coronary arteries, to evaluate the function of the ventricles, and to document the presence of pericardial effusion (fluid surrounding the heart).

Specific indications for cardiac scanning include

1. Evaluation of patients to see if they have had a myocardial infarction (heart attack). This may be done before surgery.
2. Evaluation of patients with complaints of chest pain and unclear EKG results.
3. Evaluation before and after coronary bypass surgery.
4. Quantification and surveillance of myocardial infarction (heart attack).

5. Evaluation of the function of the ventricles in patients with heart disease.

This study is free of complications. The era of noninvasive myocardial scanning is just beginning, and this test will no doubt be a vital part of the evaluation of many patients with myocardial disease.

Procedure

The nonfasting and unsedated patient is taken to the nuclear medicine department where he or she is given an intravenous injection of a radionuclide (radioactive substance). Shortly thereafter (but in less than 4 hours) a gamma-ray detector is placed over the heart. The patient is placed on his or her back and then on the side. The detector records the image of the heart and a Polaroid photo of that image is taken.

Pertinent facts

- The only part of this test that is uncomfortable is the venous puncture required with the injection of the radioisotope. This test is performed by a technician in approximately 20 minutes.
- The customary cost for this test is approximately $65.

BLOOD TESTS
Cardiac enzyme studies
Normal values

Creatinine phosphokinase (CPK): 5-75 mU/ml.
Serum glutamic oxaloacetic transaminase (SGOT): 12-36 U/ml or 5-40 IU/L.
Lactic dehydrogenase (LDH): 90-200 ImU/ml.

Purpose

Cardiac enzymes (CPK, SGOT, LDH) studies are useful in confirming a myocardial infarction (heart attack) when they are viewed in relation to the EKG, the history, and the physical examination. When the heart muscle is damaged, enzymes contained within the muscle cells are released into the bloodstream, causing increased levels within the blood. Enzyme determinations are also useful in following the course of a myocardial infarction (heart attack) and in detecting an extension of it.

CPK. The enzyme CPK is found predominantly in the heart muscle, skeletal muscle (such as arms and legs), and brain. The serum (blood) CPK level rises within 6 hours after damage to the heart cells, peaks in approximately 18 hours, and returns to normal in approximately 2 to 3 days. Because minor insults to the skeletal muscle (such as an intramuscular injection) can elevate CPK levels, the total CPK level is not reliably specific for indicating heart damage. However, the CPK can be fractionated (or broken down) into isoenzymes to measure the cardiac component of the enzyme. This provides a more specific index of cardiac muscle function.

SGOT. The enzyme SGOT (often called serum aspartate transaminase, AST) is found in very high concentrations in the heart and liver (see p. 64-65) and in moderately large amounts in the skeletal muscle, kidneys, and pancreas. After myocardial injury, the SGOT rises within 6 to 10 hours, peaks at 12 to 48 hours, and returns to normal in approximately 3 or 4 days. A characteristic rise in SGOT level occurs in more than 95% of patients with proven myocardial infarctions.

LDH. The enzyme LDH is found in many body tissues especially in the heart, liver, kidneys, skeletal muscle, brain, and lungs. The serum LDH level rises within 24 to 72 hours after myocardial injury, peaks in 3 to 4 days, and returns to normal in approximately 14 days. This makes LDH especially useful in the delayed diagnosis of myocardial infarction, (for example, in cases where the patient reports that he or she had chest pain 4 days ago). At this time this may be the only enzyme elevation apparent. Because the LDH enzyme is widely distributed throughout the body, the total LDH level is not specific for myocardial disease. LDH, like CPK, is more useful diagnostically when fractionated into isoenzymes.

Procedure

A vein is punctured and one red-top tube of blood is drawn. Usually the CPK, LDH, and SGOT enzymes are drawn daily for 3 days and then 1 week after the patient's admission.

Pertinent facts

• The only discomfort associated with this study is a needle stick.
• Frequent needle sticks are done (daily for 3 days) to assess the time elevations of the enzymes.
• The customary cost of cardiac enzyme studies is approximately $50.

Serum lipids (blood lipids; lipid profile; cholesterol, triglycerides, phospholipids)
Normal values

Total lipids: 400-1,000 mg/dl.
Cholesterol: 150-250 mg/dl.
Triglycerides: 40-150 mg/dl.
Phospholipids: 150-380 mg/dl.

Purpose

Determination of the serum lipid level provides useful data for the diagnosis and the management of atherosclerotic disease (hardening of the arteries). When lipids or fats (such as cholesterol, triglycerides, and phospholipids) are transported in the bloodstream, they are combined with proteins and are therefore called lipoproteins. Hyperlipoproteinemia refers to elevation of these lipoprotein complexes in the blood. The lipoproteins can be separated into five types determined by the major lipid (fat) elevation. Types I, III, and V are rare. Types IIa and IIb (cholesterol and triglycerides) and IV (triglycerides) are important in cardiac disease. The typing of the hyperlipoproteinemias is useful because the dietary treatment varies with the type. For example, type IV is treated primarily with a low-carbohydrate diet because carbohydrates form triglycerides. Type IIa is best treated by a reduction in dietary cholesterol.

Procedure

For this test the patient must fast for at least 12 to 14 hours after eating a normal diet for at least 2 weeks. Water is permitted. If possible, thyroid medication, contraceptives, and lipid-lowering drugs should be avoided for at least 3 weeks before testing. Two tubes (one red-top and one lavender-top) of blood are drawn from a vein.

Pertinent facts

• The diet and fasting requirements must be followed to assure accurate results for this study.
• The only discomfort associated with this test is the needle stick.
• The customary cost for the serum lipid study is approximately $35.

SPECIAL STUDIES
Electrocardiography (EKG, ECG)
Normal values

Normal rate (60-100 beats per minute), rhythm, and wave deflections.

Purpose

The EKG is a graphic representation of the electrical impulses generated by the heart during a full heart beat. These electrical impulses are conducted to the body surface where they are detected by electrode sensors placed on the patient's limbs and chest.

A 12-lead EKG provides a comprehensive view of the flow of the heart's electrical currents in two different planes. There are six "limb leads" (various combinations of electrodes on the four extremities), and six "chest leads" (corresponding to six sites on the chest) (see Fig. 1-5).

EKGs are recorded on special paper with a graphic background of horizontal and vertical lines to permit rapid measurement of time intervals (X coordinates) and voltages (Y coordinates).

The normal EKG pattern is composed of waves arbitrarily designated by the letters P, Q, R, S, and T. The Q, R, and S waves are grouped together and described as the QRS complex. The typical EKG pattern and normal time intervals are shown in Fig. 1-4. The significance of the waves and time intervals is as follows:

P wave Represents contraction of the atrium. It represents the electrical activity associated with the spread of the original impulse from the SA node through the atrium (see p. 3-4). If the P waves are absent or altered, the cardiac impulse must have originated somewhere outside of the SA node.

P-R interval Represents the time required for the cardiac impulse to travel from the SA node to the AV node (Fig. 1-4). If this timed interval is prolonged, an electrical conduction defect exists in the AV node.

QRS complex Represents contraction of the ventricle. If the QRS complex is widened, this indicates an abnormal or prolonged contraction time in the ventricles.

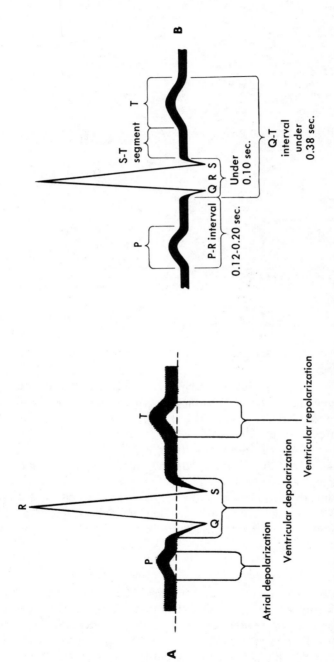

Fig. 1-4. A, Normal EKG deflection during the cardiac cycle. **B,** Principle EKG intervals between P, QRS, and T waves.

From Anthony, C.P., and Thibodeau, G.A.: Textbook of anatomy and physiology, St. Louis, The C.V. Mosby Co.

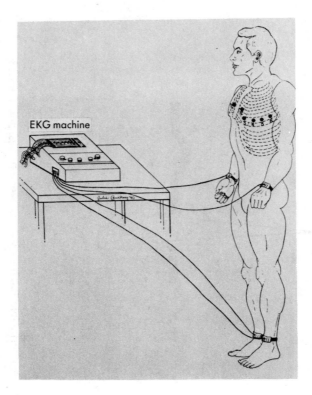

Fig. 1-5. Placement of EKG electrodes.

ST segment Represents the period between the completion of one contraction and the beginning of another contraction. This segment may be altered in patients that have angina or in patients that are in the early stages of a myocardial infarction (heart attack).

T wave Represents a return to neutral activity.

Through the analysis of these wave forms and timed intervals, valuable information can be obtained about the heart. The EKG is used primarily to identify abnormal heart rhythms (arrhythmias) and to diagnose present or past heart attacks, abnormalities in electrical conduction, and enlargement of the heart muscle (hypertrophy). It is important to note that the EKG may be normal even in the presence of heart disease.

Procedure

The patient is asked to lie on his or her back. The EKG machine is usually turned on so that it will be warmed up and ready to use after the electrodes are applied. The skin areas that will be used for the electrode placement (Fig. 1-5) are prepared by using alcohol swabs or in some cases gentle sandpaper to remove skin oil or debris. Sometimes the skin is shaved if the patient has a large amount of hair. Electrode paste is applied on the skin to ensure electrical conduction between the skin and the electrodes. The four limb leads are usually held in place by straps that encircle the extremity. Some newer machines have clamps (much like a large clothespin) that can easily be applied to the leg. The chest leads (suction cups) are applied either one at a time, three at a time, or all six at a time, depending on the type of EKG machine. These chest leads are placed in the position as indicated in Fig. 1-5.

It is very important that the patient lie still without talking when the EKG is recorded. This procedure entails no discomfort for the patient. This procedure is performed by a cardiac technician and nurse. It is done at the heart station or at the bedside.

In some cases continuous recording of the electrical activity is desired to identify intermittent abnormal heart rhythms or rates. For these patients a small portable Holter monitor can be attached to the leads and carried by the patient for 24 to 48 hours. With Holter monitoring, an EKG is recorded continuously on magnetic tape during unrestricted activity, rest, and sleep. During Holter monitoring the patient is asked to keep a record of all activities (for example, "8:00 A.M., awakened and ate breakfast").

Pertinent facts

• There is no discomfort associated with an EKG. It is important to realize that the flow of electrical current is *from* the patient. There is no danger of shocking the patient in this procedure.
• The duration of this procedure is usually 5 minutes.
• The customary cost for this procedure is $50.

Phonocardiography
Normal values

Normal heart sound.

Purpose

Phonocardiography provides a graphic display of the auditory events that occur during the heart beat. The phonocardiograph records the heart sound in a manner that resembles detection by the ear. A special microphone is placed over the heart and the cardiac sounds are electronically detected, amplified, and graphically recorded on an oscilloscope (screen).

Phonocardiography is used to identify, time, and differentiate various heart sounds and murmurs that are difficult for the human ear to detect. These sounds can be clearly defined. With this information, the physician can accurately determine what heart abnormality is causing the sound or murmur.

Phonocardiography does not replace cardiac auscultation (listening to the heart with a stethoscope). Indeed certain murmurs can be detected more readily by a skilled cardiologist using only a stethoscope. Many cardiologists use phonocardiography to document the patient's heart sounds by permanent record. Also this procedure is a valuable teaching aid for doctors of cardiology.

2. To determine the limits of safe exercise during cardiac rehabilitation of patients who are known to have heart disease.

Procedure

No patient fasting or sedation is required for phonocardiography. The patient lies on his or her back. Limb leads are attached to the patient for the simultaneous recording of an EKG (see p. 12-13). A microphone is placed over various locations on the chest, and the cardiac sounds are displayed on an oscilloscope. Polaroid pictures are taken of this display. This procedure is performed by a cardiologist or a technician in a quiet room in a cardiology clinic.

Pertinent facts

- There is no discomfort associated with this procedure. However, some patients may be bothered by the pressure of the microphone on their chest.
- The patient must lie very still during this procedure and refrain from talking while the technician is listening to the heart.
- The duration of this test is approximately 15 to 30 minutes.
- The customary cost of this test is approximately $125.

Echocardiography (cardiac echo)
Normal values

Normal position, size, and movement of the heart valves and chambers.

Purpose

Echocardiography is a noninvasive ultrasound procedure used to evaluate the structure and function of the heart. In this study, a harmless high-frequency sound wave is passed from a transducer and penetrates the organ being studied. For echocardiography, the transducer is placed over the heart, and sound waves are bounced off the heart structures and reflected back to the transducer as a series of echoes. The echoes are amplified and displayed on a screen. The tracings are then recorded on moving graph paper.

Echocardiography is useful in the diagnosis of pericardial effusion (fluid surrounding the heart), disease of the mitral valve, narrowing of the aorta, weakness of the heart muscle (cardiomyopathy), cardiac tumor, and congenital valvular heart disease. No complications are associated with this study.

Procedure

No patient sedation or fasting is required. The patient must undress to the waist. The patient lies on a bed first on his or her back and then later on the left side. The ultrasonographer (a trained technician or cardiologist) applies mineral oil or glycerine to the skin overlying the heart. This paste is used to enhance transmission and reception of the sound waves. A pencil-like probe (transducer) is then placed on the skin, held there by the technician, and then tilted into various positions to enscribe an arc that will demonstrate several areas of the heart sequentially. An EKG is recorded simultaneously during this study to time the events demonstrated by ultrasound with the cardiac cycle.

Echocardiography is usually performed in a darkened room in a cardiology clinic. It can, however, be performed at the bedside or in the emergency room in an emergency situation (for example, with suspected pericardial effusion).

Pertinent facts

- There is no pain or discomfort associated with this study.
- The duration of this study is approximately 15 to 45 minutes.
- A gel will be applied to the skin over the heart to enhance the transmission of the sound waves. After the study, the gel is removed from the chest.
- The customary cost of this study is approximately $150.

Exercise stress testing (stress testing, exercise testing, electrocardiographic stress testing)
Normal values

Negative (no symptoms or EKG abnormalities detected).

Purpose

Exercise stress testing is a noninvasive study that provides very valuable information about the heart that cannot be obtained by examination of the patient in a resting state. During this study, the EKG, the heart rate, and the blood pressure are recorded while the patient engages in some type of physical activity (stress). The three common methods of stress testing include climbing stair steps (Master Two-Step test), pedaling a stationary bicycle, and walking a treadmill.

The goal of this testing is to increase the heart rate to just below maximal levels. The maximum heart rate for adults is about 160 to 200 beats per minute. Maximum heart rates are determined according to age and sex. Tables are available for these predicted rates. Exercise tests can have single or multiple stages. With single-stage testing, the work load is held constant. For example, the patient would pedal a bike at a consistent rate for a specified amount of time. In multistage testing, the work load is increased at regular intervals until a desired level is met. For example, the incline of the treadmill may be increased at 3- to 5-minute intervals (Fig. 1-6).

Exercise stress testing is based on the principle that partially or totally occluded (blocked) arteries are unable to meet the heart's increased demand for blood during stress testing. This may result in chest pain, fatigue, shortness of breath, increase in heart rate, or a drop in the blood pressure during exercise. When any of these occurs, the test is terminated at once. When the test is terminated prematurely, the results are considered incomplete. A depression of the ST segment (see EKG study and Fig. 1-4) is the only reliable characteristic of myocardial ischemia (decreased blood supply to the heart muscle). The stress test is considered positive when the recording paper demonstrates a depression of the ST segment. The test is considered negative or normal when there are no EKG changes and the patient experiences no significant complaints or discomfort. The treadmill type of test is most frequently used today because it is the most standardized and easily reproducible of the three types of stress testing.

The indications for stress testing are the following:

1. To evaluate chest pain in a patient who is suspected of having coronary artery disease. If the pain is reproduced during the exercise stress testing, one can then infer that the pain is caused by a blocked coronary artery.

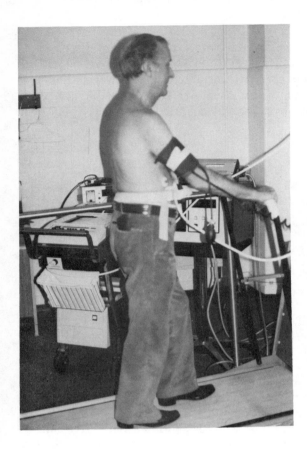

Fig. 1-6. Exercise stress testing. Patient is walking on a treadmill while blood pressure, EKG, and other vital signs are being monitored.

3. To detect exercise-related leg cramps, which indicate blockage of the arteries to the legs (intermittent claudication).
4. To detect exercise-related hypertension.

Stress testing does entail some risks, although they are uncommon. Complications may include cardiac arrhythmias and heart attack.

Procedure

The patient reports to the cardiology clinic after refraining from eating, drinking, or smoking for 4 hours. The EKG electrodes are placed on the patient and attached to a monitor. A prestress test EKG is recorded. Heart rate and respiration rate are taken as baseline values. During stress testing, the EKG and heart rate are recorded continuously by monitoring devices (Fig. 1-6). Blood pressure is recorded intermittently. A physician must be in attendance throughout the stress test to determine if the test should be terminated at any time. The test is usually terminated if the patient develops heart rhythm abnormalities on the EKG monitor, has a drop in blood pressure, or complains of worsening chest pain, exhaustion, fatigue, shortness of breath, or dizziness. After the stress test, the EKG and vital signs are recorded during the short recovery period. Stress testing is usually performed by a cardiologist or by a technician with a cardiologist in attendance.

Pertinent facts

- At least 4 hours before the test, the patient should eat a light meal without coffee or tea (stimulants) or alcohol (a depressant). A heavy meal should be avoided because heavy meals divert the blood to the stomach and intestines and then, when exercise is begun, a large portion of the remaining blood goes to skeletal muscle. A heavy meal before stress testing may cause signs of ischemia much earlier than if no meal had been eaten.
- Smoking is not permitted for at least 4 hours before the test. This is because the nicotine in cigarettes causes transient coronary artery spasm that may last up to 12 hours.
- The night before the test, the patient should get adequate sleep.
- The patient should wear loose-fitting clothes with a shirt that buttons down the front. This facilitates application of the monitoring devices. Many clinics will have the patient put on a hospital gown.
- The patient should wear comfortable, well-fitting shoes to ensure safety and stability on an inclined treadmill or stairs. Slippers are not permitted.
- Some physicians may want their patients to discontinue certain drugs before stress testing.
- During the test the patient should report any sign of chest pain, exhaustion, shortness of breath, or generalized fatigue.
- After the study the patient should rest for several hours and also avoid stimulants and extreme temperature changes.
- After the study the patient should not take a hot shower for at least 2 hours. A hot shower may cause an increase in cutaneous (skin) blood flow and lead to decreased blood pressure when standing. This may cause fainting.
- Stress testing is performed in approximately 30 to 45 minutes.
- The customary cost for this study is approximately $200.

Sample case report: chest pain (angina)

Mr. J. P., a 48-year-old man, was admitted to the coronary care unit complaining of chest pain. During the 4 months preceding admission, he noted chest pain that radiated down his neck and jaw during vigorous exercise or emotional upsets. The pain disappeared when he discontinued the activity or relaxed. The results of his physical examination were essentially normal except for a heart murmur.

STUDIES	RESULTS
Routine laboratory work	Within normal limits (WNL)
Cardiac enzyme studies	
CPK	20 mU/ml (normal: 5-75 mU/ml)
LDH	120 ImU/ml (normal: 90-220 ImU/ml)
SGOT	24 IU/L (normal: 5-40 IU/I)
Electrocardiography (EKG)	Evidence of enlargement of the left ventricle
Chest x-ray study	Within normal limits (WNL)
Phonocardiography	Murmur of aortic stenosis
Exercise stress test	ST-T segment depression after 3 minutes of walking on inclined plane

STUDIES	RESULTS
Echocardiography	Decreased movement of the aortic valve
Cardiac catheterization	
Pressures	All within normal limits except for a significant difference between the left ventricular and the aortic pressure gradient
Cineventriculography	Hypertrophy (enlargement) of the left ventricle (normal: normal-size ventricle)
Coronary angiography	90% narrowing of the left coronary artery (normal: no narrowing)
Cardiac radionuclear scanning	Scans normal except for a thallium scan, which showed a localized area of decreased uptake in the heart muscle during exercise
Serum lipid study	
Total	1100 mg/dl (normal: 400-1000 mg/dl)
Cholesterol	502 mg/dl (normal: 150-250 mg/dl)
Triglycerides	198 mg/dl (normal: 40-150 mg/dl)
Phospholipids	400 mg/dl (normal: 150-380 mg/dl)

Cardiac radionuclear scanning, electrocardiography, and serial cardiac enzyme studies ruled out the possibility of a heart attack. Stress testing and the thallium scan indicated that the patient was having exercise-related chest pain. Phonocardiography and echocardiography indicated aortic stenosis (narrowing). The cardiac catheterization demonstrated a near normal ventricular function. The ventricular to aortic pressure gradient documented an aortic stenosis, and the coronary angiography demonstrated significant narrowing of the left coronary artery. The patient's angina (chest pain) was then thought to be caused by a combination of coronary artery disease, aortic stenosis, and ventricular hypertrophy (enlargement). Open heart surgery was performed. After surgery, Mr. J.P. did well. Because the serum lipid studies showed type IIa (cholesterol) hyperlipidemia, he was placed on a low-cholesterol diet. Six months later, he was free of all symptoms and jogging 5 miles per day.

2

Diagnostic studies used to evaluate the arteries and veins

ANATOMY, PHYSIOLOGY, AND
COMMON PROBLEMS OF THE BLOOD VESSELS

There are three kinds of blood vessels: arteries, veins, and capillaries. An artery is a vessel that carries blood away from the heart (Fig. 2-1). The main artery leaving the heart is called the aorta (see Fig. 1-1). Arteries serve mainly as distributors carrying the blood to the arterioles (small arteries). Arterioles carry the blood from the arteries to the capillaries. The capillaries then transport the blood from the arterioles directly to the cells of the body. The capillaries also accept and transfer the waste products from the cells and transport the blood to venules (small veins) and then to the larger veins. The main function of the veins is to transport blood back toward the heart (Fig. 2-2). Not only do veins return blood from the capillaries to the heart, but they also can accommodate varying amounts of blood. This is important in maintaining a normal circulation. The heart acts as a pump in keeping blood moving through its special circuit of vessels, which includes arteries, arterioles, capillaries, venules, and veins. As we can see, the essential function of the entire circulatory system is that of providing blood for the needs of the cells in the body.

The major abnormality affecting either the arteries or the veins is occlusion. Veins commonly become occluded as a result of "thrombophlebitis." In this disease, which commonly affects the legs, the blood in the veins becomes clotted, and a painful, inflammatory reaction of varying degrees results. The clot worsens, and occasionally fragments of the clot can break off and travel to the lungs (pulmonary embolus). Occlusive disease of the artery, on the other hand, is commonly a result of arteriosclerosis (hardening of the arteries). Any artery can become arteriosclerotic. The more important ones are the carotid artery, which serves the brain, the coronary artery, which serves the heart, the femoral artery, which serves the leg, and the aorta, which serves the abdominal region. The atherosclerotic plaques build up and in time can block the flow of blood. Other diseases such as Buerger's disease (inflammation and obliteration of blood vessels in the extremities) and fibromuscular dysplasia (fibrous obliteration of blood

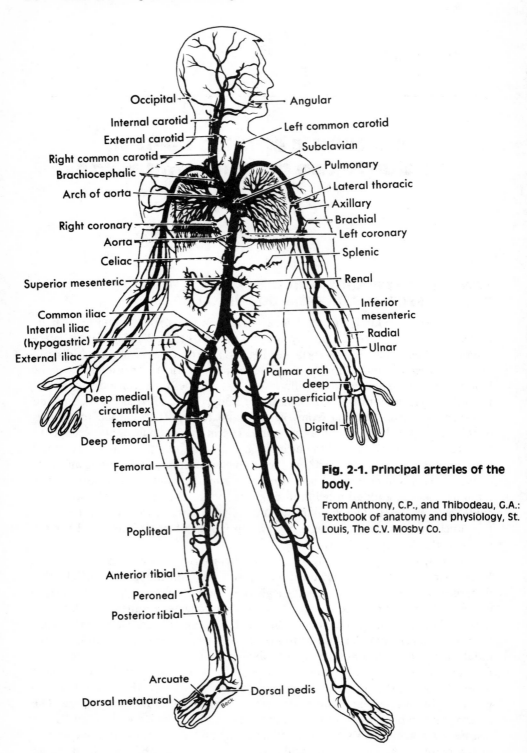

Occipital

Angular

Internal carotid

Left common carotid

External carotid

Subclavian

Right common carotid

Pulmonary

Brachiocephalic

Lateral thoracic

Arch of aorta

Axillary

Right coronary

Brachial

Aorta

Left coronary

Celiac

Splenic

Superior mesenteric

Renal

Common iliac

Inferior
mesenteric

Internal iliac
(hypogastric)

Radial

External iliac

Ulnar

Palmar arch
deep
superficial

Deep medial
circumflex
femoral

Digital

Deep femoral

Femoral

**Fig. 2-1. Principal arteries of the
body.**

From Anthony, C.P., and Thibodeau, G.A.:
Textbook of anatomy and physiology, St.
Louis, The C.V. Mosby Co.

Popliteal

Anterior tibial

Peroneal

Posterior tibial

Arcuate

Dorsal pedis

Dorsal metatarsal

Beck

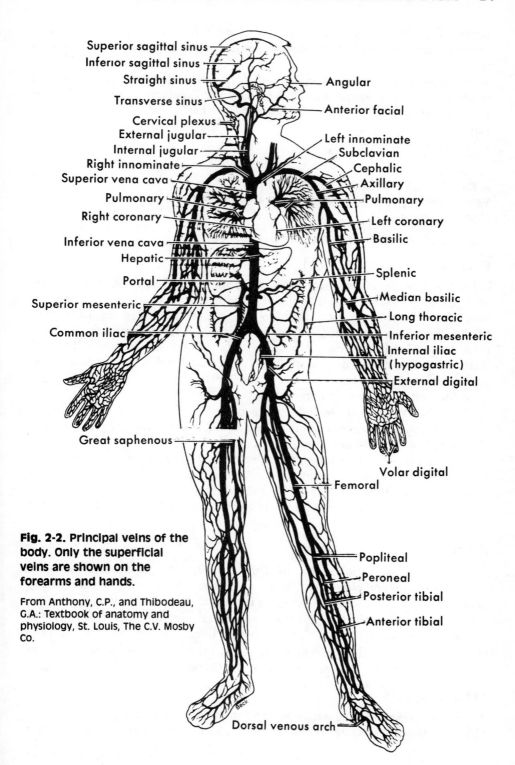

Superior sagittal sinus
Inferior sagittal sinus
Straight sinus
Transverse sinus
Cervical plexus
External jugular
Internal jugular
Right innominate
Superior vena cava
Pulmonary
Right coronary
Inferior vena cava
Hepatic
Portal
Superior mesenteric
Common iliac
Great saphenous

Angular
Anterior facial
Left innominate
Subclavian
Cephalic
Axillary
Pulmonary
Left coronary
Basilic
Splenic
Median basilic
Long thoracic
Inferior mesenteric
Internal iliac
(hypogastric)
External digital
Volar digital
Femoral
Popliteal
Peroneal
Posterior tibial
Anterior tibial
Dorsal venous arch

Fig. 2-2. Principal veins of the body. Only the superficial veins are shown on the forearms and hands.

From Anthony, C.P., and Thibodeau, G.A.: Textbook of anatomy and physiology, St. Louis, The C.V. Mosby Co.

vessels) also result in blockage of arterial blood flow. Clots formed in the heart and elsewhere (embolus) can become lodged in smaller arteries and block the flow of blood.

Traumatic lacerations and injury can affect the arteries and veins. Again the result is interruption in the continued blood flow. There are many other diseases such as varicosities, tumors, and inflammation that can affect the arteries and veins.

X-RAYS AND NUCLEAR SCANS
Venography (phlebography or venogram)
Normal values

Negative (no blood clots in the vein).

Purpose

This is an x-ray study designed to identify and locate blood clots within the venous system of the lower extremities. During this study dye is injected into the vein of the affected extremity, and x-ray films are taken. Obstruction of the flow of the dye column or filling defects within the dye-filled vein indicate that a thrombosis (blood clot) exists. A positive study confirms the diagnosis of venous thrombosis (Fig. 2-3). A normal study (negative study) makes the diagnosis of venous thrombosis very unlikely.

Complications in venography include:
1. Allergic reaction to the iodinated dye
2. Infiltration of the dye out of the veins and into the tissues, causing pain, swelling, and inflammation
3. Induction of venous thrombophlebitis (that is, the dye injection itself may cause an inflammation followed by the formation of blood clots)
4. Infection, if there is a break in sterile technique
5. Embolism, the transfer of a blood clot from one site to another within the vein

Procedure

No sedation or fasting is required for this study. The patient is taken to the x-ray department and placed lying on his or her back. Venography is most usually done to assess a vein in the leg. A needle is placed into a vein. Often this requires that the physician performing the test make a small surgical incision to insert the needle into the vein. The x-ray physician then injects an iodinated dye into the vein and takes x-ray films to follow the course of the dye up the leg. A tourniquet frequently is placed on the leg to prevent the filling of other veins on the leg.

Pertinent facts

• This study takes approximately 30 to 90 minutes to perform.
• The discomfort associated with this test is a needle stick into the vein. The dye

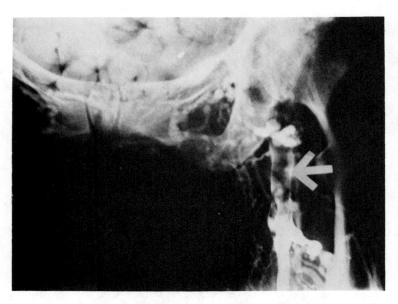

Fig. 2-3. Abnormal venogram. Arrow indicates clot within the proximal femoral vein.

itself may cause a warm flush throughout the body, but this is not as severe as with arteriography (see next study).
• Before the study is performed, the patient should be assessed for allergies to dye. If it is important that this test be performed, the patient can be placed on a special preparation (prednisone and diphenhydramine [Benadryl]) for several days before and after the test to alleviate any allergic tendencies.
• Patients who are in a considerable amount of pain before the test should be medicated so that they can lie still throughout the procedure.
• After the study, the extremity involved is carefully checked for any redness, swelling, pain, or tenderness. The patient should also report any signs of increased temperature, flushing, or chills to the physician.
• The customary cost of this study is approximately $200.

Femoral arteriography (femoral angiogram)
Normal values

Normal femoral arteries.

Purpose

Femoral arteriography allows the physician to accurately identify and locate occlusions (blockages) within the femoral arterial system. After a special tiny catheter is placed in the femoral artery (Fig. 2-1), dye is injected. X-ray films are taken immediately in timed sequence to allow radiographic visualization of the

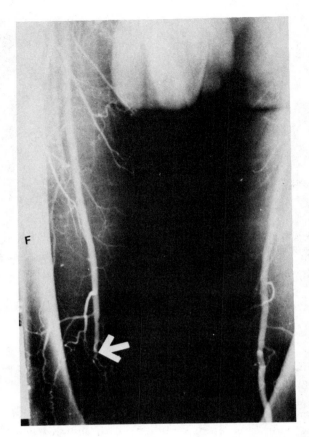

Fig. 2-4. Femoral arteriogram. White arrow indicates area of superficial femoral artery occlusion. Note normal femoral artery on right side of photograph. **F,** Femur.

arterial system of the legs. Total or near total occlusion (blockage) of the flow of dye (Fig. 2-4) may be seen in such conditions as arteriosclerotic disease, emboli, or arterial trauma (such as tearing of the vessels). Dilatation (expansion) of the femoral artery or its branches is indicative of aneurysm (a sac formed by dilatation of the walls of a blood vessel).

Femoral arteriography is usually done on patients who have symptoms and signs of vessel disease such as coldness of the extremity or no pulse in the extremity. However, emergency arteriography is needed when blood flow to an extremity has suddenly stopped. Immediate surgical therapy is needed to save the leg, and surgery is most effective when the surgeon has knowledge of the cause and location of the sudden blockage. This knowledge can be obtained only by arteriography.

Complications in this study include:
1. Hemorrhage (bleeding) at the site of the arterial puncture
2. Disruption of a fatty plaque leading to sudden occlusion of a femoral vessel
3. An allergic reaction to the dye

Procedure

Preferably, the patient is kept fasting for 8 hours, although this is not necessary. Usually sedation (meperidine [Demerol]) is ordered for arteriography. The patient is taken to the "special studies" laboratory, usually in the x-ray department, and placed on a special, movable x-ray table. The patient is asked to lie still on his or her back. The femoral artery (Fig. 2-1) on the side opposite to the affected extremity is catheterized by placing a needle and catheter into an artery. The catheter is then guided under x-ray visualization into the appropriate leg. Once the catheter is positioned in the involved femoral vessel, dye is injected and x-ray films of the thigh, calf, and ankle are taken immediately in timed sequence. This allows visualization of the femoral artery and its branches. After the x-ray films are taken, the catheter is removed and a pressure dressing is applied to the puncture site.

Pertinent facts

- Before the study the patient should be assessed for allergies to iodine dye.
- Usually the patient is kept from having anything by mouth (NPO) from midnight on the day of the study.
- Informed, written consent for this procedure is obtained by the physician before the procedure.
- As with all arteriograms, the patient will feel a discomforting and sometimes painful hot flash that usually lasts less than 10 seconds. This, along with the initial arterial puncture, is the only discomfort that the patient will experience.
- Femoral arteriography is performed by an x-ray physician (radiologist) in approximately 40 minutes.
- After the test, the patient is usually kept on bed rest for about 8 hours to allow for complete sealing of the arterial puncture site.
- After the procedure the catheter insertion site is examined for swelling, redness, bleeding, or the absence of pulses in the leg. The color and temperature of the involved extremity are compared to the color and temperature of the opposite extremity.
- After the test, the vital signs (blood pressure, pulse, respiration) are frequently checked to assess for any signs of bleeding. With bleeding, the blood pressure would decrease and the pulse would increase.
- Cold compresses may be applied to the puncture site to reduce discomfort and swelling. If the patient is having continuous, severe pain, the physician should check the site carefully because blood clots (hematomas) may be forming under the skin.
- The customary cost of this study is approximately $350.

^{125}I Fibrinogen uptake test (FUT, radioactive fibrinogen scanning, vein scanning)
Normal values

Negative (no deep-vein blood clots).

Purpose

This is a noninvasive test used to identify thrombus (blood clot) formation in the veins. Large amounts of fibrinogen are normally present at the site of blood clot formation (see Fig. 14-1). When an external source of fibrinogen is tagged with ^{125}I and given intravenously to the patient, the physician can detect the iodinated fibrinogen in the blood stream by means of a gamma-ray detector. At areas where clot formation is occurring, the ^{125}I count will be markedly increased. This test is about 80% to 90% accurate in the diagnosis of deep-vein thrombophlebitis. Although it was once thought to be able to recognize only "forming" clots, it is now known that "established" clots can be detected by an FUT. This study is also useful in the detection of early blood clots in patients who are at high risk for developing clots. There are several disadvantages of FUT as compared to conventional venography (also discussed in this chapter):

1. FUT cannot detect deep-vein blood clots in the upper thigh. This is because there is normally a high quantity of fibrinogen in this area.
2. It is necessary to wait 24 hours between the giving of ^{125}I fibrinogen and the testing of the leg for increased uptake. This is a major disadvantage when one needs to know if deep-vein thrombosis exists so that appropriate therapy can be immediately instituted.
3. Because the fibrinogen used for ^{125}I labeling is obtained from donated blood, the possibility of hepatitis transmission exists.

This test is contraindicated in the following patients:

1. Patients in whom the diagnosis of deep-vein thrombosis is needed in less than 24 hours.
2. Patients with ongoing inflammation of the leg because fibrinogen is also present in areas of inflammation and will give a false positive result.
3. Patients with large amounts of swelling in the leg that is caused by fluid retention (edema). Fibrinogen is increased in the legs of patients with a lot of edema.

Procedure

The nonfasting, unsedated patient is taken to the nuclear medicine department and an intravenous injection of ^{125}I-labeled fibrinogen is administered. The patient is then instructed to return to the nuclear medicine department 24 hours later. At that time, a Geiger counter–like detector is placed over the patient's ankles, calf, and lower thighs. The amount of ^{125}I present at these sites is recorded and compared with the amount present at the opposite leg or over the heart. If the amount of ^{125}I detected at any area is 15 times greater than that found at the area used for comparison, the test is considered positive for deep-vein blood clots.

Pertinent facts

• This test causes no discomfort other than that associated with the injection of fibrinogen into the vein.

• This procedure takes about 1 hour to complete and is usually performed by a nuclear medicine technician.
• The customary cost of this test is approximately $30.

SPECIAL STUDIES
Doppler ultrasound
Normal values

Normal veins and arteries.

Purpose

Doppler ultrasound is used to determine patency (openness) of the *veins* by detecting moving red blood cells within a vein. A transducer directs an ultrasound beam at a vein. Moving red blood cells reflect the beam back to the transducer, which then transforms the flow velocity into a "swishing" noise that is augmented by an audio speaker. If the vein is occluded, no swishing sound will be detected.

Doppler ultrasound is also used to assess the *arteries* for any occlusions or clots. By placing blood pressure cuffs on the thigh, calf, and ankle, one can measure the pressure in the various arteries of an extremity by sound waves. The extremely sensitive doppler ultrasound detector can detect even minimal blood flow.

Procedure

No fasting or sedation is required for doppler ultrasonography. Ultrasound evaluation of the arteries or the veins can be performed equally well at the bedside or in the noninvasive vascular studies laboratory. The patient is placed lying on his or her back. The ultrasound evaluation of the *veins* is performed by placing a conductive paste on the skin over the vein to be studied. The paste is used to enhance the sound transmission. The transducer probe is placed on the skin and characteristic swishing sounds are sought, indicating movement of blood within an unoccluded (unblocked) vein. The sound detector is placed on the ankle, calf, thigh, and groin. Failure to detect any sound indicates a lack of free-flowing blood within the venous system (blood clot).

Ultrasound evaluation of the *arteries* is performed by placing blood pressure cuffs on the thigh, calf, and ankle. A conductive paste is applied to the skin overlying the arteries in the thighs. Blood pressure cuffs are inflated to certain levels. The doppler ultrasound blood flow detector is placed immediately below the inflated cuff. The pressure is slowly released. The highest pressure at which the blood flow is heard (as a swishing noise) is recorded as the pressure of the artery located under the detector. The procedure is then repeated at the calf and ankle level.

Pertinent facts

• This study requires about 15 minutes to perform.
• This study is usually performed by a trained technician or a physician.
• There is no discomfort associated with doppler ultrasonography.

- The patient should avoid smoking for at least 30 minutes before the doppler study. Nicotine from cigarettes will cause constriction of the arteries and could alter the doppler ultrasound test results on the arterial studies.
- The patient will be instructed to lie very still throughout the procedure.
- After the study, the conductive lubricant is removed from the patient's skin. The legs should never be massaged when removing the paste because this could dislodge blood clots.
- The customary cost of this study is approximately $150.

Venous and arterial plethysmography
Normal values

Normal veins and arteries.

Purpose

Venous impedence plethysmography measures change in the volume of blood within the veins of the leg. A plethysmograph (a pulse-volume recorder) is placed on the leg and the volume is recorded. The venous system is then occluded above the plethysmograph with a tourniquet. The sudden increase in venous volume is then displayed on the pulse-volume recorder. When the tourniquet is released, the venous volume should rapidly return to its preocclusion level. In patients with venous thrombosis (blood clot), the venous outflow is obstructed and the volume cannot quickly return to normal.

Arterial plethysmography is performed by attaching blood pressure cuffs to the leg to display the arterial pulses. Reduction in the amplitude of a pulse wave in any of the cuffs applied indicates arterial occlusion immediately above the area where the decreased amplitude was noted. A positive result is reliable evidence of vascular occlusion. A negative result, however, does not definitely exclude this diagnosis because extensive collateralization (new blood vessel formation) can compensate for even a complete arterial occlusion.

There are no complications associated with either venous or arterial plethysmography.

Procedure

No fasting or sedation is required for either a venous or arterial plethysmography. The test can be performed equally well at the bedside or in the noninvasive vascular studies laboratory. The patient is placed lying on his or her back. For *venous* plethysmography, a large inflatable "occlusion cuff" is placed high on the patient's thigh. A second, smaller plethysmographic "monitor cuff" is placed on the calf and inflated slightly (Fig. 2-5). Normally as the patient takes a sustained deep breath, the venous volume increases because of the decreased venous return from the legs caused by the increased pressure within the abdominal and chest cavities. As the patient exhales, the venous volume decreases. These respiratory waves are displayed on a pulse-volume recorder. Diminished respiratory waves indicate venous thrombosis.

The occlusion cuff is then inflated. As the cuff is occluded, the monitor cuff records the rising venous volume and displays this on the recorder. After the

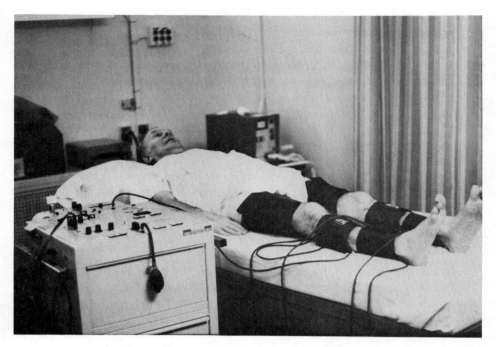

Fig. 2-5. Placement of "occlusion cuffs" for plethysmography.

highest volume is recorded, the occlusion cuff is rapidly deflated and the leg should return to its preocclusion volume within 1 second. If the return to normal volume is delayed for a prolonged period, thrombosis exists.

For *arterial* plethysmography, blood pressure cuffs are placed around the thigh, calf, and ankle as for venous plethysmography (Fig. 2-5). The blood pressure cuffs are then attached to the plethysmograph. The cuffs are minimally inflated. The arterial pulse waves are recorded on plethysmographic tape. The amplitudes of the wave in each cuff are measured and compared.

Pertinent facts

• No discomfort is associated with either arterial or venous plethysmography.
• The study requires about 15 minutes to perform.
• The study is usually performed by a trained technician.
• The customary cost of plethysmography is approximately $100.

Oculoplethysmography (OPG)
Normal values

Normal eye pulsations.

Purpose

Oculoplethysmography (OPG) is a very important test used to measure pressures in the carotid artery (see the neck area in Fig. 2-1). OPG indirectly measures blood flow in the arteries of the eye. Since the ophthalmic (eye) artery is the first major branch of the internal carotid artery, its blood flow accurately reflects carotid blood flow (the blood that eventually reaches the brain).

For this study, pressure in the eyes is measured by suction cups placed on the eye for the recording of eye pressures (Fig. 2-6). OPG is indicated in patients who have symptoms of a stroke (such as dizziness or blurred vision), carotid murmurs, and other neurologic symptoms such as dizziness or fainting. This test is often performed as a follow-up study after carotid endarterectomy (which involves cleaning out the inside of the carotid artery). This study is sometimes followed by cerebral angiography (see Chapter 6).

Ocular plethysmography is contraindicated in patients who have had recent eye surgery, patients with cataracts, and patients who have had retinal detachment. If the patient is wearing contact lenses, they should be removed before the study.

Procedure

Ocular plethysmography is usually performed in a special room designated for neurologic studies. The patient wears street clothes to the study. The patient lies on his or her back on a table or bed (Fig. 2-6). The blood pressure in both arms is taken before the test. EKG electrodes (see Chapter 1) are applied to the patient's extremities to demonstrate any abnormal cardiac rhythms or also to demonstrate blinking of the eyes during the study.

Anesthetic (numbing) eye drops are then instilled into both eyes to minimize discomfort during OPG. Small detectors are attached to the ear lobes to detect blood flow to the ear through the external carotid artery. Tracings for both ears are taken and compared. Eye cups resembling contact lenses are then applied directly on the eyeball of both eyes. Tracings of the pulsations within each eye are then recorded. A vacuum source is then applied to the suction cup. This increased pressure causes the pulse in both eyes to temporarily disappear because all blood flow to the eye is stopped. When the suction source is stopped, the blood flow then returns to the eyes. Both pulses should return simultaneously.

Pertinent facts

- The patient's eyes will burn slightly when the ophthalmic drops are applied.
- When suction is applied to the suction cup, the patient may feel a pulling sensation on the eyes.
- During the suction application, the patient may temporarily lose his or her vision. The vision will immediately return.
- The eye anesthesia wears off in approximately ½ hour.
- After the study, the vision in the eye should be unaffected. If the eyes tear, the patient should not rub the eyes for at least 2 hours after the test. The eyes should only be blotted dry.
- If the patient wears contact lenses, they should not be reinserted for at least 2 hours after OPG.
- The patient's eyes may appear bloodshot for several hours after the test.
- This test is performed by a trained technician in approximately 20 to 30 minutes.
- The customary cost of this study is approximately $125.

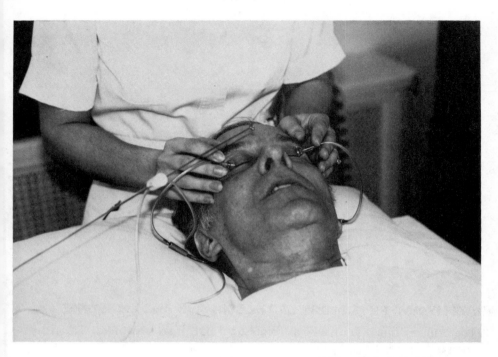

Fig. 2-6. Suction cups are ready to be placed on the eyeballs for oculoplethysmography (OPG).

Sample case report: thrombophlebitis (blood clot)

Mrs. N., a 32-year-old nursing assistant, was admitted to the hospital complaining of a painful, swollen right leg. She was otherwise in good health. On physical examination, her right leg was seen to be 1½ times the size of her left leg. The right calf was tender and there was pitting edema in that leg.

STUDIES	RESULTS
Routine laboratory work	Within normal limits (WNL)
Doppler ultrasound and plethysmographic venous studies	Occlusion of the deep venous system in the right thigh and calf (normal: no occlusion)
Venography	Same as venous studies just discussed
^{125}I fibrinogen uptake test	Increased nuclear activity in the right thigh and calf compatible with thrombophlebitis (normal: no increased uptake)

The diagnosis of acute deep-vein thrombophlebitis was made. The patient was immediately placed on heparin therapy. After full anticoagulation, she was switched to warfarin (Coumadin) (see heparin and warfarin monitoring, p. 236-237). She was discharged from the hospital on warfarin (Coumadin) therapy and prothrombin time monitoring. After 4 months, the warfarin (Coumadin) was discontinued.

3

Diagnostic studies used to evaluate the stomach and intestines

ANATOMY AND PHYSIOLOGY OF THE STOMACH AND INTESTINES

The primary function of the gastrointestinal (GI) tract is twofold. The first function is digestion (modification of consumed foods to a form that may be used by body cells). The second function of the GI tract is to eliminate waste products from the body. The organs of the GI tract form a tube extending from the mouth to the anus. The following organs comprise the GI tract: mouth, pharynx, esophagus, stomach, and intestines (Fig. 3-1).

Food enters the *mouth* and then passes through the *pharynx* to the esophagus. The *esophagus* is a 10- to 15-inch-long muscular tube that moves food by synchronous contractions through the chest cavity and into the stomach. There is a sphincter valvelike muscle (lower esophageal sphincter) at the end of the esophagus that prevents stomach acid and food from backing up into the esophagus.

The *stomach* is a J-shaped organ that stores food and secretes acids and enzymes (hydrochloric acid and pepsinogen), which mix with the food to begin the process of digestion.

Partially digested food (chyme) is expelled from the stomach and into the *small intestine,* which is a tube about 20 feet in length and 1 inch in diameter. Its coiled loops fill most of the abdomen. The small intestine is divided into three sections: the duodenum, the jejunum, and the ileum. The *duodenum* is the uppermost division and this is connected to the stomach (Fig. 3-1). As digestion of food is completed and absorption of the food products takes place, the chyme successively moves through the duodenum, the *jejunum,* and the *ileum* and into the large intestine.

The *large intestine* (colon) is the lower part of the GI tract. It is called "large" because its average diameter is 2½ inches as compared to that of the small intestine (1-inch diameter). The length of the colon is about 5 to 6 feet. The colon is divided into the cecum, ascending colon, transverse colon, descending colon, sigmoid colon, and rectum.

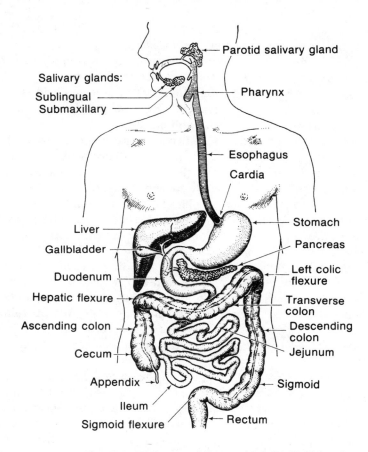

Fig. 3-1. Anatomy of the gastrointestinal tract.

From Schottelius, B.A., and Schottelius, D.D.: Textbook of physiology, St. Louis, The C.V. Mosby Co.

The first 2 to 3 inches of the large intestine is called the *cecum*. The cecum is located in the lower right section of the abdomen. The appendix extends from the lower portion of the cecum (Fig. 3-1). The *ascending colon* lies in a vertical position on the right side of the abdomen, extending upward toward the liver. The ileum joins the large intestine at the junction of the cecum and the ascending colon and there passes its material into the colon.

The *transverse colon* passes horizontally across the abdomen above the small intestine. The colon then descends vertically on the left side of the abdomen (*descending colon*). The final segment of the large intestine is the *sigmoid colon* which forms an S-shaped curve as it dips into the pelvic cavity to become the rectum.

The main function of the colon is to absorb water, secrete mucus, and eliminate waste products. Undigested materials (feces) are moved from the sigmoid colon into the *rectum*. The rectum is a vault at the last 7 to 8 inches of the GI tract that stores feces until they are evacuated from the *anus*.

The gastrointestinal system is frequently afflicted by a variety of diseases resulting in unremitting and bothersome symptoms such as abdominal pain, nausea, vomiting, diarrhea, constipation, and bleeding.

The *esophagus* can be afflicted by tumor or scarring, causing difficulty in swallowing. An inadequate lower esophageal sphincter may cause ulcers and inflammation as a result of abnormal reflux (backup) of stomach acid into the esophagus. On the other hand, a hyperfunctioning lower esophageal sphincter may not allow food to pass, as in patients with achalasia.

The *stomach* is the location of the highest concentration of digestive acids. It is little wonder therefore that this organ is frequently afflicted with peptic ulcers. Tumors and inflammation can also occur within this organ. The stomach is normally located entirely within the abdomen. In some patients, the upper part of the stomach may slide up into the chest cavity. This is called a hiatal hernia. Varices (large distended blood vessels) may occur in both the esophagus and the stomach. These are the result of the diversion of blood from the liver in patients with cirrhosis (most usually induced by excessive alcohol intake).

The *duodenum,* being so close to the acid-producing stomach, is the most common site of peptic ulcers. One must be aware that uncomplicated ulcers usually cause abdominal pain and burning. Occasionally ulcerations may be so severe as to erode a blood vessel, causing the complication of profuse gastrointestinal bleeding. Peptic ulcer erosion may also cause a hole (or perforation) in the stomach or duodenum. Both of these complications are disastrous and usually require surgical repair.

Although the *small intestine* (bowel) represents the greatest surface area of the gastrointestinal tract, it is very unusual to have disease primarily affect this organ. The small bowel does, however, frequently get twisted by abdominal scarring (adhesions). The end result is a complete or partial blockage of the bowel, frequently requiring surgical relief. The small intestine may be primarily infected by viral and flu syndromes, which interrupt the absorptive motility of the gut, causing diarrhea.

Tumor and diverticuli are the most common abnormalities that affect the *large intestine.* A diverticulum is an outpouching of the inner lining of the colon through its muscular wall. These diverticuli can be complicated by inflammation and bleeding. Inflammatory bowel disease (such as ulcerative colitis or Crohn's disease) can afflict this organ, resulting in chronic bloody diarrhea.

Finally the *rectum* and *anus* are the sites of tumors, hemorrhoids, fissures, and fistulas, all of which can create pain and bleeding.

It is the purpose of accurate diagnostic testing to identify, locate, and recognize the diseases affecting the GI tract so that appropriate and effective therapy can be instituted as soon as possible.

X-RAY STUDIES
Upper gastrointestinal series (UGI, upper GI)
Normal values

Complete and uniform filling of the esophagus, stomach, and duodenum.

Purpose

The upper GI consists of a series of x-ray films used to outline the lower esophagus, stomach, and duodenum. The purpose of this examination is to detect ulceration (Fig. 3-2), tumor, inflammation, or malposition (such as hiatal hernia) of these organs. Upper GIs are sometimes repeated to follow the healing process of ulcers.

Procedure

For this study the patient will not be able to eat or drink anything (NPO) after midnight before the test. No breakfast is permitted on the morning of the test. In the x-ray department, the patient will be asked to drink about 8 ounces of barium sulfate, which is a white chalky substance that is ingested in a "milkshake" consistency. It is usually flavored to increase its palatability. While on the x-ray table, the patient is asked to lie in several positions (such as on the abdomen, side, and back). These positional changes promote the flow of barium through the entire upper GI tract. The physician follows the barium flow with fluoroscopy (motion picture x-rays) and carefully looks for any abnormalities. "Still" x-ray pictures are

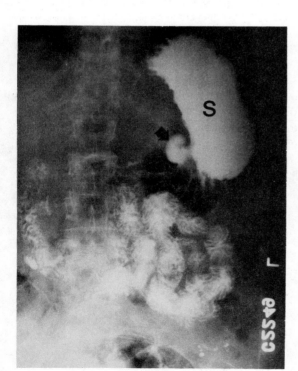

Fig. 3-2. Upper gastrointestinal series demonstrating an ulcer (black arrow) on the lesser curvature of the stomach (S).

taken intermittently for later review. When these permanent "still" pictures are taken, the patient is asked to hold his or her breath for a few moments.

Often the physician will want to follow the progression of barium through the entire small intestine. This is called a *small bowel follow-through*. For this study the patient is asked to drink additional barium mixed with saline (salt water). X-ray films are taken at timed intervals, varying from 30 minutes to 24 hours. A delay in the transit time of barium may occur with a small bowel obstruction. The barium flow may be faster in most of the diarrhea states (such as malabsorption). Small bowel follow-through studies are also helpful in identifying small bowel fistulas (abnormal connections between the small bowel and other abdominal organs or skin).

Upper GIs should not be performed if the patient is known to have a perforation (hole) in the bowel because an intense inflammatory reaction with subsequent abscess formation would occur if barium were allowed to leak out of the perforated intestine. To avoid this complication, diatrizoate methylglucamine (Gastrografin) is used when perforation is suspected. Gastrografin is water soluble and can be absorbed and eventually excreted in the urine. Upper GIs should also not be done if one has a complete bowel obstruction because the barium would not be able to progress through the intestines and would ultimately cause impaction of stool within the bowel.

Pertinent facts

- The patient must not eat or drink anything (NPO) after the midnight before the study. Food and fluid in the stomach will prevent the barium from accurately outlining the GI tract.
- There is no real discomfort with this study except for that of lying on a hard x-ray table.
- This study is performed by a radiologist (physician specializing in the interpretation of x-rays) in approximately 30 minutes. Of course the duration of the test is longer if small bowel follow-through is to be performed.
- After this study one can resume a normal diet.
- After this study the patient should check the color of the stools. They are usually light colored until all of the barium is expelled. This is important because one could become seriously constipated if the barium is retained in the bowel for a prolonged period of time (5 to 10 days). Increasing the intake of fluids will usually help. Occasionally a mild laxative or an enema may be required to prevent this complication.
- The customary cost of this test is about $75.

Barium swallow
Normal values

Uniform and consistent filling of the entire esophagus.

Purpose

This barium x-ray study provides a more thorough study of the esophagus than that provided by most upper GIs (see previous study). This study is useful in the detection of tumors, strictures (narrowing), and varicosities in the esophagus. Anatomic abnormalities (such as hiatal hernia) are easily detected. Motility abnormalities (such as achalasia and diffuse esophageal spasm) can also be detected (see Anatomy and physiology).

Procedure

The procedure for this study is similar to that of the upper GI (previous study). One cannot eat or drink after midnight on the day of this study. The patient will be given approximately 4 ounces of a flavored barium solution to drink. X-rays will be taken from the front and sides while the patient is standing. The flow of barium is followed by fluoroscopy.

This study is contraindicated if there is suspicion of esophageal perforation (see previous study).

Pertinent facts

• This study is not uncomfortable and is performed by a radiologist (x-ray physician) in approximately 15 minutes.
• The customary cost of this study is about $65.
• See Pertinent facts of the previous study.

Barium enema (BE, lower gastrointestinal series)
Normal values

Complete and uniform filling of the large intestine.

Purpose

The barium enema (BE) x-ray study consists of a series of x-ray films that visualize the inside of the colon (large intestine). Polyps (benign tumors) and cancers are readily identified by this test. Any extrinsic, noncolonic tumor or abscess (collection of pus) compressing the bowel will also be detected. Diverticula (pouches formed by protrusion of the inner lining of the bowel through the outer muscular coat of the intestines) are commonly seen (Fig. 3-3). When a diverticulum becomes infected, diverticulitis results, and this also has an appearance on barium enema. Certain forms of colitis (for example, ulcerative colitis or Crohn's disease) can be identified. The normal position of the colon is altered in children with malrotation of the intestines and in adults with volvulus. A barium enema is often used to document these problems.

Procedure

A specific preparation for a barium enema varies with each x-ray department. A typical preparation is shown below:

The day preceding the barium enema
Clear liquids for lunch and supper (no dairy products)
One glass of water or clear fluids every hour during an 8- to 10-hour period
One full bottle (10 oz) of magnesium citrate or X-Prep (potent laxatives) at 2 P.M.

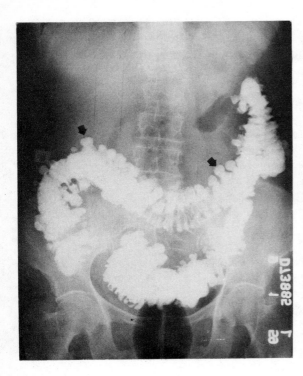

Fig. 3-3. Barium enema demonstrating multiple diverticula (arrows) in the colon.

Three bisacodyl (Dulcolax) tablets (another potent laxative) at 7 P.M.

Nothing by mouth (NPO) after midnight

The day of the barium enema

Nothing by mouth (NPO)

Enemas until the lower intestines are completely empty of all waste; that is, clear return of enema fluid

When the patient arrives in the x-ray department for this test, he or she will be given an enema containing approximately 2 to 6 cups of liquid barium sulfate. Because many patients have difficulty retaining this barium, an inflatable balloon is attached to the enema tubing and is inflated to prevent defecation. While lying on the hard x-ray table, the patient is instructed to move into various positions (stomach, back, sides) to facilitate the flow of barium through the intestine. The radiologist (the x-ray physician) follows the progress of the barium flow by fluoroscopy (motion picture x-ray images displayed on a television monitor). "Still" x-ray pictures are taken at the physician's discretion. The accuracy of the BE is increased when air is insufflated (blown into) the colon for contrast to the barium. In this study, after the bowel mucosa is outlined with barium, air is pumped into the enema tubing to enhance the outline of small lesions.

After the x-ray films are taken, the patient will be taken to a bathroom and asked to expel the barium. This may take as long as 30 minutes. After the barium is evacuated, another x-ray film is taken.

Barium cannot be used if a perforation (hole) in the bowel is suspected. If barium were to leak out of a perforated organ, an intense inflammatory reaction would occur. When a perforation is suspected, the radiologist will use a less reactive, water soluble solution (such as Gastrografin) instead of the barium sulfate.

Pertinent facts

- The preparation for this test must be strictly followed. The bowels must be free of fecal debris for the barium to accurately outline the bowel. Pieces of feces may be misinterpreted as colonic tumors.
- No eating or drinking is permitted after midnight. Food or fluid in the bowel will prevent optimal visualization of the bowels.
- The patient may want to take reading material to the X-ray department so he or she can read while attempting to evacuate the barium.
- The entire study is a little more uncomfortable than a regular enema. Some patients experience "gas pains" when air is pumped into the bowel.
- This test is performed by a radiologist in approximately 45 minutes.
- After this study, one can usually resume a normal diet. The patient should drink plenty of fluids to replace the liquid lost during the induced diarrhea before the test.
- After the test, the color of the stools (feces) should be checked. The stools will be light in color until all the barium is expelled. This is vitally important because one could become seriously constipated if barium is retained for a prolonged period of time (5 to 10 days). One may even require an enema or a laxative to remove all of the barium.
- One may need to rest after the test because the bowel-cleansing preparation is exhausting for many people, especially the elderly.
- After the test, a warm bath may be soothing for any anal discomfort caused by the test.
- The customary cost of this study is about $80.

ENDOSCOPY PROCEDURES
Gastroscopy (upper GI endoscopy)
Normal values

Normal appearing stomach and duodenum.

Purpose

This procedure allows the physician to directly visualize the esophagus, stomach, and duodenum by passing a long, flexible, lighted instrument (gastroscope) into the upper gastrointestinal tract. These organs are inspected for tumor, polyps, ulcers, inflammations, hiatal hernia, abnormally enlarged blood vessels (varices), obstructions, or ongoing bleeding.

The gastroscope has several channels through which cable-activated instruments can be inserted. With these instruments, the physician can sample abnormal tissues (biopsy), remove polyps, and even control any ongoing bleeding. Camera equipment can easily be attached to the viewing lens so that photographs can be taken.

Procedure

The patient will not be able to eat or drink anything (NPO) after midnight on the evening before the test. In the endoscopy room the patient will be positioned on a table lying on the left side. The patient will be sedated with diazepam (Valium). The patient will not be put to sleep but will feel very drowsy. Atropine will be given to decrease oral secretions. The throat will then be anesthetized (numbed) with a lidocaine (Xylocaine) spray to eradicate any gag reflex and to allow the gastroscope to pass more easily. The scope is then carefully inserted into the mouth, the esophagus, the stomach, and the duodenum while the physician is looking through the scope. Air is usually pumped into the tubing to widen the inner lumen of the gut and thereby allow better visualization.

This study frequently is not performed if voluminous bleeding is occurring in the upper GI tract. The viewing lens would be covered with blood thereby precluding adequate visualization. Gastroscopy is also not performed on anyone with abnormal esophageal diverticula (outpouching) of the esophageal wall because the scope could easily fall into the diverticulum and perforate the esophagus. Even when the upper GI tract is normal, the scope could perforate. This is a rare yet disastrous complication that nearly always requires surgical repair. Other complications may include:

1. Bleeding from the site of a biopsy
2. Regurgitation and subsequent inhalation of gastric contents into the lung, causing a severe pneumonia
3. Cessation of breathing caused by oversedation

These complications are rare. Gastroscopy is routinely performed safely and accurately.

Pertinent facts

- No eating or drinking (NPO) is permitted after midnight to ensure optimal visualization of the stomach and to preclude regurgitation of food.
- This study is not painful but may cause discomfort and gagging. The patient, however, will be sedated before the test.
- Dentures and glasses are removed before the test.
- One will be unable to talk when the scope is in the gastrointestinal tract.
- This procedure is performed by a physician in 30 minutes.
- After the study one should not eat or drink anything for about 2 to 4 hours until sensation in the throat returns. Otherwise one could choke on food or fluid.
- When the anesthesia wears off, the voice may be hoarse and one may complain of a sore throat for several days. Drinking cool fluids and gargling may relieve some of this soreness.
- For a short while after the study, one will be checked frequently for abdominal pain, and the blood pressure, temperature, pulse, and respirations will be monitored to detect any complications.
- If the patient is having this study done as an outpatient, he or she should not operate any moving vehicles until the effect of the sedation has worn off. Another adult should drive.
- The approximate cost for this study, including the physician's fee, is about $350.

Colonoscopy
Normal values

Normal appearance of the inner lining of the colon and rectum.

Purpose

Through the use of the flexible fiberoptic colonoscope, the physician can examine the entire colon (from the anus to the rectum). Colonoscopy allows the physician to visualize the inner lining of the colon far beyond the 10 inches of the colon and rectum usually seen by sigmoidoscopy (see next study). With this study the entire large intestine is examined for tumor, ulcers, inflammation, and bleeding. The colonoscope has several channels through which cable-activated instruments can be passed. Through these channels, small pieces of abnormal tissue can be removed (biopsy) for microscopic examination.

The colonoscopic examination cannot be performed if one is bleeding heavily because the physician's vision will be diminished by the blood within the colon. Perforation of the bowel and persistent bleeding from biopsy sites are rare complications of this test. However, when they occur, the situation is serious and surgical repair is usually required. Oversedation, causing cessation of breathing, is another reported yet rare complication.

Procedure

For this examination the bowels must be completely free of fecal material. Bowel cleaning regimens may vary. A typical one is listed below:

Two days before examination

Clear liquid diet is continued.

One day before examination

Clear liquid diet is continued.

Sodium biphosphate (Fleet's Phospho-Soda) is given before lunch.

Four bisocodyl (Dulcolax) tablets are given as laxatives after dinner.

Fluids are forced to avoid dehydration from diarrhea.

Day of examination

No food or fluid is allowed (NPO).

A soapsuds enema is given. If the return is not clear, a repeat enema with tap water is administered.

Before going to the endoscopy room for this study, the patient will receive injections of meperidine (Demerol) for sedation and atropine to dry up secretions. Once in the endoscopy room, an intravenous infusion (IV) is established and further medications, such as diazepam (Valium) for sedation and meperidine (Demerol) to relieve discomfort, are administered intravenously. The patient is placed on the left side and the scope is slowly inserted. Air is pumped through the scope to distend the bowel for better visualization. The scope is maneuvered through the entire lower intestine.

Pertinent facts

• The bowel-cleansing regimen must be carefully followed to allow for adequate visualization of the bowel.

- During the test, the patient will be properly draped with sheets to avoid unnecessary embarrassment.
- Most patients will describe this study as being uncomfortable. Adequate sedation will be provided.
- When air is pumped into the bowel, one may experience "gas pains."
- This study is performed by a physician in about 1 hour.
- After this study, one can resume a normal diet. Fluids should be forced to avoid dehydration caused by the preparation-induced diarrhea and fasting.
- The patient must have plenty of rest after this study. The cleansing regimen, fasting, and the medications used during this study tire the patient considerably.
- One cannot drive until the effect of the sedation has worn off.
- A warm bath is very soothing after this examination.
- The approximate cost of this procedure is about $450.

Sigmoidoscopy
Normal values

Normal appearing anus, rectum, and sigmoid colon.

Purpose

This procedure allows the physician to directly visualize the lower 10 inches of the larger intestine. Through this rigid scope, the physician can detect and biopsy tumors, polyps, and ulcers of the anus, rectum, and the sigmoid colon. *Proctoscopy* refers to examination of only the anus and rectum (about 5 inches). *Sigmoidoscopy,* which is most often performed, refers to examination of the anus, rectum, and the sigmoid colon.

The study is not performed on patients with large amounts of rectal bleeding because bleeding inhibits adequate visualization through the scope. Complications such as perforation of the colon and rectum do occur but are very rare.

Procedure

The patient will be given an enema on the night before and on the morning of the procedure. A light breakfast is usually allowed. Sigmoidoscopy is usually performed in a special room containing all necessary equipment (endoscopy room). It can also be performed at the bedside or in a doctor's office. Examination is carried out with the patient kneeling in a knee-chest position or with the patient lying on the left side with the buttocks slightly over the edge of the bed to facilitate rotation of the scope. Maximum convenience is afforded by using a special table called a "sigmoidoscopy table," which tilts the patient in the required position. The procedure begins with the physician using a finger to examine the rectum and slowly dilating the anal sphincter. Sedation is usually not required. The well-lubricated scope is then gently passed into the rectum and maneuvered to the desired depth. Air is pumped into the bowel through the scope to distend the bowel, thus providing better visualization of the colon and rectum.

Pertinent facts

- The enemas given before the study are important for cleansing the bowel so that visualization is adequate.

- No sedation is given with this study. Some discomfort and the urge to defecate will occur as the scope is passed. "Gas pains" may be experienced as air is pumped into the bowel.
- During the test the patient will be draped with sheets to prevent unnecessary exposure and embarrassment.
- Sigmoidoscopy is performed by the physician in approximately 15 minutes.
- After this study the patient can resume a normal diet.
- A warm bath is very soothing after this examination.
- The approximate cost of this procedure is about $60.

BLOOD TESTS
Carcinoembryonic antigen (CEA)
Normal values

Less than 2 ng/ml.

Purpose

CEA is a protein found to exist in the blood of patients who have certain types of cancer (such as cancer of the colon, rectum, stomach, pancreas, or breast). More recently it has been found to also exist in patients who have noncancerous disease (such as cirrhosis of the liver, ulcerative colitis, and diverticulosis). The CEA test is most commonly used to monitor the response of cancer patients to therapy. Elevated CEA levels are found to return to normal after complete surgical removal of a tumor. The increase or decrease in CEA level is an indication of progression or remission of a cancer, respectively. A rise in the CEA level is often the first sign of tumor recurrence. Therefore this study is invaluable in the follow-up of patients who have had certain types of cancer. There are many benign diseases that may also cause elevation of this protein. It is therefore not an adequate screening test for cancer. Smokers without any disease are often noted to have a fictitious elevation of CEA.

Procedure

A vein in the arm is punctured with a needle and approximately 2 teaspoons of blood is collected.

Pertinent facts

- The only discomfort associated with this study is a needle stick.
- The customary cost of this study is about $17.

Serum gastrin level
Normal values

40 to 150 pg/ml.

Purpose

This study measures the level of gastrin in the blood stream. Gastrin is a hormone produced in the stomach that stimulates the secretion of gastric acid.

Gastrin levels are mildly increased in patients with stomach ulcers and pernicious anemia and in patients who have had ulcer surgery. The gastrin level is extremely high in people with Zollinger-Ellison (ZE) syndrome (a gastrin-secreting tumor of the pancreas). Patients with ZE syndrome frequently have aggressive and complicated peptic ulcer disease requiring radical surgery. Patients whose peptic ulcers are not the result of ZE syndrome will have a normal serum gastrin level.

Procedure

A vein in the arm is punctured with a needle and approximately 2 teaspoons of blood is collected.

Pertinent facts

• The only discomfort associated with this study is a needle stick.
• The customary cost of this study is about $29.

STOOL TESTS
Stool for occult blood
Normal values

Negative.

Purpose

For this study the stool (feces) is examined for the presence of minute quantities of occult (hidden) blood. The most common cause of occult blood in the stool is a benign or malignant tumor within the gastrointestinal (GI) tract. As tumors grow in the intestines, they are subjected to repeated trauma by the fecal stream. Eventually the tumors ulcerate and bleed. This bleeding is usually minute and occult.

Occult blood in the feces can also be caused by an ulcer or inflammation anywhere along the GI tract. Even swallowed blood from a nosebleed can cause occult blood within the stool.

Procedure

It is best if the patient refrains from eating red meat for 3 days before stool testing. Red meat contains blood, which could fictitiously indicate the presence of occult blood in the stool. Stool is obtained either by asking the patient to save a stool specimen in a container or by digital examination. For digital retrieval, the physician or nurse inserts a gloved fingertip into the rectum to remove a fecal specimen. When a stool specimen is obtained at home, a small quantity of stool is smeared onto a hemoccult slide provided by the physician. The slide is sent by mail to the doctor's office. There it is processed. A special developing solution is placed on the specimen. Bluish discoloration indicates the presence of occult blood within the stool. False negatives are common, and for that reason one cannot rely completely on this test to detect ulcers or tumors in the GI tract.

Pertinent facts

• The patient should find out how many stool specimens are needed and obtain the proper number of specimen containers. Only a small amount of feces is needed.
• The stool specimen must not be contaminated with urine.
• The customary cost of this test is about $6.

SPECIAL STUDIES
Gastric analysis
Normal values

BAO: 2-5 mEq/hr.
MAO: 10-20 mEq/hr.

Purpose

For this study a tube is inserted into the stomach to determine the amount of stomach acid produced during a resting state (basal acid output, BAO) and during a stimulated state (maximal acid output, MAO). This information is useful for the following reasons:

1. To determine the location and type of ulcer. Normal or low-normal acid levels are thought to indicate a gastric (stomach) ulcer, whereas increased acid levels are indicative of duodenal ulcers. A gastric ulcer that occurs in an acid-free environment is usually a malignant (cancerous) ulcer.

2. To identify the presence of Zollinger-Ellison (ZE) syndrome. In this disease, a pancreatic tumor secretes an abundant amount of gastrin, which then stimulates the stomach to secrete acid. Therefore the stomach is never found in the resting state. In this disease, the basal acid output (BAO) level approximates the maximal acid output (MAO) level. This persistently high acid level causes serious and complicated peptic ulcer disease. Frequently, aggressive and extensive surgery is required to adequately care for this serious form of peptic ulcer disease.

3. To determine the effectiveness of antipeptic ulcer therapy. Effective medical and surgical treatment must substantially decrease the amount of acid in the stomach. Gastric analysis is performed before and after ulcer treatment. Effective therapy is indicated by a 50% reduction in the quantity of acid produced.

The usefulness of this test is now questionable in light of more recently developed and more accurate tests designed to provide similar information.

Procedure

For this study, the patient must not eat or drink anything after the midnight before the study. A nasogastric (NG) tube is inserted through the nose and into the stomach. A large syringe is attached to the NG tube and the stomach contents are withdrawn by syringe suction (aspiration). Four samples are aspirated at 15-minute intervals and placed in specimen containers, which are sent to the laboratory for BAO analysis. The patient will then receive an injection of a drug (for example, histamine or pentagastrin) that will maximally stimulate the acid output in the stomach. Eight specimens will then be aspirated at 15-minute intervals to determine MAO. The NG tube is removed after all the specimens are acquired. Patients with cardiac disease and hypertension should receive decreased doses of the acid-stimulating drug. Patients with allergies are not given histamine as this may aggravate any allergic reaction.

Pertinent facts

- Except for the initial gagging associated with the insertion of the NG tube, this test is not uncomfortable.
- One should not eat or drink anything (NPO) after midnight before the study. Food or fluid will alter gastric acid secretion and confuse the test results.
- One should not smoke the day of the study because nicotine stimulates gastric acid secretion.
- While the study is being performed, the patient should expectorate (spit out) saliva into a basin because saliva will neutralize the acid content of the stomach.
- When the histamine or pentagastrin is injected, the patient may experience flushing, increase in skin temperature, and itching. Usually the pulse rate (heart rate) will increase slightly and the blood pressure will decrease slightly.
- This study is performed by a nurse in about 3 hours.
- After this test the patient may resume a regular diet.
- The approximate cost of this study is $100.

Esophageal function studies
Normal values

Lower esophageal sphincter (LES) pressure: 10-20 mm Hg (mercury).
Swallowing pattern: normal, progressive peristaltic waves.
Acid reflux: negative.
Acid clearing: less than ten swallows.
Bernstein test: negative.

Purpose

For esophageal function studies the patient will be asked to swallow three thin spaghetti-like tubes to determine the above listed studies. Each is discussed separately below.

Lower esophageal sphincter (LES) pressure. The lower esophageal sphincter (LES) is a valve between the esophagus (swallowing tube) and the stomach. Normally this valve prevents reflux of stomach acid contents into the esophagus. When the LES pressure is abnormally diminished, stomach acid can flow from the stomach and into the esophagus. A bitter taste or heartburn may be experienced by the patient. This disorder is called "gastroesophageal reflux" in the adult and "chalasia" in infants.

If, on the other hand, sphincter pressure is increased, as in patients with achalasia, food cannot pass easily into the stomach. These patients have difficulty in swallowing and feel as though food "gets stuck" in the midchest area.

Swallowing pattern. Normal swallowing requires synchronous and propulsive waves of muscle contraction in the esophagus. The pattern of these waves are recorded on a graph. Asynchrony of these swallowing waves occur in patients with "diffuse esophageal spasm."

Acid reflux. Stomach acid reflux is the primary component of "gastroesophageal reflux." Patients who have an incompetent LES will regurgitate stomach acid into the esophagus. This acid is measured by a fourth tube (pH probe), which is placed into the esophagus.

Acid clearing. Normally patients can completely clear an acid solution from the esophagus in less than 10 swallows. Patients with decreased esophageal motility (for example, achalasia) require a greater number of swallows to clear the acid.

Bernstein test. This test is simply an attempt to reproduce symptoms of gastroesophageal reflux. If a patient complains of discomfort (similar to the original complaints) when an artificial acid solution is placed in the esophagus, the test is considered positive.

Procedure

For this study one may not eat or drink anything after midnight before the test. The patient will probably be taken to a specially equipped room that contains appropriate instrumentation for this study. The patient will then be asked to swallow three very thin tubes (Fig. 3-4). The other ends of the tubes are connected to a special machine that records and measures pressures. First, the *lower esophageal sphincter (LES) pressure* measured. Then with all tubes in the esophagus, the patient is asked to swallow. With normal esophageal contraction, the *swallowing wave pattern* will be recorded as a successive rapid rise and fall in pressure.

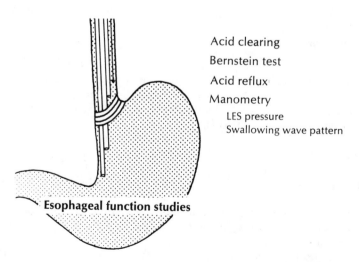

Acid clearing
Bernstein test
Acid reflux
Manometry
  LES pressure
  Swallowing wave pattern

Esophageal function studies

Fig. 3-4. Esophageal function studies demonstrating placement of the manometry tubes and pH probe within the esophagus.

The tubes are then advanced into the stomach and the patient is asked to swallow a fourth tube (pH indicator) into the esophagus. The stomach will then be filled with approximately one third of a cup of dilute hydrochloric acid. If *gastroesophageal reflux* occurs, acid will be detected by the pH indicator within the esophagus. Next, all the tubes are returned to the esophagus. Dilute hydrochloric acid is instilled through them. *Acid clearing* is determined by counting the number of swallows necessary to completely clear the acid from the esophagus. Finally, the *Bernstein test* is performed by alternately instilling hydrochloric acid and water through the tubes into the esophagus. The patient will not be told which solution is being infused. If one complains of discomfort while the acid is infusing, it is considered a positive Bernstein test. If the patient does not recognize any discomfort, the Bernstein test is considered negative. The tubes are then removed and the test is completed. A normal diet is allowed after this test.

Pertinent facts

- Surprisingly the entire study is not uncomfortable despite some initial gagging when these tubes are swallowed.
- The patient cannot eat or drink (NPO) after midnight before the test because one could inhale regurgitated stomach contents into the lungs during the study and thereby cause a severe pneumonia.
- One should not take any sedatives before the test because patient cooperation is essential. Swallowing and sphincter pressures can be affected by sedation.
- This study is performed by a technician in about 30 minutes.
- The customary cost of this study is about $60.

Sample case report: colon cancer

An 85-year-old man with previously normal bowel function began to complain of constipation, rectal bleeding, and pencil-like stool. The results of the physical examination were negative.

STUDIES	RESULTS
Routine laboratory testing	Normal except for a decreased hemoglobin and hematocrit
Examination of stool for occult blood	Positive
Carcinoembryonic antigen (CEA) test	33 ng/ml
Sigmoidoscopy	No tumor seen
Barium enema (BE) study	Stricture or narrowing in the left side of the colon
Colonoscopy	Tumor in the left side of the colon
Colonoscopic biopsy	Adenocarcinoma

The elevated CEA level and the occult blood in the stool indicated serious colon or rectal disease. Because the sigmoidoscopy was normal, the disease was suspected to being beyond the reach of the sigmoidoscope. The barium enema study demonstrated narrowing in the left side of the colon, which could have been caused by infection, infestation, or neoplasm. Adenocarcinoma of the colon was diagnosed by means of the biopsy done during colonoscopy. The patient had surgery to resect the left side of his colon. After surgery his CEA level returned to normal. On examination 3 years later, no evidence of disease was found.

4

Diagnostic studies used to evaluate the liver, gallbladder, bile ducts, and pancreas

ANATOMY, PHYSIOLOGY, AND DISEASES THAT AFFECT THE LIVER, GALLBLADDER, BILE DUCTS, AND PANCREAS

The liver, gallbladder, bile ducts, and pancreas are listed together because of their anatomic proximity (Fig. 4-1), their closely related functions, and the similar symptoms caused by the diseases that affect these organs.

The liver is the largest gland in the body and occupies most of the space in the right upper part of the abdomen. The primary functions of the liver are:

1. Formation and excretion of bile. *Bile* is a collective term that includes bile salts, bilirubin, and other digestive materials. *Bile salts* mix with ingested fatty foods to provide absorption of fat from the gastrointestinal tract. *Bilirubin* is an example of the excretory products of the liver. After red blood cells are about 120 days old, they are destroyed. The spleen is the major organ that destroys these aged blood cells. Within the red blood cell is a substance called hemoglobin. The heme (oxygen-carrying) portion of the hemoglobin is broken down and chemically modified to form bilirubin. Breakdown and modification occur within the liver. Jaundice is the yellow discoloration of the skin caused by abnormally high blood levels of bilirubin. There are many diseases that result in jaundice (discussed later).
2. Modification and storage of ingested carbohydrates, protein, and fats.
3. Normal breakdown of many endogenous (within the body) substances such as hormones.
4. Detoxification and breakdown of a variety of ingested drugs.
5. Formation of several important factors involved in blood clotting.
6. Filtration and detoxification of many commonly occurring harmful substances that normally exist within the body.

The gallbladder and bile ducts are collectively termed the "biliary system." The bile ducts are separated into hepatic, cystic, and common bile ducts (Fig. 4-1). These are the conduits through which bile flows into the gastrointestinal sys-

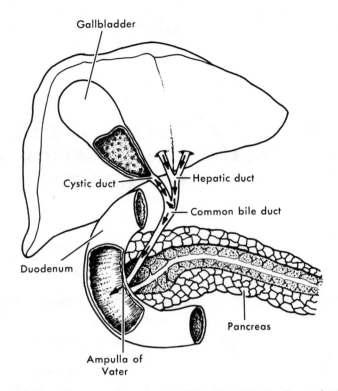

Fig. 4-1. Normal anatomy of the liver, gallbladder, bile ducts, and pancreas.

From Given, B.A., and Simmons, S.J.: Gastroenterology in clinical nursing, St. Louis, The C.V. Mosby Co.

tem for excretion. Bile leaves the liver, where it is made, via the right and left hepatic ducts. It then flows via the cystic duct to the gallbladder where it is stored. When fatty food is ingested, bile salts within the bile are required for digestion. The gallbladder then contracts, and bile flows through the cystic duct and into the common bile duct. The common bile duct carries the bile through the substance of the pancreas and enters the upper part of the small intestine (duodenum). There is a sphincter of Oddi that surrounds the common bile duct at the point it enters the duodenum. This sphincter is hormonally controlled to regulate bile flow into the gut.

The most common disorder associated with the biliary system is gallstones. Gallstones are a result of precipitation of bile within the gallbladder. This precipitation forms a small nidus (nucleus), around which more and more bile crystals will gather and finally form a stone. These gallstones can lodge within the cystic duct and thereby prevent the excretion of bile from the gallbladder. When the patient eats fatty food, the gallbladder contracts against the obstructing stone, and colicky pain is experienced. If the exit of the gallbladder is blocked long enough, the gallbladder can become inflamed, resulting in acute cholecystitis. Symptoms of this condition usually include right upper abdominal pain, nausea, and vomiting.

Gallstones can sometimes leave the gallbladder via the cystic duct and become lodged within the common bile duct. The excretion of bile into the gastrointestinal tract can be blocked off. In this situation, the patient will become jaundiced (yellow). Tumors within the gallbladder, bile ducts, pancreas, or duodenum also can obstruct the outflow of bile from the liver. This too will cause jaundice. Occasionally, the liver itself can be the cause of jaundice. A diseased liver cannot excrete the bile into the hepatic ducts fast enough, and jaundice results. Hepatitis is the most common example of primary liver disease. Tumors that spread into the liver also can interrupt the normal function of the liver and result in inadequate excretion of bile and jaundice. Poor liver function is common in newborn children, in whom the enzymes required for normal bilirubin handling are often not present in adequate quantities. In a short period of time, however, these enzymes do become available, and the jaundice disappears.

The pancreas lies directly adjacent to the stomach and the duodenum (Fig. 4-1). Part of the common bile duct passes directly through the substance of the pancreas. One can see that tumors of the pancreas can easily obstruct the common bile duct and cause jaundice. Like the liver, the pancreas is a complex and multifunctional organ. These functions include (1) the production and secretion of many hormones such as insulin, (2) the production and secretion of many digestive enzymes such as lipase and amylase, and (3) the production and secretion of natural antacids used to neutralize stomach acid. Thousands of little glands within the pancreas excrete their digestive enzymes and neutralizing products into small pancreatic ducts that ultimately lead to one large pancreatic duct. This large pancreatic duct enters the duodenum at about the same area as the common bile duct. This area within the duodenum is known as the ampulla of Vater (Fig. 4-1). In addition to tumors of the pancreas, as previously mentioned, the most common disease affecting this organ is pancreatitis. Pancreatitis is inflammation of the pancreas, which can result from several causes. Alcohol ingestion and blockage of the ducts at the ampulla of Vater by gallstones are the two most common causes of pancreatitis. Pancreatitis results in severe epigastric pain associated with nausea and vomiting. Cysts may also grow from within and around the pancreas. These cysts may be a result of inflammation or tumor.

X-RAYS AND NUCLEAR SCANS
Oral cholecystogram (gallbladder series, GB series)
Normal values

Normal visualization of the gallbladder with no evidence of gallstones.

Purpose

The oral cholecystogram provides x-ray visualization of the gallbladder after ingestion of iodinated x-ray dye tablets. Normal visualization of the gallbladder requires concentration of the dye within the gallbladder. The following factors are necessary to obtain an adequate concentration of dye within the gallbladder for x-ray detection:

1. The patient must take the correct number of tablets (usually 6 tablets).

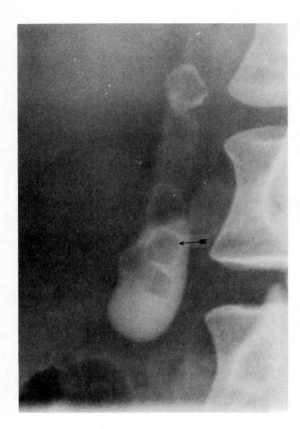

Fig. 4-2. Oral cholecystogram showing gallbladder filled with stones (arrow).

2. There must be adequate absorption of dye from the GI tract. Vomiting or diarrhea will preclude normal absorption.
3. The patient must not eat any fatty meals. Ingestion of a meal that contains a high quantity of fat causes the gallbladder to empty and thereby eliminates the dye from the bile ducts.
4. The liver must be capable of handling and excreting the dye tablets into the gallbladder. Patients with primary liver disorders (such as hepatitis) cannot be expected to excrete the dye into the gallbladder.
5. The cystic duct entering the gallbladder must be patent. Normally the dye is excreted from the liver and through the hepatic ducts (see Anatomy and physiology). It then enters the gallbladder through the cystic duct. A gallstone obstructing the cystic duct (as occurs in an acute gallbladder attack) will prevent the dye from entering the gallbladder.
6. The gallbladder must have the capability of concentrating the dye. A chronically infected and inflamed gallbladder that contains gallstones is unable to concentrate this dye.

On x-ray film taken about 12 hours after the dye tablets are ingested, the gallbladder is seen as a small bag filled with white dye materials. Gallstones are visualized as dark rounded shadows within this gallbladder (Fig. 4-2). Tumors or polyps within the gallbladder occasionally can be seen as similar dark shadows in an otherwise normal dye-filled gallbladder.

If the gallbladder is not visible after the patient has taken the appropriate number of dye pills, the test is often repeated using a double dose of dye. This is to ensure that an adequate amount of dye has been ingested. If after that double dose, the gallbladder still does not appear, one can safely assume that the gallbladder is chronically inflamed as a result of long-standing gallstones. When properly performed, the oral cholecystogram is considered a very accurate and reliable test for indicating gallstones. However, occasionally small gallstones can be missed.

Procedure

On the evening before the test, the patient is given Telepaque (iodine-containing tablets). Usually this is given 1 or 2 hours after eating a low-fat dinner. The patient is allowed only water until bedtime. Thereafter the patient is asked not to eat or drink until the test is completed.

On the morning of the test, the patient goes to the x-ray department. An x-ray technician takes several films of the right upper part of the abdomen. The patient may be asked to lie on his or her back or side. After the initial x-ray, the patient is asked to drink a substance that contains a large quantity of fat. Normally this causes emptying of the gallbladder. X-ray films are then repeated to ensure that the gallbladder has the capability of emptying and expelling the dye. The x-rays are interpreted by a radiologist. There is no need for sedation, and this test can be performed on an outpatient basis. There are no complications associated with this test. The test should not be performed on patients who are known to have iodine allergies. They may develop an allergic reaction to the dye tablets.

Pertinent facts

- The patient should be assured that there is no pain or discomfort associated with this test.
- It is important that the patient follow the instructions carefully to ensure visualization of the gallbladder.
- On the evening before the test, the patient should not eat a fatty meal.
- Approximately 12 hours before the test the patient must ingest six dye tablets. Tablets are taken one at a time at 5-minute intervals. Water can be used to swallow the pills.
- If the patient is known to be allergic to iodine, the physician should be notified before the pills are taken.
- If vomiting or diarrhea occurs after taking the pills, the physician should be notified.
- Fatty meals should be avoided after the pills are taken.
- Some patients may complain of pain on urination following the gallbladder tests. This is a result of urinary excretion of the dye.
- The test takes about 30 minutes to perform.
- The customary cost is approximately $60.

Intravenous cholangiography (IVC)
Normal values

Open bile ducts without evidence of gallstones.

Purpose

In this study intravenous (IV) x-ray dye is excreted by the liver into the bile ducts. In contrast to the oral cholecystogram, in which only the gallbladder is filled, intravenous cholangiography (IVC) allows for visualization of the hepatic and common bile ducts (Fig. 4-1) along with occasional filling of the gallbladder. The IVC is used to demonstrate gallstones, stricture (narrowing), or tumor of the bile ducts. Visualization of the bile ducts does not require concentration of the dye within the gallbladder. Therefore this test is helpful in studying the bile ducts for gallstones in patients who have previously had their gallbladder removed. This is also helpful in patients who cannot tolerate oral administration of the iodine-containing tablets.

Procedure

The day before the examination, laxatives such as bisacodyl (Dulcolax) tablets are given to the patient. A normal diet is allowed. From the midnight before the exam, the patient is asked not to eat or drink anything (NPO). In the morning the patient is taken to the x-ray department and instructed to lie on his or her back. An intravenous injection of iodinated x-ray dye is administered. X-rays are taken of the right upper part of the abdomen at various time periods up to 8 hours. The dye is usually seen in the hepatic ducts and then later in the common bile ducts. Subsequent x-rays will show dye flowing into the duodenum. Duct obstruction caused by stones, stricture, or tumor will interrupt this normal sequence. The study is usually performed on patients who are admitted to the hospital. The study is performed by a radiologist. The test should not be performed on patients who have an allergy to iodine, nor should it be performed on patients who have a diseased liver, which is unable to adequately excrete the dye into the bile ducts.

Pertinent facts

- The test is not associated with any significant discomfort. Minimal pain occurs with the intravenous injection because the dye causes a burning sensation when it is injected.
- It is important that the patient take the laxatives the day preceding this study to preclude the possibility that feces may block visualization of the bile duct.
- The patient should avoid eating or drinking (NPO) after the midnight before the test.
- It is important that any iodine allergy be reported to the physician before the administration of dye.
- The duration of this study can vary anywhere from 1 to 8 hours.
- Some patients report pain on urination after the injection of dye. This is because the kidneys excrete the dye into the urine.
- The customary cost of the procedure is $60.

Operative cholangiography

An operative cholangiogram is performed by injecting the common bile duct with x-ray dye during surgery. Usually this is done during a cholecystectomy (gallbladder removal).

Purpose

The purpose of this test is to see if gallstones have been emptied from the gallbladder into the common bile duct. If stones are found in the common bile duct, the operation must be extended to include removal of the gallstones from the common bile duct. The operative cholangiograph also provides a "road map" of the duct system for the surgeon so that inadvertent injury to the bile ducts can be prevented.

T tube cholangiography
Normal values

No stones in the common bile duct.

Purpose

A **T**-shaped tube is placed in the common duct of patients who require opening of the bile duct for removal of the stones. Before that tube is removed, dye is injected through the end of the T tube that exits the body, and x-rays of the right upper part of the abdomen are taken. If no retained gallstones are evident on this study, the T tube can be safely removed. If there are stones still present in the common bile duct, the tube is left in place with the hope that the stones can be removed through the tube tract.

Procedure

The patient is kept from having anything by mouth (NPO) after midnight on the day of the test. No laxatives are required. In the x-ray department, x-ray dye is injected into the end of the T tube that is outside the body. X-ray pictures are taken as the bile ducts fill with dye.

Pertinent facts

- No discomfort is associated with the test.
- One should be observant for chills and fever after the test. If this occurs, the physician should be notified immediately.
- The duration of this procedure is approximately 15 minutes. There is no need for sedation.
- The test can be performed on outpatients or on in-hospital patients.
- Occasionally a patient may develop a fever as a result of the injection of dye, which may instigate a bile duct infection.
- The customary cost is $50.

Cholescintigraphy (PIPIDA scan or DISIDA scan)
Normal values

No gallstones.

Purpose

Because of the relative inaccuracy of ultrasound and oral cholecystogram in detecting an acutely inflamed gallbladder caused by gallstones, a nuclear material called technetium-99m iminodiacetic acid (PIPIDA or DISIDA) has been recently produced. Shortly after this material is injected into the patient's bloodstream, it is taken up by the liver and excreted into the hepatic duct. From the hepatic duct it flows through the cystic duct and into the gallbladder. Some of it, however, does flow into the common bile duct and into the duodenum. This follows normal bile flow (Fig. 4-1). The flow of this new radionuclear material can be seen with the use of a gamma camera similar to that used in liver scanning. A gamma detector (Geiger counter) is placed over the right upper part of the patient's abdomen. Radionuclear counts are detected and a dynamic representation of the gallbladder and bile ducts is created on a Polaroid or x-ray film.

If the cystic duct is blocked by a gallstone (as occurs in patients with acute gallbladder inflammation), the PIPIDA or DISIDA material will flow into the hepatic ducts, but will not be able to flow through the cystic duct into the gallbladder. This is definite evidence of acute cholecystitis (gallstones). If the visualization of the gallbladder is delayed, this may indicate partial obstruction of the cystic duct from a gallstone or persistent and intermittent low-grade inflammation of the gallbladder (also caused by gallstones). Obstruction of the common bile duct (Fig. 4-1) can also be detected by this study. When the common bile duct is obstructed by gallstones, there appears to be no flow of the PIPIDA or DISIDA material into the duodenum.

Procedure

The patient is asked to refrain from eating and drinking at least 2 hours and preferably longer before the test. The patient is then asked to lie on his or her back and a gamma camera (Geiger counter) is placed over the right upper part of the abdomen. After an intravenous injection of Technetium-labeled PIPIDA or DISIDA, serial scintiphotos are obtained at 1, 5, 30, 45, 60 and 90 minutes. In normal individuals there is visualization of the liver, common bile duct, gallbladder, and duodenum within that time period. However, if any one of these structures is not identified, delayed views up to 4 hours may be obtained. The ability of the gallbladder to contract, which is evidence of gallbladder function, can be evaluated after the ingestion of a fatty meal.

The test is performed in the nuclear medicine department of the hospital. It can be performed on an outpatient or inpatient basis. There should be some reservation to perform this study on a pregnant woman; however, it is not truly considered to be injurious to an unborn child. The test is usually performed by a radionuclear medicine technician and interpreted by a radiologist or nuclear medicine specialist. There is no need for sedation.

Pertinent facts

- The test is not uncomfortable other than the small needle stick associated with the intravenous injection of the radionuclear material.
- The patient is asked to refrain from eating 2 to 4 hours before the test. Because this test is frequently done on patients who have acute abdominal pain, it is common that the patient has not eaten for this period of time.
- The test usually takes about 90 minutes.
- The customary cost of this test is approximately $100.
- It must be recognized that as of this writing, not all hospitals have the capability of performing this test. Soon, however, the test will be widely used in the evaluation of patients for gallstones.

Percutaneous transhepatic cholangiography (PTHC)
Normal values

Open nondilated, nonobstructed bile ducts.

Purpose

By passing a needle through the skin and into the liver, bile ducts can be injected with x-ray dye (Fig. 4-3). Bile ducts and occasionally the gallbladder can be visualized and studied for partial or total obstruction caused by gallstones, benign strictures, cysts, and malignant tumor. Other methods of visualizing the gallbladder and bile ducts require that the patient have normal liver function. This test, however, can be performed in patients whose liver function is severely compromised. This is the definitive test used to elucidate the cause of jaundice in adults. As stated previously, there are many causes for jaundice. These may include bile duct obstruction (gallstones, stricture, or tumor) or primary liver disorder (hepatitis). In the jaundiced patient, if no bile duct obstruction is seen on PTCH, it is safe to conclude that the jaundice is a result of primary liver disorder.

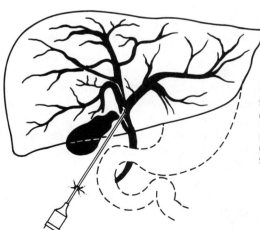

Fig. 4-3. Percutaneous transhepatic cholangiogram (PTHC).

From Given, B.A., and Simmons, S.J.: Gastroenterology in clinical nursing, St. Louis, The C.V. Mosby Co.

Procedure

The patient is asked not to eat or drink after the midnight before the study. An intravenous infusion of water is instituted. Usually the patient is premedicated with sedatives and taken to the x-ray department where he or she is placed lying on the back on an x-ray table. The skin on the upper right hand side of the abdomen is injected with a numbing medication such as lidocaine (Xylocaine). With the use of immediate fluoroscopic x-ray imaging (an x-ray movie machine), a very thin needle is advanced into the liver through which the physician attempts to withdraw bile. The appearance of bile through the needle indicates that a bile duct has been entered. X-ray dye is then injected and x-ray films are immediately taken of the bile ducts.

The test usually takes about 1 hour, during which time the patient is asked to lie still. There are many potential complications associated with this test, such as leakage of bile out of the liver and into the free abdominal cavity. This will cause severe pain and possibly subsequent abscess formation. Also the needle may lacerate a blood vessel, resulting in serious bleeding within the abdomen. Both of these complications may require surgical repair. Finally, a severe infection may result from the injection of dye within an infected bile duct. When the test is performed by an experienced radiologist, these complications are fortunately uncommon. The test should not be performed in patients who have an allergy to iodine. Also, if a patient is known to have abnormal blood clotting ability, the clotting mechanism should be corrected before performing this test. In patients who have recently had an upper GI or a barium enema, the test should be performed only after appropriate bowel cleansing regimens are used. The dye within the gut may interrupt the visualization of the dye within the bile ducts.

Pertinent facts

- Usually this test is not associated with significant pain. Repeated sticks may be required to gain access to the bile ducts, and mild pain may be experienced.
- It is not uncommon to have a minimal amount of blood or bile leak from the liver into the abdominal cavity. As a result, patients frequently may experience some right upper abdominal or shoulder pain.
- Iodine allergies should be reported to the physician before the test.
- Written and informed consent is usually obtained before performance of this test.
- This test is routinely performed on inhospital patients.
- There may be a need for immediate surgical intervention to control hemorrhage or bile leak. It is for that reason that blood is frequently typed and crossed and held ready in case the patient requires transfusion and surgery.
- In a patient whose bile duct is obstructed, frequently a catheter can be placed in the bile duct and used to drain bile from the obstructed bile duct. This can markedly improve the jaundiced patient's medical condition.
- After the test, the patient is usually observed for signs of infection or hemorrhage.
- This test takes about 1 hour.
- The customary cost is $100.

Computerized tomography (CT scan) of the liver, bile ducts, and pancreas
Normal values

Normal appearing liver, bile ducts, and pancreas.

Purpose

Computerized tomography (CT) is a noninvasive yet very accurate x-ray procedure used to diagnose diseases and abnormalities in just about any organ within the body. In this instance we will limit the discussion to the liver, bile ducts, and pancreas. The CT scan has the ability of detecting tumors, cysts, infection (abscess), and abnormal positions of the liver. Dilated bile ducts caused by obstructing tumors or gallstones within the duct can also be detected by this highly accurate recent x-ray development. Tumors, cysts, and inflammation of the pancreas (pancreatitis) can now be easily recognized by computerized tomography. The pancreas is an organ that, before the development of the CT scan, was very difficult to study. As a result, many tumors of the pancreas went unrecognized until the symptoms of pancreatic cancer became unremitting and the chance of cure was near zero. At present we are recognizing this disease earlier in its course. This is primarily because of the development and use of the CT scan.

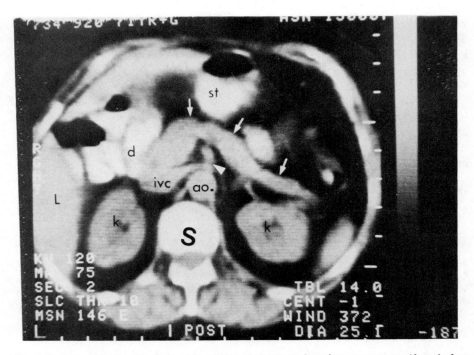

Fig. 4-4. Computerized tomogram of the abdomen showing a cross-sectional view of the abdomen at the level of the pancreas. st, Stomach; d, duodenum (both the stomach and the duodenum contain dye); L, liver; k, kidneys; ivc, inferior vena cava; ao, aorta; S, spine; arrows indicate pancreas.

Computerized tomography produces an image that results from passing x-rays through the patient's abdomen at many angles. The variation in the thickness of each tissue allows for a variable-rate x-ray penetration. The varying rates of x-ray penetration are given a numerical value called a coefficient, which is digitally computed to shades of gray, which are then displayed on a television screen as thousands of dots creating the shades of gray. The final display appears as an actual photograph of the anatomic area sectioned by the x-rays (Fig. 4-4). This study is only two dimensional (that is, front to back), but if one looks at a series of cross-sectional views from the foot to the head, a three-dimensional appearance can be created. This allows one to examine the liver, pancreas, and bile ducts in great detail. Tumor may be represented as a localized mass with a coefficient much different than its native tissue. Inflammation may be demonstrated as an enlarged yet normal appearing organ. Cysts will be demonstrated as a hollow structure within the organ to be examined. The radiation exposure that the patient incurs with this procedure is minimal.

Procedure

Often the patient is kept fasting for 4 hours before the test. Sedation is rarely required and is given only to those patients who cannot remain still during the length of the procedure (especially small children). The patient is taken to the radiology department and is asked to remain motionless while lying on his or her back. Motion will cause blurring and streaking of the final picture, which will inhibit accurate interpretation. An encircling x-ray camera (body scanner) takes pictures at various levels, usually 1 to 4 cm apart. Television equipment allows for immediate display. The images are recorded by a Polaroid type or x-ray type of camera.

Occasionally x-ray dye is administered by mouth or via an enema to opacify the gastrointestinal tract for easier recognition. Frequently an injection of x-ray dye is given to the patient. This assists in delineation of the kidneys from the rest of the organs. As a result, it is important to notify the physician if an iodine allergy exists.

Pertinent facts

- The test is painless. One occasionally feels mildly claustrophobic when asked to lie motionless in the machine.
- The patient should refrain from eating for 4 hours before the test. The dye may cause nausea and vomiting.
- This procedure takes about 30 to 45 minutes to perform.
- It is important to recognize that not all hospitals have computerized tomography machines. Often it is required that patients be transported from one facility to another to have this test performed.
- The customary cost of this is $240.

Liver scan (radioisotope liver scan)
Normal values
Normal size, shape, and position of the liver.

Purpose
This procedure is used to outline and detect any changes within the liver. A minimal dose of a radionuclear material (usually technetium-99 sulfur-labeled albumin colloid) is given intravenously. Later, a gamma-ray detecting device (Geiger counter) is passed over the right upper portion of the abdomen. This records the distribution of the radioactive particles collected within the liver. The spleen can also be visualized by the detector when the technetium-99 sulfur is used. The final result is usually a Polaroid- or x-ray-type picture of the liver and spleen. Abnormalities such as tumor, cyst, hematomas (collection of blood), abscesses, and tubercular granulomas will not take up the nuclear material. The result then is a defect among an otherwise homogeneous uptake of nuclear material within the liver and spleen. Liver enlargement along with cirrhosis and hepatitis can also be demonstrated by this study.

It is important to recognize this scan can only demonstrate abnormalities that are larger than 1 inch in diameter. False negative results can occur in patients with lesions smaller than 2 centimeters. Also this scan can be incorrectly interpreted in patients who have cirrhosis because of the distortions that commonly occur in these people.

Procedure
No special preparation is required. Trace amounts of a radionuclear material are injected intravenously. Thirty minutes later a gamma-ray detecting device (Geiger counter) is slowly passed over the patient's right upper part of the abdomen. The patient is asked to lie on his or her stomach, back, and right and left sides. This allows visualization of all surfaces of the liver. The procedure is performed in the nuclear medicine department by a trained technician. The results are interpreted by a physician specifically trained in nuclear medicine. Because only trace doses of radioisotopes are used, no precautions need be taken against radioactive exposure. This test can be performed on an outpatient basis. A liver scan should not be performed in pregnant women because, although the radionuclear dose is minimal, this may be harmful to an unborn child.

Pertinent facts
- The only discomfort associated with the test is the needle stick required for intravenous injection of the radionucleotide.
- One must remember that the dose of radioisotope is minimal and there should be no fear of radioactive exposure.
- The test takes about 1 hour.
- The customary cost is $70.

ENDOSCOPY
Endoscopic retrograde cholangiopancreatography (ERCP)
Normal values

Normal bile and pancreatic ducts.

Purpose

Like percutaneous transhepatic cholangiography, ERCP is used to inject x-ray dye into the bile ducts. This allows examination of these ducts for evidence of stones, benign strictures, cysts, and malignant tumors. Likewise the pancreatic duct can be injected with x-ray dye and subsequently examined for similar diseases that will affect this organ. This test is especially helpful in detecting the cause of jaundice. If no abnormality within or around the bile duct is detected in the jaundiced patient, one can assume that the problem lies primarily within the liver, and surgery is not indicated. However, if the jaundice is shown to be caused by disease within the bile ducts, surgery is indicated to relieve it.

Procedure

The patient is asked to refrain from eating or drinking (NPO) after the midnight before the day of examination. Commonly the patient is premedicated with

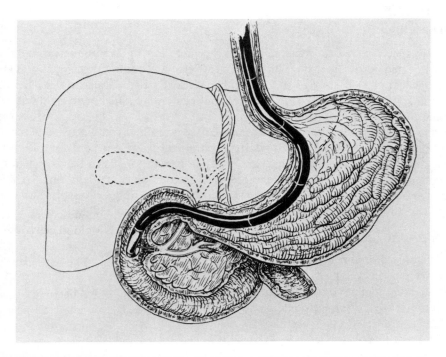

Fig. 4-5. Endoscopic retrograde cholangiopancreatogram (ERCP). The scope is passed through the mouth and down into the duodenum. Note a small catheter being advanced into the pancreatic biliary ducts.

a sedative. The test is usually performed in the x-ray department. A flexible gastroscope (see previous discussion of gastrosopy, p. 39-40) is passed through the mouth into the esophagus, stomach, and duodenum. Through an accessory lumen within the scope, a small catheter is passed into the bile duct or the pancreatic duct (Fig. 4-5). X-ray dye is then injected and x-ray pictures are taken.

As in gastroscopy, the possibility of perforating the esophagus, stomach, and duodenum exists in ERCP. This occurs very rarely. A second complication is serious infection caused by injection of dye into an infected bile duct. Commonly the patient is given an antibiotic before this test in the attempt to avoid infection. The accurate and safe performance of this procedure requires an experienced endoscopist, who is a physician specifically trained to pass the scope and perform this test. ERCP requires significant cooperation from the patient. It should not be performed with patients who are incapable of cooperating with the physician. This test usually requires the patient to be admitted to the hospital.

Pertinent facts

- The test takes about 1 hour. During this time the patient will be asked to lie on his or her back motionless on a hard x-ray table. Remaining still for this period of time is frequently uncomfortable. There is surprisingly little other discomfort associated with this test except for the initial gag that occurs when the endoscope is passed.
- Usually written and informed consent is required before this procedure.
- The patient is premedicated with sedation to more easily tolerate the procedure.
- The patient is frequently monitored after the test to ensure no complications have occurred.
- The customary cost is approximately $125.

BLOOD TESTS
Serum bilirubin test
Normal values

0.1-0.3 mg/dl.

Purpose

Bilirubin is the end product of hemoglobin breakdown. As described in the discussion of anatomy, hemoglobin normally exists within red blood cells. When the red blood cell is over 120 days old, it is usually destroyed by the spleen. The free hemoglobin is then broken down by the liver to bilirubin. The liver excretes this bilirubin as a component of bile. Bile is excreted via the bile ducts into the intestines. Elevation of bilirubin causes the skin and other tissues to become yellow. There are two components to bilirubin, conjugated and unconjugated. Abnormal elevation of bilirubin is a result of one or both of these components. A determination of which of these components is elevated will assist the physician in determining the cause of the jaundice. There are well over 100 diseases that can result in jaundice. Common causes of conjugated bilirubin elevation include obstruction of the bile duct from gallstone or tumor, primary liver disorders (such as hepatitis), or advanced cirrhosis. Common causes of increased levels of unconjugated bilirubin are Rh factor incompatibility in the newborn and congenital enzyme deficiencies.

Procedure

Approximately 1½ teaspoons of blood is withdrawn from a vein in the arm of an adult. In infants, the heel is punctured for the collection of blood. This blood is usually obtained by a laboratory technician. This can be performed on an outpatient in the laboratory or at the bedside.

Pertinent facts

• The only discomfort associated with this test is the needle stick.
• The cost of this study is $12.

Liver enzyme tests
Normal values

Serum glutamic oxaloacetic transaminase (SGOT): 5-40 IU/L.
Serum glutamic pyruvic transaminase (SGPT): 5-35 IU/L.
Lactic dehydrogenase (LDH): 90-200 ImU/ml.
Alkaline phosphatase
  Adults: 30-85 ImU/ml.
  Children and adolescents:
    Less than 2 years: 85-235 ImU/ml.
    2-8 years: 65-210 ImU/ml.
    9-15 years: 60-300 ImU/ml (Active bone growth).
    16-21 years: 30-200 ImU/ml.
5′-Nucleotidase: 0-1.6 Units.

Purpose

The liver is the home of many enzymes. The purpose of these chemicals (enzymes) is to speed up the chemical organic reactions that occur within a cell. These enzymes (SGOT, SGPT, LDH, alkaline phosphatase, and 5′-nucleotidase) are stored and used within the liver cell. Injury or disease affecting the liver cells will cause those cells to die. With cellular death, there is a release of these intracellular enzymes to the bloodstream, creating an abnormal elevation of the enzyme level in the blood. Some of these enzymes are also produced in the cells of organs other than the liver (such as the lung, kidney, and muscle). Injury or disease of these other organs will also cause abnormally elevated blood levels of these enzymes. Therefore although elevation of these enzymes is found in diseases of the liver, it is not specific for the liver alone.

SGOT, SGPT, and LDH. Diseases affecting the liver cell (such as hepatitis or Reye's syndrome) will cause very high serum levels of SGOT, SGPT, and LDH. The alkaline phosphatase and 5′-nucleotidase levels will show only minimal elevation.

LDH and SGOT levels can also be increased when diseases affect the heart, lungs, and kidneys. SGPT, however, is made only in the liver. Unlike LDH and

SGOT then, the SGPT, when elevated, very strongly incriminates the liver as the site of disease. LDH and SGOT are much less specific.

Alkaline phosphatase and 5'-nucleotidase. With obstruction of the bile ducts (caused by tumors, gallstones, structure, cysts, or congenital malformations), the alkaline phosphatase and 5'-nucleotidase levels will increase more than tenfold. The SGOT, SGPT, and LDH, however, will be only minimally elevated. Other diseases (such as dead bowel, bone fractures, or bone tumors) along with normal bone growth in children, can cause elevated levels of alkaline phosphatase. Like SGPT, however, 5'-nucleotidase is located only in the liver cell. Its elevation then incriminates only the liver as the site of disease. Again this is much more specific than alkaline phosphatase. For example, if the patient has obstructive bile ducts, one can expect elevation of alkaline phosphatase and 5'-nucleotidase. If, however, the patient has a bone disorder, only the alkaline phosphatase will be elevated. However, it is possible to fractionate (separate) the components of alkaline phophastase (and for that matter LDH). These different components are called isoenzymes, and each isoenzyme comes from a specific organ. Therefore fractionation of the isoenzymes can differentiate liver disease from other organ disease.

Procedure

A quantity equal to several teaspoons of blood is extracted from a vein in the arm. No special patient preparation is required. This is usually performed by a laboratory technician either at the bedside or in the laboratory. Of course there is no need for sedation before the testing.

Pertinent facts

• The only discomfort associated with this test is the needle stick.
• Many patients who have liver disease also have abnormalities in the blood clotting function. As a result it is important that one ensure adequate control of bleeding at the venous puncture site.
• The cost of this study is approximately $15.

Serum protein tests
Normal values

Total protein: 6-8 g/dl.
Albumin: 3.2-4.5 g/dl.

Purpose

One way to assess liver function is to measure the products that are synthesized by it. One of these products is protein, especially albumin. Albumin is a portion of the total protein within the body. When disease affects the liver cells, the cells lose their ability to make albumin. As a result the blood level of albumin drops markedly. However, because previously made albumin will stay in the blood 12 to 18 days, severe impairment of liver albumin synthesis will not be recognized until after that period has lapsed. Albumin is just one component of total protein level. Therefore the measure of total protein is a rather indirect and inadequate indication of liver function. Measuring the level of albumin is much more reliable. There are other causes for decreased serum albumin level. Certain kidney disorders (such as nephrotic syndrome) result in excessive urinary losses of albumin, which cause a diminished blood level of serum albumin.

Procedure

The procedure is similar to that mentioned in liver enzyme test (see previous study).

Pertinent facts

• The cost of this test is approximately $11.

Hepatitis B antigen study (hepatitis-associated antigen [HAA], Australian antigen)
Normal values

No evidence of the hepatitis antigen within the bloodstream.

Purpose

Hepatitis is an inflammation of the liver cell caused by a virus. There are two common viruses that cause this disease. Hepatitis A is most frequently transmitted orally and is known to cause "infectious hepatitis." Hepatitis B is most frequently transmitted by blood transfusions and is most closely associated with what is called "serum hepatitis." It is now known that both types of hepatitis can be transmitted either orally or via contaminated blood. There is no test capable of detecting hepatitis A virus, which usually causes a benign limited form of hepatitis. Hepatitis B virus (also called the dane particle) may cause a severe unrelenting form of hepatitis, which may even end in liver failure and death. Several tests are available to detect and document the presence of this hepatitis virus. Among the antigens and antibodies used in these tests are:

1. Australian antigen or hepatitis-associated antigen (HAA). The dane particle is the infecting virus and is made up of an inner core surrounded by an outer capsule. Both parts of the virus are foreign and therefore will stimulate antibody reaction. It is the capsule or surface that was originally called Australian antigen or HAA. Detection of this antigen is the most commonly and easily performed test to detect hepatitis. Usually the level of this surface antigen in the serum returns to normal 12 weeks after a bout of hepatitis. If it persists in the blood, the patient is considered to be a carrier of hepatitis.
2. Hepatitis B core antigen. Very little presently is known about this antigen.
3. Hepatitis B e antigen. The persistent presence of this antigen in the blood indicates a severe form of hepatitis that is progressive and often fatal.
4. Antihepatitis B surface antibody. This is an antibody against the capsule of the dane particle (previously discussed) and is elevated in patients who have hepatitis B. This antibody appears in almost 80% of the patients with hepatitis B and is manufactured by the patient to fight the invading virus. Con-

centrated forms of this agent constitute the hyperimmune globulin given to patients who have come into contact with patients infected with hepatitis B (such as medical staff who have inadvertently stuck themselves with needles previously used on patients who have had hepatitis B).
5. Antihepatitis B core antibody. When this antibody is persistently present in the blood, it indicates the patient is a carrier for hepatitis B.

Procedure

This test, like the previously mentioned tests, can be performed in the laboratory or at the bedside. A quantity equal to a few teaspoons of blood is removed from a peripheral vein by needle puncture. A technician usually performs this function. Most of this testing is performed by a technique called radioimmunoassay. Frequently the hospital does not have the capabilities to perform this test in its own laboratory and sends the blood to central laboratories for analysis. No special patient preparation is required to perform this test.

Pertinent facts

• It must be noted that in patients who are suspected to have hepatitis, the medical team will take great precautions to avoid inadvertent exposure to the patient's blood.
• The only discomfort associated with this study is the needle stick.
• The cost of this test is approximately $35.

Serum amylase test
Normal values

56-190 IU/L.
80-250 Somogyi units/dl.

Purpose

The serum amylase test is an easily and rapidly performed test used to detect acute inflammation of the pancreas. Amylase is normally secreted from pancreatic cells and into the pancreatic duct. The pancreatic duct empties into the duodenum (See Anatomy at the beginning of this chapter and Fig. 4-1). Once in the intestine, it aids in digestion of carbohydrates. Damage to these pancreatic cells caused by inflammation (pancreatitis) or pancreatic duct obstruction (as in pancreatic carcinoma) will cause an outpouring of this enzyme into the blood vessels and lymph vessels surrounding the pancreas. As a result, there is an abnormal rise in the blood level of amylase that will occur within 12 hours after the onset of pancreatic disease. Amylase is rapidly cleared by the kidney, and these abnormal blood levels can return to normal within 48 to 72 hours. Severe and ongoing inflammation, duct obstruction, or persistent pancreatic duct leakage will cause rather prolonged elevated amylase levels. Although amylase is a sensitive test for pancreatic disorders, it is far from being specific. Many disease processes other than pancreatic disorders can cause elevation of blood amylase levels. Examples would include inflammation of the salivary glands, inflammation of the gallbladder, perforation (hole) in the bowel, and ectopic pregnancy.

Procedure

Similar to the liver enzyme blood tests.

Pertinent facts

• The cost of this test is approximately $16.

Serum lipase test
Normal values

0-110 U/L.
0-1.5 U/ml.

Purpose

The most common cause of an elevated blood or serum lipase level is acute inflammation of the pancreas. Lipase is an enzyme secreted by the pancreas into the duodenum to break down ingested fats. Like amylase (see previous test), lipase appears in the bloodstream following damage to the pancreas. Since lipase is produced only in the pancreas, elevated levels of this enzyme are much more specific in indicating disease of the pancreas.

In acute pancreatitis, elevated lipase levels usually parallel serum amylase levels. However, the lipase levels rise 24 to 48 hours after the onset of pancreatic disease and remain elevated for as long as 5 to 7 days. In comparison to amylase then, lipase peaks later and remains elevated longer. Therefore serum lipase levels are useful in the late diagnosis of acute pancreatitis. Serum lipase can also be elevated in patients with pancreatic carcinoma.

Procedure

See liver enzyme tests (p. 64-65).

Pertinent facts

• It is best to perform this test before the patient has eaten breakfast. Water is permitted.
• The cost of this test is approximately $16.

URINE TEST
Urine for amylase levels
Normal values

3-35 IU/hr or 6-30 Wohlgemuth U/ml, or up to 5000 Somogyi U/24 hr.

Purpose

(See serum amylase test). Because amylase is rapidly cleared by the kidneys, disorders affecting the pancreas will cause elevated amylase levels in the urine. As stated before, the serum amylase may rise only transiently in acute inflammation of the pancreas. This serum level frequently returns to normal in 1 to 2 days after the onset of disease. Levels of amylase in the urine, however, remain elevated for 7 to 10 days after the onset of disease. This fact is important if one is to make the diagnosis of inflammation of the pancreas in patients who have had symptoms for 3 days or longer. Like the serum amylase levels, amylase levels in the urine can be elevated in many other nonpancreatic disorders, but the urine levels are higher in patients who have primary pancreatic diseases.

Procedure

There is no preparation required for this test. Generally any plastic urine container can be used. It should, however, be thoroughly cleaned before use. Generally, a timed 2-hour or 24-hour urine collection is required. The specimen is refrigerated or kept on ice during the collection period. The specimen is then taken to the laboratory where analysis is carried out by a laboratory technician.

Pertinent facts

- It is very important that all urine be saved during the directed time. The collection period begins *after* the patient empties his or her bladder and discards that specimen. All subsequent urine is collected, including the one at the end of the collection period.
- If some urine is lost, this may lead to inaccurate test results.
- The customary cost of this study is approximately $12.

SPECIAL TESTS
Ultrasound of the liver, gallbladder, and pancreas
Normal values

Normal liver, gallbladder, bile ducts, and pancreas.

Purpose

In diagnostic ultrasound, a harmless, high-frequency sound wave is emitted and penetrates the organ being studied. The sound waves bounce back from the organ to a sensor (transducer), and by electronic conversion they are arranged into a pictorial image of that organ. A realistic Polaroid picture of the organ studied is obtained (Fig. 4-6).

Ultrasound is useful in detecting cystic structures of the liver such as benign cysts, hepatic pus collections (abscesses), or dilated intrahepatic bile ducts. It is also capable of detecting solid liver tumors that may arise primarily within the liver or may represent metastatic tumors from a malignancy elsewhere in the body. The gallbladder can also be examined by ultrasound for the presence of gallstones or tumors. In relation to the pancreas, ultrasound examination is used to establish the diagnosis of cancer, cyst, inflammation, or abscesses. Frequently follow-up ultrasound studies can be used to monitor the resolution of benign pancreatic diseases, such as inflammation, and to document the response of a tumor to therapy.

Procedure

For examination of the gallbladder, the patient must be kept from having anything by mouth (NPO) on the day of examination. This is to ensure that the gallbladder is at maximum size for the test. If the patient were to eat, the gallbladder

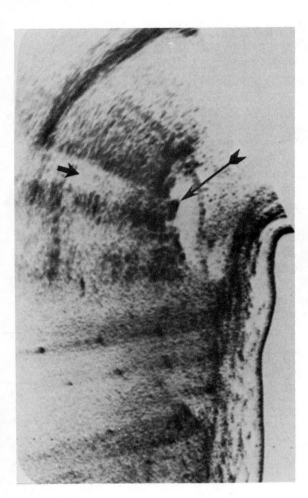

Fig. 4-6. Ultrasound image of the gallbladder. Long arrow points to stone in the gallbladder. Short arrow indicates areas behind the gallbladder not penetrated by ultrasound because of the gallstones.

would empty its bile and become very small. A small gallbladder is more difficult to detect by ultrasound. Fasting, however, is not required for ultrasound of the liver or pancreas.

The ultrasonographer, usually a radiologist or ultrasound technician, applies mineral oil or glycerine to the skin overlying the area to be studied. This paste is used to enhance transmission and reception of the sound waves. The transducer is moved along the skin in a vertical and then a horizontal manner. The depth-in-intensity recording of these sound waves produces a truly anatomic photograph of the section being examined. Combined views allow for three-dimensional examination of the organ studied. Ultrasound is noninvasive, has no side effects, and can safely be performed on pregnant patients. Because ultrasound is almost totally reflected by air-filled organs, this study cannot be used diagnostically if the patient's intestines are filled with large quantities of gas. Also, since barium also reflects the sound wave, ultrasound examination should be performed before any barium x-ray studies are done.

No sedation is routinely required in the performance of this test. The accuracy of this test depends on the ability of the technician to obtain good ultrasound films and on the ability of the radiologist who interprets those films.

Pertinent facts

- If the gallbladder is to be examined, the patient is asked to refrain from eating or drinking (NPO) as of the midnight before the test. Fasting is not required for ultrasound study of the other organs.
- This test is painless and takes about 15 minutes for its performance.
- The test can be performed on an outpatient or on an inpatient basis.
- If a barium study has been carried out within 2 days of this study, the physician should be notified so that the ultrasound test can be rescheduled, if so ordered. Barium may interfere in the transmission and reflection of sound waves.
- The gel applied in performing the test may be removed after the test is carried out.
- The customary cost of this test is approximately $85.

Liver biopsy
Normal values

Normal liver tissue.

Purpose

Liver biopsy is a simple and valuable method of diagnosing primary liver disease. For this study, a specially designed needle is inserted through the skin of the abdomen and then into the liver. A piece of liver tissue is removed for microscopic examination. Liver biopsy is used in the diagnosis of liver disorder (such as cirrhosis, hepatitis, drug reactions, and tumor). It is performed in patients with the following conditions:

1. Unexplained enlargement of the liver
2. Persistent elevated liver enzyme levels (see liver enzyme test)
3. Suspected liver tumor
4. Unexplained jaundice
5. Suspected less common primary liver diseases

Procedure

Before this study, prothrombin time, partial thromboplastin time, and platelet counts (see Chapter 14) are performed to ensure adequate blood clotting in the event a small blood vessel is punctured. The patient's blood is also typed and crossmatched so that blood can be available for transfusion if necessary. The patient must be admitted to the hospital for the test. He or she is kept from having anything by mouth (NPO) from midnight on the day of examination. Sedation is administered 30 to 60 minutes before the study. The patient is placed on the back, and the skin overlying the right upper part of the abdomen is cleansed and anesthetized with a numbing medicine. Occasionally a small ¼-inch incision is made in the skin. The patient is asked to breathe out and hold his or her breath. This reduces the possibility of a collapsed lung. The physician then rapidly induces the biopsy needle into the liver, obtains liver tissue, and then immediately withdraws the needle. The tissue is then sent to the pathology laboratory for microscopic examination. A small dressing is placed over the needle insertion site. The patient is then placed on his or her right side to provide pressure at the biopsy site. The entire procedure is usually performed at the bedside in about 20 minutes.

Although liver biopsy is generally considered a safe procedure, complications do exist. These include:

1. Bleeding caused by inadvertent puncture and laceration of a blood vessel within or surrounding the liver
2. Infection caused by inadvertent laceration of a bile duct with leakage of bile into the abdominal cavity
3. Collapse of the lung caused by improper placement of the needle upward into the adjacent chest cavity

The incidence of these is markedly diminished when this study is performed by an experienced and skilled physician.

The test should not be performed in patients who are unable to cooperate with the physician. Patients with an impaired blood clotting system should be excluded from having this test. Patients who are known to have obstruction or blockage of their bile ducts should also not undergo biopsy because they have a high chance of bile leakage and subsequent infection.

Pertinent facts

- Informed and written consent is usually required.
- It is vitally important that the patient lie very still during this procedure and hold his or her breath during the biopsy.
- The patient must be prepared to go to surgery in the event that bleeding or serious bile leakage occurs.
- The patient will be observed closely for several hours after the test.
- This test is moderately uncomfortable.
- The customary cost is approximately $70.

Sweat electrolyte test (sweat chloride test)
Normal values

Sodium: less than 70 mEq/L (abnormal value is more than 90 mEq/L).
Chloride: less than 50 mEq/L (abnormal value is more than 60 mEq/L).

Purpose

Patients with cystic fibrosis have an increased salt (sodium and chloride) content in their sweat. This fact forms the basis of this test, which is both sensitive and specific for this disease. Cystic fibrosis is an inherited disease characterized by abnormal secretion of the glands within the lungs, intestines, pancreas, bile ducts, and skin (sweat glands). Sweat, induced by electrical current or drugs, is collected, and the sodium and chloride content is measured. The degree of abnormality is, however, in no way an indication of the severity of the disease. It merely indicates that the patient has or does not have the disease. It is commonly used in children who have recurrent lung infections or diarrhea or demonstrate a failure to thrive. This test is not reliable, however, during the first few weeks of infancy. Almost all patients with cystic fibrosis have sweat sodium and chloride contents two to five times greater than normal values.

Procedure

No food or fluid restrictions are necessary. The test is usually performed in a laboratory or at the bedside by an experienced technician. A low level of electrical current is applied to the test area (the thigh in infants, the forearm in older children). Electrodes are applied to the skin after being saturated with chemicals (pilocarpine and bicarbonate). These electrodes are strapped onto the test area and a low-level electrical current is begun and continued for 10 to 12 minutes. The electrodes are then removed and paper discs are placed over the test area. From these paper discs, the chloride and sodium content is determined. There is no need for sedation. This test can be performed on an outpatient or an inpatient.

Pertinent facts

- This test takes about 1 to 1½ hours to perform.
- The electrical current is small, and no discomfort or pain is associated with its delivery.
- The customary cost is approximately $20.

Sample case report: gallstones

Shortly before admission to the hospital, Mrs. R, a 44-year-old mother of seven children, began to complain of right upper abdominal pain that was associated with nausea and vomiting. She noticed that her skin was becoming progressively yellow. She was found to have mild right upper abdominal tenderness when the abdomen was examined.

STUDIES	RESULTS
CBC, electrolytes, glucose, and BUN determination	Normal
Total serum bilirubin	3.8 mg/dl (normal: 0.1-1 mg/dl)
Liver enzyme test	
SGOT	46 IU/L (normal: 5-40 IU/L)
SGPT	40 IU/L (normal: 5-35 IU/L)
LDH	228 mIU/ml (normal: 90-200 mIU/ml)
Alkaline phosphatase	885 mIU/ml (normal: 30-85 mIU/ml)
Total serum protein test	7.2 g/dl (normal: 6 to 8 g/dl)
Serum albumin test	4.2 g/dl (normal: 3.2 to 4.5 g/dl)
Oral cholecystogram	Nonvisualization of the gallbladder
Cholescintigraphy	Stone obstructing the cystic and common bile duct
Ultrasound examination of liver, bile ducts, and gallbladder.	Dilated bile ducts with the presence of gallstones within the gallbladder
Endoscopic retrograde cholangio-pancreatography (ERCP)	Dilated common bile duct containing a gallstone
Percutaneous transhepatic cholangiography (PTHC)	Dilated bile duct containing gallstones

Because of the combination of the increased level of bilirubin and alkaline phosphatase with a minimally elevated level of SGOT and LDH, obstruction of the bile duct was suspected as the cause of this patient's jaundice. The normal protein level indicated some liver function was still present. The oral cholecystogram, cholescintigraphy, and ultrasound all indicated that gallstones were blocking the cystic dust. ERCP and PTHC, however, indicated that gallstones also were causing blockage of the common bile duct. The patient underwent a removal of the gallbladder and removal of gallstones from the common duct. The patient's postoperative course was uneventful. She soon returned to a normal color and no longer had any symptoms of abdominal pain, nausea, or vomiting.

Sample case report: pancreatitis

Mr. D, a 52-year-old man, was admitted to the hospital complaining of severe pain in the upper midportion of the abdomen, which radiated to his back. The pain started the day before his admission and was associated with nausea and vomiting. He was found to be mildly dehydrated and his abdominal examination indicated significant tenderness in the upper abdomen.

STUDIES	RESULTS
Routine laboratory studies	Within normal limits (WNL)
Serum amylase test	650 IU/L (normal: 56-190 IU/L)
Two-hour urine amylase	1240 IU/L (normal: 3-35 IU/L)
Serum lipase test	240 units/L (normal: 0-110 units/L)
Ultrasound examination of the pancreas	Edematous and enlarged pancreas
Computerized tomogram of the abdomen	Diffusely enlarged and swollen pancreas
ERCP	Normal pancreatic duct

The diagnosis of pancreatitis was quite certain in light of the elevation of both serum and urine amylase levels and also of the lipase level. Alcohol and gallstones are the two most common causes of pancreatitis. However, this patient denied drinking alcohol and a previous gallbladder study excluded gallstones. Because cancer of the pancreas can also cause inflammation of the pancreas, cancer had to be excluded as the cause of this patient's problem. Ultrasound and computerized tomography indicated that the pancreas was enlarged; however, no definite tumor was seen. The normal ERCP eliminated the possibility of a pancreatic cancer. The patient was treated by intravenous infusion of water and asked to eat nothing by mouth (NPO). The inflammation of the pancreas soon resolved and the cause of this problem was found to be drug induced. The drug was a well known diuretic that was discontinued. He had no further problems.

5

Diagnostic studies used to evaluate the lungs

ANATOMY, PHYSIOLOGY, AND DISEASES OF THE LUNG

The lungs are elastic, saclike structures located within the chest cavity. There is one lung on either side of the chest. The outer surface of the lung is enveloped in a protective membrane called the pleura. This covers each lung and also lines the inner chest wall. Between the lung and the chest wall is a space called the pleural space (Fig. 5-1). There is a small amount of fluid that lubricates the pleural space, thus preventing any friction between the lungs and the chest wall. The outer lining of the lung may become inflamed as a result of a viral or bacterial infection. This is called pleuritis. The symptom associated with pleuritis is severe chest pain with deep breathing. Infection, tumor, and trauma are common causes of large amounts of fluid developing within the pleural space. This is called "pleural effusion."

Each lung is divided into subsections called lobes. The right lung has three lobes (upper, middle, and lower); the left has two lobes (upper and lower). Each lobe is further divided into segments. Each lung segment has its own bronchiole (air tube) and pulmonary arteriole (which carries blood to the segment) and is drained by its own pulmonary venule (which carries blood from the pulmonary segment). These small air tubes, arterioles, and venules are branches of the main bronchus, pulmonary artery, and pulmonary vein, respectively. These larger structures enter the lung at its root called the hilus. Air travels through the nose, trachea, bronchus, and bronchiole to end up in the alveoli (tiny air spaces) (Fig. 5-1). Each alveolus is in close proximity to a pulmonary arteriole and venule. Together the alveoli and their blood supply form the basic unit of the lung system where exchange of oxygen (good air) and carbon dioxide (bad air) ultimately takes place. The human lung contains approximately 3 million of these small basic units. Viruses, bacteria, or fungi can infect the alveoli, creating pus within them. This is most commonly referred to as pneumonia. As a result of pneumonia, air cannot be exchanged appropriately. Pneumonia is a serious infection that requires prompt antibiotic treatment.

The upper airway includes the nose, the throat, and the vocal cords. The

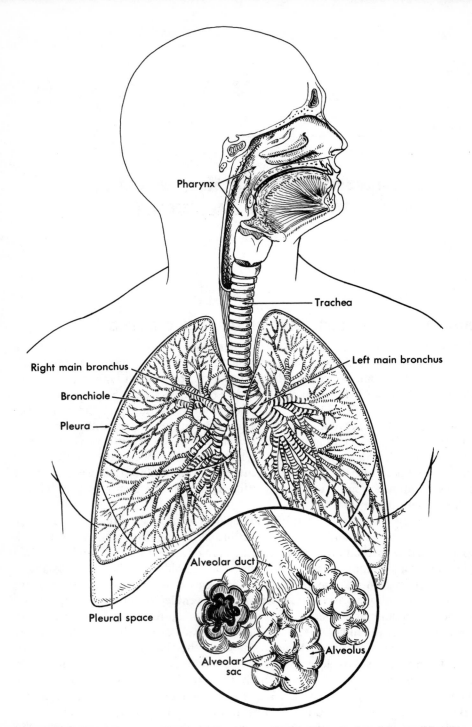

Fig. 5-1. Normal anatomy of the pulmonary system: pharynx, trachea, and lungs. The inset shows the grapelike alveolar sacs where air and blood exchange oxygen and carbon dioxide through the thin walls of the alveoli. Capillaries (not shown) surround the alveoli.

From Anthony, C.P., and Thibodeau, G.A.: Textbook of anatomy and physiology, St. Louis, The C.V. Mosby Co.

lower respiratory tract includes the trachea and the bronchi (Fig. 5-1). The bronchus and larger bronchioles are most commonly afflicted with cancer. Occasionally, however, tumors may arise from the very small lung bronchioles or even from the lining of the lung. Infrequently, tumors do arise within the trachea. Chronic obstructive pulmonary disease is a disease of the small lung bronchioles. These bronchioles collapse easily and are filled with secretions. As a result, it is very difficult to remove the air from the lungs (exhale). Air that is breathed in (inhaled) becomes trapped within the lung, causing "hyperinflation" of the lungs. This air creates a "dead space," and appropriate movement of air cannot occur.

Ventilation

The process of ventilation includes two phases, inspiration and expiration. During inspiration the diaphragm, which is the muscle that separates the chest cavity from the abdominal cavity, contracts. This, along with contraction of the intercostal muscles (the muscles between each rib), causes the chest cavity to enlarge and thereby lowers the pressure within the chest to below atmospheric pressure. Air is then drawn into the lungs. During expiration, the same muscles relax, causing the chest cavity to decrease in size. The pressure within the chest then becomes greater than atmospheric pressure, and air flows from the lungs into the atmosphere. The stimulus for breathing is controlled by the brain.

Pulmonary circulation

Almost the entire amount of blood that passes through the right side of the heart goes to the lung and comes into close contact with the alveolus (Fig. 5-1). It is here that the alveolus (breathing unit) comes into contact with the pulmonary capillaries (blood unit). This is where oxygen and carbon dioxide exchange occurs.

X-RAYS AND NUCLEAR SCANS
Chest x-ray
Normal values

Normal lungs and surrounding chest structures.

Purpose

The chest x-ray is important in the complete evaluation of the heart and lungs. This test is a routine part of the general evaluation of all adult patients. Much information can be provided by this x-ray study. One can identify or follow (by repeated chest x-ray studies) the following:
1. Tumors of the lung or chest wall (primary or metastatic) (Fig. 5-2)
2. Inflammation of the lungs (pneumonia), the pleural lining (pleuritis), or the lining of the heart (pericarditis)
3. Fluid accumulation within the pleural cavity (effusion) or within the lung itself (pulmonary edema as the result of congestive heart failure)
4. Excessive abnormal air collection within the lung (chronic obstructive pulmonary disease) or within the pleural cavity (pneumothorax)

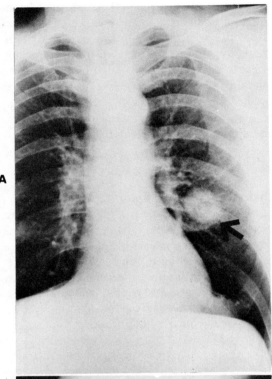

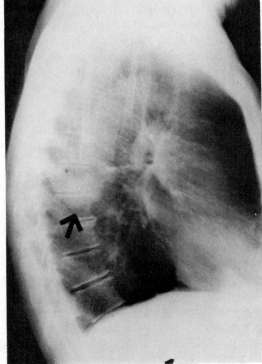

Fig. 5-2. Chest x-ray film showing tumor (arrow) in the left lung. A, Posterior—anterior (back to front) view. B, Lateral (side) view.

5. Fractures of the ribs, sternum (breast bone), or shoulder blades (scapula)
6. Hiatal hernias (part of the stomach is abnormally displaced within the chest)

Procedure

Chest x-ray studies are performed in the radiology department. They can, however, be done at the bedside when critically ill patients cannot leave the nursing unit. A portable chest x-ray camera is used in this instance. The patient's clothing is removed down to the waist. A gown or drape is put on the patient. Objects such as necklaces, watches, and pins must be removed. They will show up on the x-ray film and obscure visualization of part of the chest.

Most chest x-ray films are taken with the x-ray camera at a distance of 6 feet from the patient. The patient is usually standing. The sitting or reclining position can also be used. A picture is taken with the x-rays passing through the back of the body to the front of the body. Next, a lateral view with the x-rays passing through the patient's side is taken (Fig. 5-2). In some instances, a third view is taken with the x-ray passing from front to back. Various slanted or angled pictures can be taken in specific instances. Occasionally "decubitus" films are taken with the patient lying on his or her side. This is done to localize fluid collections.

After the patient is correctly positioned, he or she is asked to take a deep breath and hold it until the x-ray film is taken. The x-ray technician will then tell the patient to breathe again. X-ray films are taken by a radiology technician. This can be performed on an outpatient or on an inhospital patient.

Pregnant patients must protect their abdomen from exposure to the x-rays. Too much exposure to x-ray can be harmful to an unborn child especially in the early months of pregnancy. However, if such a study is required in a pregnant woman, a lead shield is placed over the abdomen. Normally there is some scatter of x-rays to other parts of the body during x-ray tests. It is for that reason that it is wise to place a lead shield over the ovaries or testes of all patients.

Pertinent facts

- The patient must remove all clothing above the waist. Jewelry and any metal objects should be removed.
- The patient will be asked to take in a deep breath and then "hold it." This will ensure the maximum inflation of the lungs.
- Any movement at the time the x-ray is taken will blur the film.
- Premenopausal patients who are not presently menstruating should wear a metal apron (lead shield) over their abdomen. This is to prevent x-ray exposure to a fetus in unsuspected early pregnancy.
- Men and women should cover their testes and ovaries, respectively. This is to prevent radiation-induced abnormalities that may lead to congenital (occurring at birth) abnormalities in future children.
- The test is painless and takes only a few minutes for completion.
- The customary cost is approximately $47.

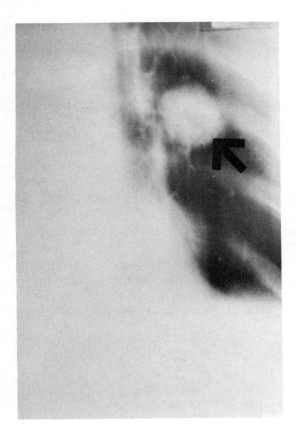

Fig. 5-3. Tomogram of left lung. Arrow indicates a "solid" tumor.

Chest tomography
Normal values

Normal lungs.

Purpose

Tomography is a technique of x-ray examination of the lungs by which a sequence of x-ray films, each representing a "slice" of the lung, is taken. Usually, films are made at ½-inch intervals throughout the entire lung. Tomography permits examination of a single layer or plane of lung that would otherwise be obscured by the surrounding lung on an ordinary film (Fig. 5-3). For tomography, the x-ray camera on one side of the patient and the film on the other side of the patient are rapidly moved in opposite directions while the x-ray picture is being taken. This technique effectively blurs out all tissue planes except that plane or slice being studied (Fig. 5-3). Tomography is often a helpful adjunct to a routine chest x-ray study for several reasons:

 1. It more clearly delineates a known lung abnormality such as a tumor margin (a tumor with sharp margins is more likely to be benign than a

tumor with shaggy margins) or a central core (a lung mass that has a hollow center is more likely to be an infected abscess than a tumor).

2. Many structures such as the root of the lung, trachea, and other central chest structures are not clearly seen on routine chest x-ray. Tomography more clearly visualizes these structures.

3. Some metastatic tumors whose primary tumor site exists outside the lung may be missed on routine chest x-ray films and can only be seen on certain tomographic "cuts" of the lung.

Procedure

The nonfasting patient goes to the x-ray department as for a routine chest x-ray (see preceding discussion). With the patient remaining completely still, an x-ray camera is rapidly moved to and fro, while the x-ray film is moved in the opposite direction. This movement is so fast and so slight that it is unrecognizable by the naked eye. The excursions of these movements regulate the plane of tissue photographed. The patient is usually lying on his or her back. The test is usually performed by a technician and interpreted by a radiologist.

Pertinent facts

- This is a painless study.
- Chest tomography takes about 15 minutes for its completion.
- The customary cost is approximately $55.

Computerized tomography (CT) of the chest
Normal values

Normal lungs, heart, great vessels, and mediastinum.

Purpose

Computerized tomography, as stated earlier in this book, is a noninvasive yet very accurate x-ray procedure used to diagnose disease and abnormalities in just about any organ of the body. The CT scan has the ability to detect tumors, cysts, and infection (abscesses) of the lungs, heart, and other mediastinal structures, which include the trachea, the lymph nodes, the thymus gland, the esophagus, and the great vessels leading from the heart. The computerized tomography machine produces an image that results from passing x-rays through the patient's chest at many angles. The variation in and thickness of each tissue within the chest allows for a variable rate of x-ray penetration. The varying rates of x-ray penetration are then given a numerical value called a coefficient, which is digitally computed to shades of gray. These are displayed on a television screen as thousands of dots in various shades of gray. The final display appears as an actual photograph of the anatomic area sectioned by the x-ray.

This study is only two dimensional (that is, front to back), but if one looks at a series of cross-sectional views from the top of the lung to the bottom of the lung, a three-dimensional appearance can be created. This allows complete examination of all the organs within the chest. Tumors may be represented as a localized mass with a coefficient much different than its native tissue. Inflammation may be demonstrated as an enlarged and abnormal-appearing area within an organ. Cysts or abscesses will be demonstrated as a hollow structure within the organ to be examined. The radiation exposure that the patient has received during this procedure is minimal.

The computerized tomography is much more accurate in detecting tumors that were previously hidden by alternate techniques (such as routine chest x-ray and chest tomography).

Procedure

Sedation is rarely required and is given only to those patients who cannot remain still during the length of the procedure (especially children). The patient is taken to the radiology department and asked to remain motionless while lying on his or her back. Motion will cause blurring and streaking of the final picture, which will inhibit accurate interpretation. An encircling camera (body scanner) takes the pictures at various levels, usually 1 to 4 cm apart. Television equipment allows for immediate display of the images, and they are then recorded on a Polaroid or x-ray type of film. The procedure takes about 30 to 60 minutes to perform. X-ray dye is usually injected into the bloodstream to visualize the blood vessels within the chest. Also the patient is asked to drink x-ray dye so that the swallowing tube (esophagus) will be visualized. Patients who are known to be allergic to x-ray dye should not be given the dye injection.

Pertinent facts

- The test is uncomfortable in that the patient is asked to lie on a hard table for 30 to 45 minutes.
- Occasionally the patient becomes claustrophobic within the body scanner.
- It is important to recognize that not all hospitals have a computerized tomography machine. The patient may be transported from one facility to another to have the test done.
- Because the CT scanner is computerized, it must be in a cool, controlled environment. As a result, the patient may be cold during the procedure. The patient is allowed to bring a sweater or warm blanket.
- The customary cost is approximately $200.

Pulmonary angiography
Normal values

Normal arteries to the lung without evidence of clot.

Purpose

With the injection of x-ray dye, the arteries of the lung (pulmonary arteries) can be studied. This test is most commonly used to detect pulmonary embolism, which is an obstruction of one of the smaller pulmonary arteries caused by an embolus. The embolus is usually a blood clot formed in the veins of the lower extremities of the legs or pelvis. Part or all of the blood clot breaks loose from its origin and travels through the heart and into the lungs. Here it is lodged in one of the smaller pulmonary arteries and is called a pulmonary embolism. Blood flow to that part of the lung ceases. As a result, the patient develops chest pain and serious shortness of breath and may even go into shock. In addition, pulmonary angiography is used to detect a variety of congenital and acquired abnormalities of the lung blood vessels.

The complications associated with this test are:
1. Irregular heart beats
2. Severe allergic reaction to the x-ray dye
3. Death as a result of transferring an unstable patient from the intensive care unit to the x-ray department where this test takes place

Procedure

Preferably, the patient is kept from eating or drinking (NPO) anything as of the midnight before the test. He or she is sedated with narcotics. In the special procedure room of the x-ray department, the patient is asked to lie on an x-ray table. The groin area is cleansed and draped in a sterile manner. A long, thin catheter is placed into the femoral vein (the major vein in the groin) and then passed to the heart and into the pulmonary artery. The passage is made easier by directly visualizing the progress of the catheter via fluoroscopy (a motion picture x-ray usually displayed on a television monitor). With expertise, the angiographer (usually a radiologist) can manipulate the catheter into the pulmonary artery where dye is then injected. X-ray films of the chest are immediately taken in timed sequence. This allows all vessels to be visualized by the injection. If a defect in normal blood flow is detected, there is strong evidence that the patient has suffered a pulmonary embolus. This study is performed only on inpatients.

Pertinent facts

- During the actual injection of dye material, the patient will feel a severe burning and feel "flushed" throughout the body. This is transient and disappears in seconds.
- The test takes about 1 hour to perform.
- It is mildly uncomfortable to lie on a hard table for 1 hour.
- If the patient is known to have an allergy to x-ray dye, this should be reported to his or her physician at once.
- It is common to obtain a written and informed consent before this procedure is carried out.
- The patient will be sedated to decrease discomfort associated with the study and to ensure a relaxed patient.
- After the procedure, the site of the venous needle stick in the groin should be observed for evidence of persistent bleeding.
- The customary cost is approximately $600.

Lung scanning
Normal values

No evidence of pulmonary embolism.

Purpose

This radionuclear test is used to identify defects in the blood flow to the lungs. It is used in patients who are suspected of having suffered a blood clot to the lungs (pulmonary embolism). Technetium 99m-labeled aggregates of a protein (such as albumin) are injected into the patient's vein. Because the size of the aggregate is larger than the smallest blood vessel in the lung, they become temporarily lodged in the tiny blood vessels of the lungs. A gamma-ray–detecting device (Geiger counter) is passed over the patient's chest while the patient is lying on his or her back, stomach, and sides. This gamma camera records the distribution of these aggregates within the lung.

A homogeneous uptake of particles that fill all the small blood vessels within the lung conclusively eliminates the possibility that a pulmonary embolus has occurred. If there is a defect in an otherwise smooth and diffusely homogeneous pattern, an embolism should be suspected. Unfortunately, other serious pulmonary lung diseases (such as pneumonia, emphysema, and fluid within the chest) will cause a similar defect. One can see that although the scan is sensitive (easily recognizes disease entities), it is not specific, because many different diseases can cause the same abnormal results on lung scan.

Procedure

The unsedated, nonfasting patient who is suspected of having a pulmonary embolism is taken to the nuclear medicine department. Sometimes this department is within the x-ray department. An intravenous injection of a radionuclear-tagged aggregate is given into a vein of the arm. While the patient lies in the appropriate position, a gamma-ray camera is passed over the patient's chest and records the nuclear counts on an x-ray- or Polaroid-type film (Fig. 5-4). This is done with the patient lying on the back, stomach, and both sides. The results are interpreted by a physician trained in diagnostic nuclear medicine. The amount of radiation the patient receives is minimal.

This test should be interpreted with significant reservation when the patient is known to have concomitant lung disease (such as pneumonia, emphysema, fluid in the chest, or a lung tumor). These problems will definitely give the false impression that a pulmonary embolism exists when in fact the abnormality in the test is a result of the pneumonia or other disease. As always, a pregnant patient should avoid unnecessary radiation. As a result, it may be wise to perform this test selectively for fear of injury to the unborn child.

Pertinent facts

- This test is relatively painless. The only discomfort is the needle stick for injection.
- The test lasts for about 30 minutes.
- The customary cost is approximately $75.

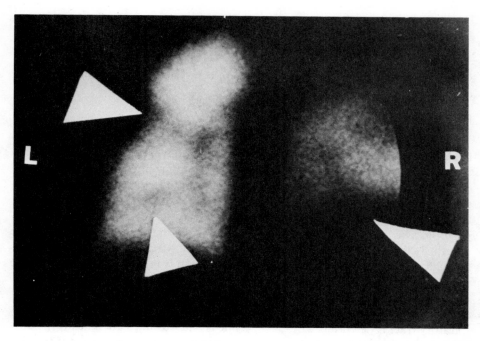

Fig. 5-4. Lung scan (posterior view). Pointers indicate areas of decreased blood perfusion. The right side is worse than the left.

ENDOSCOPY
Bronchoscopy
Normal values

Normal larynx, trachea, and bronchus.

Purpose

Bronchoscopy permits direct visualization of the voice box (larynx), trachea, and bronchi by a flexible fiberoptic-lighted bronchoscope. Diagnostic uses of the bronchoscope include direct visualization of the tracheobronchial tree for abnormalities (such as tumors, inflammation, and strictures).

The flexible fiberoptic-lighted bronchoscope has a second lumen through which cable-activated instruments can be used for taking and removing biopsy specimens of suspected tumors. Also this second lumen can be used to obtain bronchial washings and sputum for cytology and cultures (see pp. 89-91).

The bronchoscope can also be used as a treatment in the following manner:
1. The removal of retained lung secretions that the patient is incapable of coughing up
2. The control of bleeding in areas within the bronchus
3. The retrieval of swallowed foreign bodies (most commonly food) that mistakenly go down into the trachea
4. Placement of radiation seeds in patients with unresectable lung tumor

Possible complications of bronchoscopy include:
1. Spasm of the vocal cords or bronchus, resulting in difficulty breathing
2. Bleeding from biopsy sites

Complications are rare when this procedure is performed by an experienced endoscopist.

Procedure

The patient is kept from having anything by mouth (NPO) after midnight on the day of the bronchoscopy. Fiberoptic bronchoscopy is performed by a surgeon or a pulmonary specialist at the bedside or in an appropriately equipped endoscopy room. Narcotics are given for sedation shortly before this study. The patient's nose and mouth are numbed by a lidocaine (Xylocaine) spray before insertion of the bronchoscope. The patient is placed in the sitting or semirecumbent position. The bronchoscope is then inserted through the nose into the back of the mouth. It is then passed through the vocal cords. After the bronchoscope goes through the vocal cords, more numbing medication is injected through the scope to completely numb the trachea and bronchus. This prevents the cough reflex. The bronchoscope is then passed further, well into the trachea, bronchi, and first and second branch bronchioles. Systematic examination of the entire lower respiratory tract is performed. Biopsy specimens and washings are taken if the doctor deems it necessary. Patients who are severely short of breath cannot tolerate this procedure well.

Pertinent facts

- It is important that the patient eat nothing by mouth (NPO) the day of the study to prevent the possibility of vomiting. If one were to vomit during the test, there is a significant chance that one could breath in (aspirate) the vomitus contents and have a very severe pneumonia.
- Usually, informed written consent is required.
- Sedation will be given to prevent any anxiety or any unusual discomfort.
- It is important that the patient remove his or her glasses or contact lenses and dentures.
- After numbing medication is injected into the trachea and bronchi, there is an early severe, yet transient, desire to cough. Coughing is permissible and will not injure the patient.
- It is important to realize that there will be no difficulty breathing during the procedure.
- After bronchoscopy, the patient is not allowed to eat or drink anything until the numbing medicine in the throat has worn off. Usually this takes about 2 hours. The patient who eats or drinks before that time could unknowingly aspirate the food or drink and develop a severe pneumonia.
- If biopsies (pieces of tissue) were removed, a small amount of blood streaking within the sputum is expected. A large amount of bleeding, however, is disconcerting.
- Occasionally the patient will be asked to collect the sputum after this procedure. This is because secretions are loosened by bronchoscopy, and these secretions may contain cells that may be diagnostic of a possible lung tumor.

- Bronchoscopy is not terribly uncomfortable. The procedure takes about 30 minutes to perform. There is some initial gagging reflex and some initial cough reflex. This is not usually a major problem and is well controlled with a numbing medication.
- The customary cost is approximately $350.

Mediastinoscopy
Normal values

No abnormal mediastinal tumors or lymph node tissue.

Purpose

Mediastinoscopy is a procedure in which a lighted viewing instrument is inserted through a small midline incision made at the lowest portion of the neck. The scope is passed into what is called the mediastinum, which is the middle part of the chest and contains many lymph nodes, large blood vessels, and the heart. Primary tumors can originate anywhere within the mediastinum. More commonly, however, because the lymph nodes within the mediastinum receive the lymphatic drainage from the lungs, the assessment of these mediastinal lymph nodes can provide the diagnosis of such diseases as cancer of the lung, tuberculosis, or sarcoidosis. Therefore mediastinoscopy is used in establishing the diagnosis of a variety of diseases that occur within the chest.

In addition, mediastinoscopy is employed to "stage" lung cancer and to determine the operability of the tumor. Patients who are suspected of having a lung cancer and whose cancer has spread (metastasis) to the mediastinal lymph nodes, are usually considered incurable by surgery. These people would best receive treatment other than surgery. Approximately 35% of all patients with lung cancer who are examined by mediastinoscopy are indeed found to have metastasis of the tumor to the lymph nodes within the mediastinum.

The possibility of inadvertently puncturing the swallowing tube (esophagus), the windpipe (trachea), or the large blood vessels leading from the heart exists. This is a rare occurrence if the test is performed by an experienced surgeon. If the puncture were to occur, however, immediate surgery on the chest would be required.

Procedure

Mediastinoscopy is a surgical procedure performed in the operating room. The patient is asked not to eat or drink anything (NPO) after the midnight before the test. In the morning the patient is given sedation approximately 1 hour before the study is to begin. The patient is brought to the operating room, and a small incision is made in what is called the suprasternal notch (lowest aspect of the neck) and the mediastinoscope is then passed through this neck incision and into the midpart of the chest. After the mediastinum is examined and any suspected abnormal tissues are biopsied, the scope is withdrawn and the incision is closed by stitches. Admission to the hospital is always required for the performance of this test and for observation after the test.

Pertinent facts

- An informed and written consent is required.
- The patient's blood will be typed and cross matched (see Chapter 14) for several units of blood in the event that a complication occurs that may require immediate surgery in the chest.
- The test is not uncomfortable other than the needle stick required for an intravenous infusion before being put to sleep. After the procedure, the patient may complain of a "sore throat" for a day or two.
- The test usually takes about 45 minutes to complete.
- The customary cost is approximately $600.

BLOOD TEST
Arterial blood gas analysis (ABGs)
Normal values

pH: 7.35-7.45.
P_{CO_2}: 35-45 mm Hg.
HCO_3 (bicarbonate): 22-26 mEq/L.
P_{O_2}: 80-100 mm Hg.
Oxygen saturation: 95%-100%.

Purpose

A sample of blood is drawn and used to assess and manage respiratory and metabolic (kidney) disturbances.

pH. The pH is the hydrogen ion (H+) concentration expressed as a negative logarhithm (p). Because it is a negative log rhythm, pH is *inversely proportional* to the actual hydrogen ion (acid concentration). Therefore as pH increases, the hydrogen ion concentration decreases; and as pH decreases, the hydrogen ion concentration increases. The pH is used to measure acidity and alkalinity. Acidity is determined when the pH is less than 7.35. Alkalinity, or base, can be defined when the pH is greater than 7.45.

P_{CO_2}. P_{CO_2} is a measurement of a partial pressure of CO_2 (carbon dioxide) in the blood. P_{CO_2} is referred to as the *respiratory* component in acid-base determination because this value is primarily regulated by the lungs. For example, respiratory acidosis (increased P_{CO_2}) could be a condition caused by drug overdose, which depresses breathing. Another common example would be pneumonia, which affects air exchange. An example of respiratory alkalosis (decreased P_{CO_2}) would be hyperventilation. This often occurs when someone breathes very quickly in response to some upsetting experience.

HCO_3. The bicarbonate ion is a measure of the metabolic (kidney) component of the acid-base equilibrium. The bicarbonate ion is referred to as the *metabolic* or kidney component of acid-base determination because this value is largely controlled by the kidneys. If the body needs more base, the kidneys would retain the bicarbonate ion. If there is an excess amount of base in the body, the kidney would then excrete the bicarbonate ion. An example of metabolic acidosis (decreased bicarbonate) would be uncontrolled diabetes mellitus. An example of metabolic alkalosis (increased bicarbonate) would be sodium bicarbonate overdosage.

Po$_2$. The Po$_2$ is an indirect measurement of the oxygen content of the arterial blood. The Po$_2$ would be decreased in patients whose lungs are unable to carry oxygen to the blood because of problems such as pneumonia, chronic obstructive lung disease, or other serious lung diseases.

Oxygen saturation. This value indicates the percentage of hemoglobin that is saturated with oxygen. As previously stated, hemoglobin carries the oxygen within the bloodstream. When 95% to 100% of the hemoglobin carries oxygen, the tissues are provided with an adequate amount of oxygen.

After the arterial blood is drawn, these different values will permit the physician to determine the acid-base condition of the patient, and whether the problem is caused by a respiratory or a kidney problem. Based on these results, the physician can more effectively treat the patient in such ways as administering oxygen, putting the patient on a respirator to allow better ventilation of the lungs, or giving the patient medication (such as sodium bicarbonate).

Procedure

For this study, arterial blood is obtained. (Remember that venous blood is used for most studies.) Arterial blood is obtained wherever pulses can be felt. Common sites that are used are the radial artery in the wrist, the brachial artery in the arm, and the femoral artery in the groin area. The site that will be used is cleansed with povidone-iodine (Betadine) or alcohol. The needle is attached to a syringe and inserted into the artery. Approximately 1 teaspoon of arterial blood is withdrawn. After the blood is drawn, pressure must be applied for several minutes to the site to prevent bleeding. ABGs are drawn by a laboratory technician, a nurse, or a physician. For these studies, the blood is drawn at the bedside or in the laboratory.

Pertinent facts

- These tests are more painful than a routine needle stick into the vein. This is because the arteries lie deeper beneath the skin than do the veins; therefore the needle must be put more deeply into the tissues.
- The duration of this procedure is approximately 5 to 10 minutes.
- The customary cost for ABGs is approximately $25.

SPECIAL TESTS
Sputum studies
Normal values

Culture and sensitivities (C&S): Normal throat organisms.
Acid-fast bacilli (AFB): No tuberculosis bacilli seen.
Cytology: Normal cells, no tumor cells.

Purpose

Study of the patient's sputum (that is, the products of an effective deep cough) can provide valuable information in the diagnostic evaluation of a patient with lung disease.

Culture and sensitivities (C&S). Sputum cultures are obtained to determine the presence of bacteria in patients with suspected pneumonia. Pneumonia is an infection of the small air spaces within the lung. This infection is usually caused by a bacterium. Pus develops at the infection site and fills part or all of the lung, thus limiting the air space available for breathing. It is important to identify the bacteria and to determine the antibiotic to which it is most sensitive. The results of this test then indicate the appropriate medicine that the patient should be given. Sputum studies for culture and sensitivity should be done before antibiotic therapy is begun. If antibiotics are initiated before the culture is taken, the bacteria may not grow on the culture medium. This would then cause a false negative result, indicating that the patient is not infected when indeed he or she is.

Acid-fast bacilli. Sputum collections for the examination for acid-fast bacilli (AFB) are usually ordered when tuberculosis is suspected. After taking up a dye such as fuchsin, *Mycobacterium tuberculosis* (the cause of tuberculosis) is not decolorized by an acid alcohol. That is, *Mycobacterium tuberculosis* is considered to be acid-fast and is seen under the microscope as a red rod-shaped organism. If this bacillus is seen, the patient is considered to have active tuberculosis and should be treated appropriately.

Cytology. Tumors within the lung frequently shed cells into the sputum. When the sputum is gathered, the cells are then examined under a microscope. If the test is positive, malignant cells are seen, indicating a lung tumor is present. If only normal cells are seen, and no malignant cells are seen, either no malignancy exists or the tumor is not shedding cells. Therefore a positive test indicates malignancy and a negative test means essentially nothing.

Procedure

Sputum specimens are usually collected when the patient awakes in the morning and before he or she eats or drinks. Only sputum that has come from deep within the lung should be collected. At least 1 teaspoon of sputum must be collected in a sterile, wide-mouthed sputum container. (This will be given to the patient by the laboratory where the sputum is to be analyzed.) Sputum is usually obtained by having the patient cough after taking several deep breaths. If the patient is unable to produce a sputum specimen, coughing can be simulated by lowering the head below the body or by asking the patient to inhale a special aerosolized solution. Other methods used to collect sputum include placing a catheter through the nose and into the trachea and then applying suction to that catheter and collecting the specimen. A second method is to obtain the secretions through the bronchoscope (see Bronchoscopy). A less commonly used form is to puncture the trachea with a needle and inject a solution. As this solution loosens the secretions and the patient begins to cough, appropriate sputum specimens can then be aspirated through that needle. For cytology or AFB determinations, sputum is usually collected on three separate occasions.

The sputum can usually be collected on an outpatient basis. There is no discomfort associated with the collection unless invasive methods are required to obtain sputum. The sputum collection container is provided by the physician or the laboratory.

Pertinent facts

• It is important that the sputum be coughed up from deep within the lungs. Saliva is not considered appropriate as sputum.

- The patient should have the specimen container at his or her bedside. This allows for easy collection on arising.
- The patient should rinse his or her mouth with water before the sputum is collected. Toothpaste or mouthwash should not be used because they may affect the viability of the bacteria or cells.
- Sputum collection can be done on an inpatient or outpatient basis. If the collection is made on an outpatient basis, the specimen should be brought to the laboratory as soon as possible. Delay in the delivery of the sputum may significantly affect the results.
- The customary cost is approximately $45.

Pulmonary function studies (forced vital capacity [FVC], forced expiratory volume in 1 second [FEV$_1$], maximal midexpiratory flow [MMEF], and maximal voluntary ventilation [MVV])
Normal values

The normal or predicted value of FVC, FEV$_1$, MMEF, and MVV depends on the height, weight, and sex of the patient. When the patient's volumes or flow rates are 100% of the predicted value, this represents good pulmonary function. Values less than 50% indicate poor lung function.

Purpose

Pulmonary function studies routinely include determination of the forced vital capacity (FVC), forced expiratory volume in 1 second (FEV$_1$), maximal midexpiratory flow (MMEF), maximal voluntary ventilation (MVV), and arterial blood gas analysis (discussed as a separate test [see p. 88]). Pulmonary function studies are performed for several reasons:

1. Evaluation before an operation. When planned thoracic (chest) surgery will result in loss of functional lung tissue (as in removal of part or all of the lung), there may be a risk of lung failure. If the pulmonary function before an operation is already severely compromised by other disease (such as chronic obstructive pulmonary disease), these patients would not be considered candidates for lung resection. A lung resection in this type of patient may end in death.
2. Evaluation of response to bronchodilator therapy. Some patients with chronic obstructive pulmonary disease have a spastic constricting component to their obstructive disease, which may respond to long-term use of drugs that cause opening (dilatation) of the airway. Pulmonary function studies performed before and after the use of these drugs (bronchodilators) will identify that group of patients.
3. Differentiation between restrictive forms of chronic obstructive pulmonary disease (such as pulmonary fibrosis) and obstructive forms (such as emphysema, bronchitis, or asthma).

FVC. FVC is the amount of air that one can forcefully exhale after maximally inflating the lungs. This volume is decreased below the expected value in patients with either obstructive or restrictive pulmonary disease.

FEV$_1$. FEV$_1$ is the volume of air expelled during the first second of the forced vital capacity. In patients with obstructive disease, airways are narrowed, and therefore the resistance to airflow is high. As a result, not much air can flow out in 1 second, and FEV_1 will be reduced below the predicted value. In restrictive lung diseases such as fibrosis of the lung, the lung is restricted from maximally inflating, even though there is no obstructive component increasing airway resistance. Therefore in these patients, the FEV_1 is decreased, not because of airway resistance, but because the amount of air originally inhaled is less. One should therefore measure FEV_1 in relation to the total FVC. If the patient has the capability of breathing out 80% of the FVC within the first second yet has a decreased FVC, this patient is considered to have restrictive lung disease. In obstructive disease, the ratio of FEV_1 over FVC is below 80%. It is the FEV_1 measurement that will reliably improve with bronchodilator therapy if a spastic component to the obstructive lung disease exists.

MMEF. MMEF is the maximum rate of airflow through the airway during forced expiration. This test is independent of the patient's effort or cooperation. MMEF is reduced below the expected value in obstructive lung disease and is normal in patients who have restrictive lung disease. If it is below 60 liters per minute, surgery carries a prohibitive mortality risk.

MVV. MVV, formerly called maximal breathing capacity (MBC), is the maximal volume of air that the patient can breathe in and out during 1 minute. It is decreased below the expected value in both restrictive and obstructive pulmonary disease.

Procedure

The unsedated patient is asked to breathe into a sterile cylinder that is connected to a computerized machine able to measure and record the desired values. This is usually performed in a pulmonary function laboratory of most hospitals. It can be done on an inpatient or an outpatient basis. The patient is asked to inhale as deeply as possible and then to breathe out as much air as possible. With this, the spirometer computes the FVC, FEV_1/FVC ratio, and the MMEF. Next the patient is asked to breathe in and out as deeply and as frequently as possible for 15 seconds. The total volume breathed is recorded and multiplied by four to obtain the MVV. The test is usually repeated after bronchodilator pulmonary therapy.

The test is usually performed by an inhalation therapist or technician. Patients who are in pain should not undergo this test because they are unable to cooperate by breathing deeply. Also patients whose age or mental status prevent them from fully cooperating should not have this test because the test results would be inaccurate and may be misleading.

Pertinent facts

- The patient must be sure that he or she understands completely the instructions given to him or her by the inhalation therapist.
- One must be assured that the supply of air will not be inadequate during this test.
- The patient should not use any bronchodilator drugs or smoke for 6 hours before this test. Occasionally patients with severe lung disease may be completely exhausted after the test. However, there is no discomfort associated with this test.

- The duration of the test is about 10 minutes.
- The customary cost is approximately $88.

Tuberculin skin test (tuberculin skin test with purified protein derivative [PPD])
Normal values
Negative (that is, a skin reaction less than 5 mm).

Purpose
Although this test is used to detect tuberculosis infection, it is unable to detect whether the infection is active or dormant. For this test, a purified protein derivative (PPD) of the bacterium that causes tuberculosis is injected intradermally (into the skin). This bacterium is not live but simply a protein part of the bacterium. Usually an intermediate strength (0.1 ml or 5 tuberculin units) of PPD is used. If the patient is or has been infected with tuberculosis, his or her immune cells will remember this infection and recognize the PPD. The result is a local inflammatory skin reaction where the PPD has been injected. If, on the other hand, the patient has not been or is not infected with tuberculosis, no reaction will occur. If no reaction occurs and the physician still strongly suspects tuberculosis, a "second strength" PPD (100 to 250 tuberculin units) can be used. If still no reaction occurs, the patient most certainly does not have or has not had tuberculosis.

A word of caution should be mentioned concerning a positive PPD reaction. If a patient with a particular complaint has a positive PPD reaction, this does not necessarily mean that active tuberculosis is the cause of the complaint. It may only mean that the patient has had tuberculosis in the past that is now dormant and not causing any problems. The patient's complaints may be caused by a disease quite different from tuberculosis.

The PPD test can also be used as part of a series of skin tests done to assess the immune system. If the immune system is nonfunctioning because of poor nutrition or chronic illness (such as cancer or infection) the PPD test will be negative despite the fact that the patient has had an active or dormant tuberculosis reaction in the past. It has been well established that surgery is associated with a greater mortality in patients whose immune system is not competent.

When a patient who is known to have or has had active tuberculosis receives a PPD test, the local reaction may be so severe as to cause a complete loss of skin around the injected area. This may require surgical repair. When these patients are eliminated from PPD testing, the test has essentially no complications. There is no chance that one can get active tuberculosis from this test because no live organisms are injected.

Procedure
A nurse prepares the inner aspect of the arm with alcohol and then injects a small amount of PPD into the skin of the arm. The test site is then marked with indelible ink. A nurse or physician reevaluates the test site 48 to 72 hours later for swelling or hardening. If the thickened, swollen area measures more than 10 mm (slightly over ½ inch), the test is considered positive, and it is thought that the pa-

tient is or has been infected with tuberculosis. Measurements between 5 and 10 mm are considered doubtful, and results less than 5 mm are labeled negative.

Patients who are known to have active tuberculosis should not have a PPD test. As previously stated, these patients will have a very severe reaction that will probably result in a severe local reaction. Likewise, patients who have been immunized with bacille Calmette Guerin (BCG) (a tuberculosis immunization) should not be given PPD. These patients will develop a severe reaction similar to those who have had tuberculosis. The test can be performed both on outpatients and inpatients. No sedation is required.

Pertinent facts

- It is important that the patient understand that he or she cannot contract tuberculosis from this test.
- If the patient is known to have tuberculosis or has received a BCG immunization, he or she should notify the physician immediately. The PPD will be cancelled.
- It is important that the results of this test be read by a nurse or a physician within 48 to 72 hours of the initial reaction.
- If the test is positive, it is helpful to recheck the injection site 4 to 5 days later to be certain that a severe skin reaction does not occur.
- The needle used for injection is very small. The quantity of material injected also is very small. As a result, this injection hurts much less than most needle sticks.
- The customary cost is approximately $10.

Sample case report: lung cancer

Mr. N., a 63-year-old man, had a long history of cigarette smoking. He had a chronic cough but more recently had noticed blood-streaked sputum. The results of his physical examination were normal.

STUDIES	RESULTS
Routine laboratory tests	Normal
Chest x-ray films	A suspected tumor mass in the left lower lung field
Tomogram of the chest	Solid mass in the left lower lung field
Sputum studies for cytology, acid-fast bacilli, culture and sensitivity (C & S)	Positive for cancer cells; no acid-fast bacillus. Culture: normal throat flora
Bronchoscopy	Tumor partially obstructing the airway to the left lower lobe
Biopsy from bronchoscopy	Cancer
Mediastinoscopy	No spread of tumor to the lymph nodes
Pulmonary function studies	
Forced vital capacity (FVC)	3400 cc (predicted: 3800 cc)
Forced expiratory volume in 1 second (FEV_1)	2600 cc (predicted: 3000 cc)
Maximal midexpiratory flow (MMEF)	340 L/min (predicted: 360 L/min.)
Maximal volume ventilation (MVV)	120 L/min (predicted: 130 L/min.)

Arterial blood supply (ABG)

pH: 7.41 (normal: 7.35-7.45)
P_{O_2}: 70 mm Hg (normal: 80-100 mm Hg)
P_{CO_2}: 30 mm Hg (normal: 35-45 mm Hg)
HCO_3^- 24 mEq/L
(normal: 22-26 mEq/L)

The mass seen in the lung on x-ray examination and tomography was considered to be malignant based on the sputum cytology study and the bronchoscopy results indicating cancer. Mediastinoscopy showed no tumor had spread to the mediastinal lymph nodes. If these lymph nodes had contained tumor, the cancer would have been considered inoperable. Pulmonary functions before the operation indicated the patient could tolerate an aggressive surgical approach to remove the lung, tumor, and some surrounding lung tissue. Part of his left lung was surgically removed. After surgery, Mr. N. had no problems. He died of unrelated problems 6 years after his operation.

Sample case report: pulmonary embolism (blood clot to lungs)

Mrs. K, a 68-year-old woman, fell on the ice while shopping. She was brought to the local hospital where a fracture of her hip was diagnosed and repaired. She had been doing well until her sixth day after surgery, when she complained of a sudden onset of right-sided chest pain, shortness of breath, and feeling as though her heart were skipping a beat (palpitations).

Physical examination revealed her to be very short of breath and scared. Her pulse rate was elevated. Her heart was normal except for a rapid heartbeat.

STUDIES	RESULTS
Routine laboratory work	Normal
Chest x-ray study	A white area on the right side of her chest
LDH determination (see Chapter 4)	600 ImU/ml (normal: 90-200 ImU/ml)
SGOT determination (see Chapter 4)	33 IU/L (normal: 5-40 IU/L)
EKG (see Chapter 1)	Severe right-sided heart strain
Arterial blood gas analysis (ABG)	pH 7.4 (normal: 7.35-7.45)
	P_{CO_2}: 22 mm Hg (normal: 35-45 mm Hg)
	P_{O_2}: 48 mm Hg (normal: 80-100 mm Hg)
	HCO_3: 23 mEq/L
	(normal: 22-26 mEq/L)
Lung scan	Multiple defects; right side worse than left; strongly suggestive of blood clot to the lungs (pulmonary embolus)

In light of the clinical findings, a blood clot (pulmonary embolism) was highly suspected. The white spot on the chest x-ray indicated that a pulmonary embolus or pneumonia had occurred. The lung scan was compatible with the pulmonary embolus. The trend of elevated LDH in the presence of a normal SGOT is considered classic for pulmonary embolus. The arterial blood gas level indicates the severe lack of oxygen compatible with a significantly serious blood clot to the lungs. This patient was placed on a blood thinner called heparin for a few days. Thereafter, the patient was begun on an oral form of blood thinner called warfarin (Coumadin) and discharged. She had no further problems and warfarin was discontinued after 6 months.

6

Diagnostic studies used to evaluate the brain and nerves

ANATOMY, PHYSIOLOGY, AND COMMON PROBLEMS OF THE BRAIN AND NERVES

The nervous system may be divided conveniently into three areas:
1. The central nervous system, consisting of the brain and the spinal cord
2. The peripheral nervous system, which includes the cranial and spinal nerves
3. The autonomic nervous system, made up of the sympathetic and parasympathetic nerves

Since the diagnostic procedures discussed in this chapter relate primarily to the brain and the spinal cord, this brief discussion of anatomy and physiology is limited to these areas.

The brain is encased and protected by the bony skull, which is a composite of several bones (frontal, parietal, occipital, and temporal). At the base of the skull is the foramen magnum, through which the spinal cord passes. Numerous small openings in the skull permit the passage of cranial nerves and blood vessels. The skull can be fractured by a severe blow to the head. Also, this is not an uncommon site for tumor metastasis (especially from breast cancer and myeloma).

The brain is divided into the cerebrum, cerebellum, and the brain stem (Fig. 6-1). The *cerebrum* is the largest part of the brain. It is divided into two hemispheres, each consisting of four lobes. The *frontal* lobe, located anteriorly, contains nerves that primarily affect the emotional responses, attitudes, and thought processes. The *parietal* lobe, located in the midcentral area, contains nerves associated with sensation and motion. The *temporal* lobe is located on the side (laterally) of the frontal and parietal lobes. It contains the hearing center. The posterior part of each cerebral hemisphere is called the *occipital* lobe, which is primarily concerned with visual perception.

The *cerebellum* is located just below the occipital lobe (Fig. 6-1). It is primarily responsible for the control and coordination of skeletal function and spatial equilibrium.

The *brain stem* extends from the cerebral hemisphere through the foramen magnum, where it then becomes the *spinal cord*. The brain stem includes the mid-

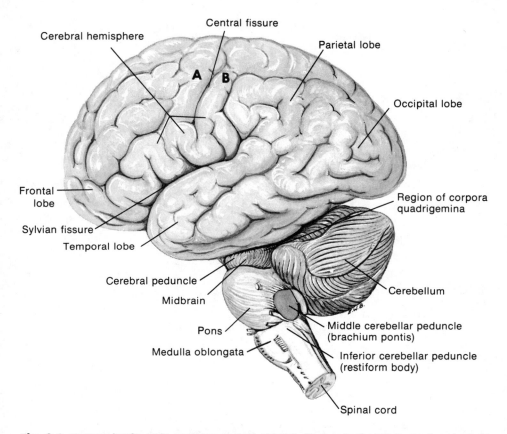

Fig. 6-1. Human brain as it appears on left side. A, Precentral and, B, postcentral convolutions.

From Schottelius, B.A., and Schottelius, D.D.: Textbook of physiology, St. Louis, The C.V. Mosby Co.

brain, pons, and medulla oblongata (Fig. 6-1) and neurologically controls breathing, heart rate, blood pressure, and consciousness. The actual brain tissue itself can be afflicted by primary benign or malignant tumors and even metastatic tumors. Inflammation (encephalitis) is most commonly caused by a virus, yet bacterial infections can and do occur. Scarring after infection or oxygen deprivation can be devastating, resulting in palsy or retardation.

The vertebral column (Fig. 6-2) supports the head and protects the spinal cord. The spinal cord, which is contained within the spinal canal, is about 18 inches long and approximately the width of a finger. The spinal cord is a direct continuation of the medulla oblongata. It contains the motor and sensory relay fibers to and from the higher centers within the cord and the brain (Fig. 6-2). Trauma and tumor are the major serious diseases affecting the spine and the spinal cord. Any unremitting pressure placed on the cord, whether it be a simple disc, fractured bone, or tumor, will cause varying degrees of numbness, weakness, or paralysis.

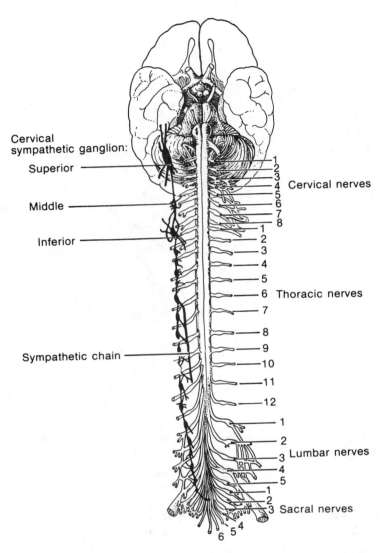

Fig. 6-2. Ventral view of brain and spinal cord with spinal nerves.

From Schottelius, B.A., and Schottelius, D.D.: Textbook of physiology, St. Louis, The C.V. Mosby Co.

Because the brain and spinal cord are vital yet delicate organs, they are well protected by three membranes called meninges (dura mater, arachnoid, and pia mater). The *dura mater* is the dense fibrous outer layer. The *arachnoid* lies next to the dura mater. The *pia mater* is that layer most closely adherent to the brain and spinal cord. The space between the arachnoid and the pia mater is called the subarachnoid space. Within this space, cerebrospinal fluid (CSF) circulates. Infection of the fluid involving the meninges is called meningitis. The result of this severe infection depends on the infecting agent and can vary from mild stiff neck to a progressive, unremitting downhill course ending in death. Tumors, most usually benign meningiomas, can arise from these membranes.

Cerebrospinal fluid (CSF) is formed within the brain from the blood that circulates through the brain. The function of the CSF is to cushion and support the brain and spinal cord within the skull and the vertebral column. This fluid acts as a "shock absorber" and therefore reduces the impact of trauma to the central nervous system. CSF also carries nutrients to various areas of the brain and spinal cord. The average person has approximately 150 ml CSF.

The brain has a dual blood supply that is provided by the carotid artery and the vertebral artery. This double blood supply serves to protect the brain from tissue necrosis (death) in the event of occlusion or blockage of one of the vessels to the brain. If the secondary blood supply is not adequate, a full-blown stroke syndrome will develop. The patient is left with varying degrees of numbness and paralysis. Transient ischemic attacks are small strokes that quickly resolve without deficit. These are a warning that a full-blown stroke is imminent.

Unique to the brain is the blood-brain barrier. This prevents the free movement of particles from the blood into the brain tissue.

X-RAYS AND NUCLEAR SCANS
Skull x-ray
Normal values

Normal skull and surrounding structures.

Purpose

X-ray of the skull allows one to visualize the bones that make up the skull, and the nasal sinuses, in addition to any cerebral calcification. The study is indicated in patients in whom abnormalities are suspected in any of these structures. Fractures of the skull (Fig. 6-3), tumors of the skull, and problems with the nasal sinuses (such as hemorrhage, infection, or tumor) can easily be seen on the skull x-ray. Skull x-rays also may allow one to detect blood clots or brain tumors, which cause a shift of the structures of the brain to one side. There are no complications to this study when it is used appropriately and selectively.

Procedure

The unsedated patient is taken to the radiology (or x-ray) department and placed on the x-ray table. Metal objects (such as bobby pins, barrettes, and earrings) and dentures must be removed because they will obscure visualization of part of the skull. Front, back, side, and other special views are taken. Skull x-ray films are taken by a radiologic technician and interpreted by a radiologist.

Pertinent facts

- Skull x-ray is painless and requires only a few minutes for its completion.
- The patient must remove all objects above the neck. Metal objects and dentures will prevent x-ray visualization of the structures they cover.
- The customary cost of this study is approximately $40.

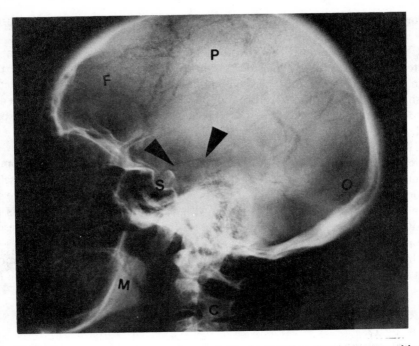

Fig. 6-3. Side view of skull x-ray. Pointers indicate fracture line in temporal bone. F, Frontal bone; P, parietal bone; O, occipital bone; S, sella turcica; M, mandible; C, cervical vertebrae.

CAT scanning (computerized axial tomography [CAT], computerized axial transverse tomography [CATT], electronic musical instrument [EMI] scanning)
Normal values

Normal brain.

Purpose

Computerized axial tomography (CAT) of the brain represents the most significant advance in diagnostic study of the brain in the last 50 years. This remarkable study, which may be performed with or without dye injection, consists of a computerized analysis of multiple x-ray films taken of the skull and brain tissue in successive layers to provide a three-dimensional view of the contents of the skull. The CAT x-ray image provides a view of the head as if one were looking down through its top. The variation in density of each tissue type allows for variable penetration of the x-ray beam. An attached computer calculates the amount of x-ray penetration of each tissue (coefficient) and displays this as shades of gray. This image is placed on a television screen and photographed. The final result is a pictorial series of actual anatomic sections of the brain and skull.

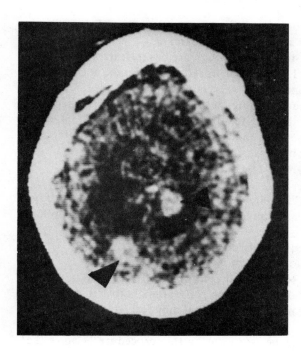

Fig. 6-4. Computerized axial tomogram (CAT scan) of head. Black pointers indicate tumors within brain.

CAT scanning is useful in the diagnosis of brain tumors (Fig. 6-4), infarction, hydrocephalus, bleeding, arteriovenous (AV) malformation, and abnormal displacement of the contents of the skull. Visualization of tumors or any pathologic process that destroys the blood-brain barrier can be enhanced by the intravenous (IV) injection of an x-ray dye. CAT scans may be repeated frequently to monitor any healing process.

In many cases, CAT scanning has eliminated the need for more invasive procedures such as cerebral arteriography (also discussed in this chapter) and pneumoencephalography. There are no complications associated with CAT scanning other than the possibility of an allergic reaction to the dye. The amount of radiation incurred during CAT scanning is comparable to that incurred during a routine skull x-ray series. The final picture is immediately available in the form of an x-ray or Polaroid film. CAT scanning is performed by a technician.

Procedure

The patient is usually kept fasting for 4 hours before the study. Sedation is required only for young children and other patients who cannot remain still during the procedure. Wigs and hairpins are removed from the patient's head. The patient lies on his or her back on an examining table with the head resting in a snug-fitting rubber cap within a water-filled box. The patient's head is enclosed only to the hair line (as in a hair dryer). The face is not covered and the patient can see out of the machine at all times. Sponges are placed along the side of the head to ensure that the patient's head does not move during this study. Any movement will cause computer-generated artifacts to appear on the image produced. The patient is instructed not to talk or sigh during the scanning.

The scanner passes a small x-ray beam through the brain from one side to the other. The machine then rotates 1 degree; the procedure is repeated at each degree through a 180-degree arc. The machine is then moved down about 0.5 to 2 cm, and the entire procedure is repeated through a total of about 3 to 7 "slices," or planes. This procedure requires about 15 to 30 minutes. Usually an iodinated dye will then be used. An IV line is started and the iodine dye is then administered through it. The entire scanning process is repeated.

Pertinent facts

- This is a painless procedure. The only discomfort associated with this study is lying very still on a table. Occasionally the patient may become claustrophobic or uncomfortable during this study.
- Hospitalization is not required for this procedure.
- The patient can wear street clothes during this study.
- This study is performed by a technician in approximately 45 to 60 minutes.
- The patient should not eat or drink anything for 4 hours before this study because the x-ray dye may cause nausea. The patient may feel facial flushing during the dye injection.
- Wigs, hairpins, or clips cannot be worn during this procedure because they hamper visualization of the brain.
- If the patient is allergic to iodine, the iodine x-ray dye used for this study should not be given before the test unless the patient has received antiallergy medication.
- During this study, the patient must lie very still. Even talking or sighing may cause artifacts on the computer image.
- During the procedure, the patient may hear a clicking noise as the scanner machine moves around the head. Some patients describe this sound like that of a washing machine. The patient will not be able to feel the scanning machine rotate.
- No special care is required after the procedure. The patient can resume all activities.
- Patients who did receive a dye injection should increase their fluid intake after the study. This is because the dye is excreted by the kidneys.
- Usually only larger hospitals and university medical centers have CAT scanning devices. Transportation arrangements may have to be made for patients in smaller facilities.
- The CAT scan equipment is usually kept cool to allow the computer to function better. It is helpful for the patient to bring a sweater or blanket in case the room temperature is too uncomfortable.
- The customary cost of this study is approximately $350.

Myelography
Normal values

Normal spinal canal.

Purpose

By placing an x-ray dye into the subarachnoid space (of the spinal canal), the contents of the spinal canal can be outlined on x-ray film. Tumors, herniated discs, and arthritic bone spurs can readily be detected by this study. These lesions will be seen as a narrowing of the spinal canal or as varying degrees of obstruction to the flow of dye within the spinal canal (Fig. 6-5). The entire canal can be examined. This test is indicated in patients with severe back pain or with neurologic signs that could possibly incriminate the spinal canal as the location of injury or disease. Because this test is usually performed by lumbar puncture (also discussed in this chapter), all of the potential complications of that procedure exist.

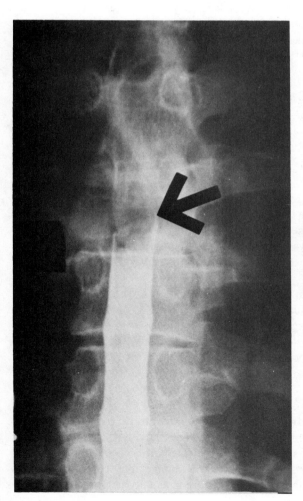

Fig. 6-5. Abnormal myelogram. Obstruction of the dye column at high lumbar level (arrow) is caused by a tumor compressing the canal.

Procedure

A lumbar puncture is performed as described later in this chapter (p. 112-113). Approximately 3 teaspoons of cerebrospinal fluid (CSF) is withdrawn and approximately 3 teaspoons or more of x-ray dye is injected into the subarachnoid space of the spinal canal. With the needle in place, the patient is then placed on his or her stomach while the table is tilted head down. A foot support and shoulder brace or harness keeps the patient from sliding off the table. The column of dye is followed under fluoroscopy (moving x-ray pictures). Representative still x-ray films are taken. Any obstruction to the flow of dye is evident, and the location of the abnormality is determined. When the test is completed, the needle is removed, a sterile dressing is applied, and the patient returns to the ward on a stretcher and will require bed rest.

Pertinent facts

- See Lumbar puncture also discussed in this chapter.
- Examining time for myelography is approximately 45 minutes.
- Usually food and fluid are not permitted for 4 hours before this study to prevent any vomiting during this study.
- The customary cost of this study is approximately $200.

Cerebral angiography (Cerebral arteriography)
Normal values

Normal blood flow to the brain and normal blood vessels in and around the brain.

Purpose

Cerebral angiography provides x-ray visualization of the cerebral blood vessels after the injection of a dye into one of the main arteries leading to the brain (Fig. 6-6). This procedure is used for the detection of abnormalities of the cerebral circulation such as aneurysms (a sac formed by dilatation of the walls of a blood vessel), occlusion (blockage), arteriovenous (AV) malformations, or tumors.

Cerebral angiography is an invasive procedure and is therefore associated with complications. These include:

1. Shock caused by an allergy to the iodinated dye
2. Hemorrhage or bleeding at the site used to enter the artery
3. Stroke caused by the dislodgement of a fatty plaque or clot, which can interrupt the blood supply to part of the brain.

Procedure

The patient is usually kept from having anything by mouth (NPO) after midnight on the day before cerebral angiography. The patient is usually sedated with atropine to dry secretions and meperidine (Demerol) to decrease pain 30 minutes before the test. He or she is taken to the angiography room usually located in the radiology department. This procedure is usually performed with the

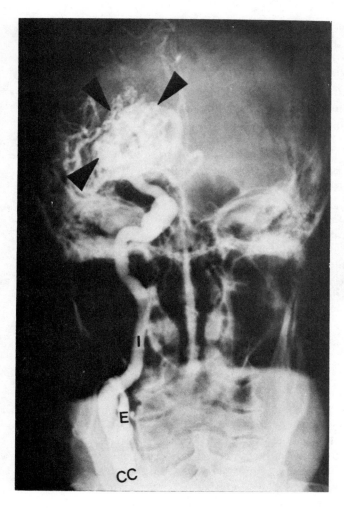

Fig. 6-6. Cerebral angiogram. Black pointers indicate large blood vessel deformity. CC, Common carotid artery; E, external carotid artery; I, internal carotid artery.

patient under local anesthesia. General anesthesia (putting the patient to sleep) is reserved for the confused or extremely restless patient.

The puncture site is determined by the clinical problem under investigation and by the personal preference of the physician performing the study. Usually the artery in the groin is used. The skin site is numbed with an anesthetic such as lidocaine. A needle is placed into the selected artery and then a catheter is placed as the needle is withdrawn. Under fluoroscopy (moving x-ray pictures), the catheter is passed into the desired artery to the brain. The x-ray dye is then injected and the flow of blood through the brain is seen.

The patient is required to lie quietly on his or her back or side during this study. When the dye is injected, the patient will feel a severe, transient, burning sensation and flush. After the x-ray films are completed, the catheter is removed and a pressure dressing is applied over the puncture site. This procedure is performed by an angiographer (x-ray physician).

Pertinent facts

- During the dye injection, the patient will feel a severe, transient, burning sensation and flush. The only other discomfort associated with this study is from the arterial needle stick needed for the dye injection. Most patients are very frightened about this procedure.
- If the patient is allergic to dye, this study will be performed only after appropriate antiallergy medicine is administered.
- Usually a signed consent form must be completed before the study is begun.
- After the study, the blood pressure, pulse, and respirations are monitored frequently to assess any of the complications that can ensue from this study.
- After this study, the patient is usually kept on bed rest for 12 to 24 hours. This allows complete sealing of the arterial puncture site. During this time, the involved extremity should be extended and immobilized. Pulses in the involved extremity are frequently checked.
- An ice bag can be applied to the puncture site to reduce swelling and pain.
- After the study, the patient can usually resume a regular diet. Fluids are usually encouraged to help excretion of the dye from the kidneys.
- The customary cost of this study is approximately $700.

Brain scan
Normal values

No areas of increased radionucleotide uptake within the brain.

Purpose

Brain scanning allows one to detect abnormalities within the brain by scanning of the patient's brain after the intravenous (IV) administration of a radionuclear material. This study is routinely performed on patients who have frequent and severe headaches, stroke syndrome, seizure disorders, or other major neurologic complaints. Normally the blood-brain barrier does not allow the blood to come in direct contact with the brain tissue. Commonly used radioisotopes are unable to cross this blood-brain barrier. However, when abnormalities such as tumor, hemorrhage, or infarction occur, the normal barrier may be disrupted. The isotopes are then preferentially localized or concentrated in these abnormal regions of the brain. A Geiger counter recognizes this relative increase in radioactive material through the intact skull and graphically displays this brain feature (Fig. 6-7). The precise cause of the disruption of the blood-brain barrier can be any number of pathologic processes. Unfortunately, the brain scan is not a specific indicator as to exactly what the disease process is. Study of the location, size, and shape of the abnormality, along with the timing of the scan, may help one specify the disease.

The injection of isotopes followed by immediate scanning can be used to detect changes in the dynamics of the brain blood flow by comparing one side of the brain to the other. For example, an occlusion of the blood vessels on one side of the brain is characterized by a decreased flow rate on that particular side of the brain. This noninvasive study is essentially without complications.

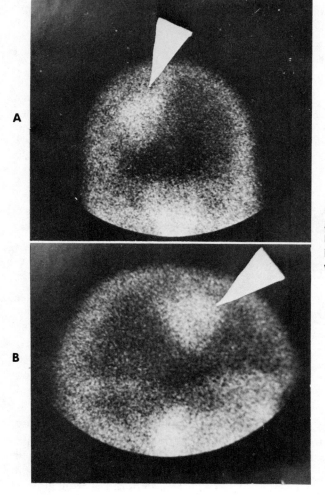

Fig. 6-7. Brain scans. **A**, Anterioposterior view. **B**, Lateral view. White pointers indicate tumor seen in both views.

Procedure

The nonfasting, unsedated patient is given a potassium chloride capsule 2 hours before the IV injection of the radioisotope. The potassium chloride prevents an inordinate amount of the radionuclear material uptake by the brain, which would simulate a pathologic condition. Shortly after the injection of the radioisotope, the patient is placed on his or her back, side, and stomach while the Geiger counter is placed over the head. The radioisotope counts are anatomically displaced and photographed.

When cerebral flow studies are performed, the patient is placed on his or her back and injected with isotopes, and the counter is immediately placed over the head. The counts are anatomically recorded in timed sequence to follow the isotope during the first flow through the brain. Another scan may be obtained later for identification of any pathologic tissue. Brain scanning is performed by a technician in the nuclear medicine department and interpreted by a physician specially trained in radionuclear material.

Pertinent facts

- No discomfort is associated with the study other than that associated with the IV puncture required for the injection of the radioisotope.
- The duration of this study is approximately 30 to 45 minutes.
- The radioactive material will all be excreted from the body within 24 hours.
- There is no danger of radioactive contamination by feces or urine. Only trace doses of radionuclear dye is administered.
- The customary cost of this study is approximately $80.

SPECIAL STUDIES
Electroencephalography (EEG)
Normal values

Normal frequency, amplitude, and characteristics of brain waves.

Purpose

The electroencephalogram (EEG) is a graphic recording of the electrical activity generated by the brain. Brain waves are detected by electrodes in a manner similar to the EKG recording of electrical impulses generated by the heart (see Chapter 1). The EEG electrodes are placed on the scalp overlying multiple areas of the brain to detect and record electrical impulses produced within the brain. Moving graph paper is used. Considerable sophistication is necessary for interpreting the frequency, amplitude, and characteristics of the brain waves (Fig. 6-8).

This study is invaluable in the investigation of epilepsy. Patients with brain abnormalities (such as hemorrhage, abscess, tumor, or infarction) will have abnormally slow EEG waves recorded by the electrodes overlying the abnormal areas. EEGs are also used to determine brain death in comatose patients. Brain death must be determined by two "flat" line EEG recordings of the brain at least 24 hours apart.

Procedure

The patient is instructed to shampoo his or her hair on the night before the study. No oils, sprays, or lotions may be used. The patient should not fast before the study. Coffee, tea, and cola are not permitted on the morning of the procedure. Anticonvulsant medications such as phenytoin (Dilantin) and phenobarbital are rarely discontinued before the study because of the risk of seizures. Only a limited amount of sleep is allowed on the night before this study.

The EEG is usually performed in a specially constructed room that is shielded from outside disturbances (electrical, auditory, or visual). EEGs can, however, be done at the bedside if the patient is too ill to be moved. The patient is placed lying on his or her back in a bed or on a reclining chair. Sixteen or more electrodes are applied to the scalp with electrode paste in a uniform pattern over both sides of the head. One electrode may be applied to each earlobe as a ground.

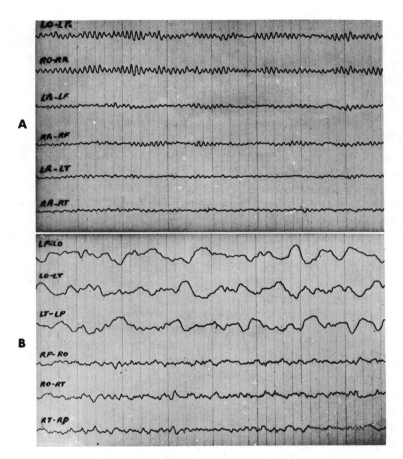

Fig. 6-8. Electroencephalographic (EEG) recordings. **A,** Normal brain waves. **B,** Irregular brain waves in a patient with a brain tumor.

From Conway Rutkowski, B.L.: Carini and Owen's neurological nursing, St. Louis, The C.V. Mosby Co.

After the electrodes are applied, the patient is instructed to lie still with his or her eyes closed. The technician continuously observes the patient during the EEG recording for any movements than can alter the results. Approximately every 5 minutes, the recording is interrupted to permit the patient to move if desired. In addition to the resting EEG, a number of "activating" procedures can be performed:

1. The patient is asked to hyperventilate (breathe deeply 20 times a minute for 3 minutes). This may induce some abnormalities that would otherwise go undetected.
2. Photostimulation is induced by flashing a light over the patient's face with the patient's eyes open or closed. This is important because some seizure activity can be stimulated by a flashing light.
3. The sleep EEG may be performed to aid in the detection of some abnormal brain waves that are seen only if the patient is sleeping (such as certain types

of epilepsy). The sleep EEG is performed after orally administering a sleeping medication to the patient. The recording is performed while the patient is falling asleep, while the patient is asleep, and while the patient is waking up.

After the study, the electrode paste and the electrodes are removed. The patient is returned to the unit or goes home. This study is performed by an EEG technician.

Pertinent facts

- Other than the fatigue caused by missing sleep on the night before the test, there is no discomfort associated with this study. The sleep time of the patient is generally shortened on the night before the test. Adults should not sleep more than 4 to 5 hours, and children not more than 5 to 7 hours. This is done because it allows the patient to relax and possibly fall asleep during the study.
- Many patients fear that the EEG can "read the mind" or detect senility. Some patients fear that the EEG is a form of electric shock therapy. These ideas are false. Another false belief among some patients is that needles are stuck into their head for this study. The electrodes are flat discs of metal that are placed on top of the electrode paste.
- The flow of electrical current for this study is *from* the patient. Therefore no current will be delivered to the patient.
- The patient's hair must be washed on the night before this study. No oils, sprays, or lotions should be used, because these can cause movement of the scalp electrodes and therefore distort the EEG picture.
- The physician will determine if any medications are to be discontinued before this study.
- The patient should not fast before the study. Fasting can cause a low blood sugar, which can modify the EEG pattern. Coffee, tea, and cola are omitted on the morning of the study because of their stimulating effect.
- During the recording of the EEG, the patient's activities should be minimal if any. Movement (including opening of the eyes) will create interference and alter the EEG recording.
- After the study, the patient's hair should be shampooed to remove the electrode paste.
- After the study, safety precautions should be observed to make sure the effect of any sleeping medication has worn off. If the patient is having this study done as an outpatient, another adult should accompany the patient and provide transportation home after the study.
- The customary cost of this study is approximately $50.

Lumbar puncture and cerebrospinal fluid (CSF) examination (LP, spinal tap, spinal puncture)
Normal values

Pressure: Less than 200 mm H_2O.
Color: Clear and colorless.
Blood: None.
Cells: No red blood cells; less than 5 white blood cells/cu mm.

Culture and sensitivity (C&S): No organisms present.
Protein: 15-45 mg/dl CSF.
Glucose: 50-75 mg/dl CSF or greater than 40% of the blood glucose levels.
Cytology: No malignant cells.
Serology for syphilis: Nonreactive.

Purpose

By placing a needle in the subarachnoid space of the spinal column (see Anatomy, physiology, and common problems), one can measure the pressure of the space and obtain spinal fluid for examination. This examination may assist in the diagnosis of brain or spinal cord tumor, hemorrhage, meningitis, encephalitis, and degenerative brain disease. The lumbar puncture may also be used therapeutically to inject medications and to administer spinal anesthesia. Examination of the cerebrospinal fluid (CSF) usually includes evaluation for the presence of blood, bacteria, and malignant cells along with measurement of glucose and protein present. The color is noted and tests are performed to detect syphilitic organisms.

Pressure. By attaching a sterile manometer (Fig. 6-9) to the needle used for the lumbar puncture, the physician can measure the pressure within the subarachnoid space of the spinal cord. A pressure over 200 mm of water is considered abnormal. As discussed in the anatomy and physiology section, the subarachnoid space surrounding the brain freely connects to the subarachnoid space of the spinal cord. Therefore any increase in intracranial pressure (because of tumor, hemorrhage, or edema) will be directly reflected as an increase at the lumbar site.

Color. A red tinge to the CSF indicates the probable presence of blood in the fluid. This blood may be present because of bleeding in or around the brain or spinal cord. Cloudy fluid indicates infection (that is, meningitis).

Blood. Blood within the CSF may indicate bleeding into the subarachnoid space. One must be aware that the spinal tap itself may cause some bleeding.

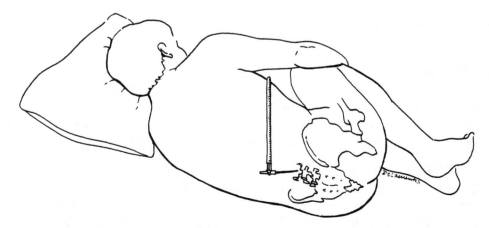

Fig. 6-9. Lumbar puncture. The patient is placed in the fetal position. A manometer is attached to the spinal needle to record pressure recordings.

Cells. The number of red blood cells is merely an indication of the amount of blood present within the CSF. The presence of white blood cells may indicate an infection (such as meningitis). Except for a few lymphocytes, it is abnormal to have any white blood cells in the CSF.

C&S. Organisms that cause meningitis or brain abscess can be cultured from the CSF. These may include bacteria, fungus, or tuberculosis organisms.

Protein. Normally very little protein is found in the CSF. Because protein is a large molecule, it does not normally cross the blood-brain barrier (that is, leave the bloodstream and enter the CSF). However, some diseases can alter the permeability of the barrier, and protein may leak into the CSF. Infection, inflammation (such as meningitis), or tumors may cause an increase in the protein content within the CSF.

Glucose. The glucose level in the CSF is decreased far below the blood glucose level when there is an increase in the number of white cells within the CSF. A low CSF glucose level usually indicates infection.

Cytology. By examining the cells in the CSF, one can determine if a malignancy is present somewhere in the central nervous system. Often, however, tumors do not shed cells and no cells are seen within the CSF.

Serology for syphilis. Late-stage syphilis affects the central nervous system and may be diagnosed by performing one of the commonly available syphilis tests on the spinal fluid.

•   •   •

Complications of lumbar puncture include
1. Persistent leak of CSF, causing severe headache.
2. Introduction of bacteria into the CSF during the procedure, causing meningitis.
3. Laceration of the spinal cord caused by an inaccurately placed needle. This could result in weakness or loss of sensation.
4. Bleeding, resulting from the puncture of one of the blood vessels surrounding the spinal cord.
5. Herniation of the brain from the cranial vault and into the upper spinal canal. This happens only in patients who have an increased pressure inside the skull.

Procedure

No fasting or sedation is required for a lumbar puncture. This study is a sterile procedure that can easily be performed at the bedside by a qualified physician. The patient is placed lying on his or her side with the arms and legs brought together (a fetal position, Fig. 6-9). It is important that the lumbar area be flexed as much as possible to ensure bowing of the spine. This creates more space between the vertebrae for needle insertion. A local anesthetic (usually 1% lidocaine) is injected into the skin after the site has been cleansed with an antiseptic. Next, a spinal needle is placed through the skin and into the spinal canal. The spinal needle can then be attached to a sterile manometer and the opening pressure is recorded (Fig. 6-9). Next, three sterile test tubes are filled with about 2 teaspoons of

CSF and sent for appropriate testing. Finally, the closing pressure is recorded.

After the procedure, the spinal needle is removed and finger pressure is placed over the area of the needle insertion. An adhesive bandage can be placed over the puncture wound. The patient is then placed on his or her stomach with a pillow under the abdomen to increase the pressure inside the abdominal cavity. This indirectly increases the pressure in the tissues surrounding the spinal canal. The patient is encouraged to drink large quantities of fluid in the attempt to avoid a spinal headache. The patient is asked to maintain bed rest for about 6 to 12 hours.

Pertinent facts

- Most patients will describe this test as being uncomfortable. This is because of a feeling of pressure felt when the needle is inserted. Some patients may also complain of shooting pain in their legs. This is caused by the needle touching the spinal nerves to the leg.
- The duration of this procedure is approximately 20 to 60 minutes.
- If properly performed, the insertion of the needle into the spinal canal will not cause paralysis because the needle is inserted below the level of the spinal cord.
- Usually written consent for this procedure is obtained before the test.
- During the procedure, the patient must lie very still. Any movement can cause injury.
- Before the study, the patient should empty his or her bladder and bowels if possible. If these organs are distended, they could possibly be punctured with a misdirected needle stick.
- After the procedure, the patient requires bed rest with his or her head flat. The patient may turn from side to side. The patient is encouraged to drink fluid.
- The customary cost of this procedure is approximately $100.

Nerve conduction studies (electroneurography)
Normal values

No evidence of nerve injury or disease.

Purpose

Nerve conduction studies allow a physician to detect and locate peripheral nerve injury or disease. By initiating an electrical impulse at one site of a nerve and recording the time required for that impulse to travel to a second site of the same nerve, one can determine the conduction velocity (speed) of an impulse in that nerve.

This procedure is performed by placing a shock-emitting device above the area of the nerve to be evaluated and placing a recording electrode over the muscle innervated by that specific nerve. Both the time from the shock to the muscle contraction and the distance from the stimulating electrode to the recording electrode are precisely measured. The distance per unit of time, measured from the shock to the muscular contraction, is called the *conduction velocity*.

The normal value for conduction velocity varies from one nerve to the next.

There is also an individual variation. For these reasons, it is always best to compare the conduction velocity of the afflicted side to the opposite side. In general the range of normal conduction velocity will approximate 50 to 60 meters per second.

Procedure

No fasting or sedation is required or desired for this study. The patient is usually taken to a nerve conduction laboratory in a physician's office or in a physical rehabilitation department. However, the machine is portable, and the study can also be performed at the bedside. Nerve conduction studies are usually performed by a neurologist or physical therapist. The results are interpreted by a physician. The patient is placed in whatever position is determined best for studying the area of suspected nerve injury or disease. A recording electrode is placed on the skin overlying the muscle innervated solely by that nerve. A reference electrode is placed nearby. All skin-to-electrode connections are assured by using electrical paste. The nerve is then stimulated by a shock-emitting device. The time between the nerve impulse and the muscular contraction is measured on a special machine that automatically calculates conduction velocity.

Pertinent facts

- This test is uncomfortable in that a mild electric shock (comparable to that obtained in most household electrical outlet accidents) is required for nerve impulse stimulation.
- This test takes about 15 minutes to perform.
- After the nerve conduction study, the electrode gel is removed from the skin.
- The approximate cost for this test is $300.

Electromyography (EMG)
Normal values

No evidence of nerve or muscle abnormality.

Purpose

Electromyography (EMG) is used to detect muscular disorders. By placing a recording electrode into a muscle, one can monitor the electrical activity of that muscle in a way very similar to electrocardiography (see Chapter 1). The electrical activity of the muscle is displayed on a special screen as an electrical wave form. An audioelectrical amplifier can be added to the system so that both the appearance and the sound of the electrical activity can be analyzed and compared simultaneously.

When the patient is at rest, the EMG records no electrical activity in the normal muscle. As the patient begins to contract the muscle slowly, electrical wave forms are then displayed on the screen. With stronger and stronger contractions, more and more muscle fibers contract, and increasing numbers of wave forms appear on the display. This is representative of good, strong, well-functioning skeletal muscle.

Spontaneous involuntary muscular twitches (such as fibrillation and contraction) can be detected during EMG. When seen, these waves indicate injury or disease of the nerves innervating that muscle. A reduced size of the electrical wave form is indicative of some muscular disorder (such as muscular dystrophy). A progressive decrease in amplitude of the electrical wave form is classic for myasthenia gravis.

Procedure

No fasting or special preparation is required for this study. Although EMG can be done at the bedside, the patient is usually taken to the EMG laboratory. The position the patient is placed in depends on the muscle being studied. A small needle that acts as a recording electrode is inserted into the muscle being examined. An electrode is placed nearby on the skin surface. The patient is then asked to keep the muscle still. The oscilloscope screen display is then viewed for any evidence of spontaneous electrical activity. Next, the patient is asked to contract the muscle slowly and progressively. The electrical wave forms are then examined for number and form. EMG is performed by a physical therapist, physiatrist, or neurologist. The results are interpreted by the physician.

Pertinent facts

- Because the needle used for this study is very small, its placement into the muscle is relatively painless.
- The duration of this study is approximately 20 minutes.
- The customary cost for this study is approximately $150.

Sample case report: seizure disorder

Johnny C., a 12-year-old boy, began to complain of frequent headaches 4 months before his hospital admission. On the day of his admission, he had a major seizure that was observed by his parents. During the seizure, he lost both bowel and bladder control.

STUDIES	RESULTS
Routine laboratory work	Within normal limits (WNL)
Skull x-ray	No evidence of skull fracture
Lumbar puncture:	
Pressure	250 mm water (normal: less than 200 mm water)
CSF examination	All normal except the following:
Protein	120 mg/dl (normal: 15-45 mg/dl)
cytology	Questionably malignant cells
Electroencephalography (EEG)	Slowing of the wave pattern in the posterior portion of the brain (normal: regular, rhythmic, electrical waves)
Brain scanning	Increase in radioactivity in the posterior aspect of the brain (normal: normal, homogeneous, and minimal uptake of radioactive material)

STUDIES	RESULTS
Cerebral angiography	Tumor vessels in the posterior aspect of the brain (normal: normal vessels)
CAT scanning	A soft tissue mass arising out of the cerebellum and invading the occipital lobe of the cerebrum

The skull x-ray ruled out the possibility of a skull fracture as the cause of the boy's problems. Lumbar puncture excluded the possibility of meningitis or hemorrhage. However, the high protein count and the questionable cells indicated a possible tumor. EEG located an area of nonspecific abnormality of the posterior aspect of the brain. Brain scanning, cerebral angiography, and CAT scanning all indicated a tumor in the posterior aspect of the brain.

Because of the above findings, the patient underwent a craniotomy (opening of the skull). An invasive tumor was found to be arising from the patient's cerebellum, invading the occipital lobe of the brain. The tumor could not be removed. After surgery, the patient was given phenytoin (Dilantin), and radiation therapy was administered to the involved area. A chemotherapy regimen was administered. The patient's tumor did not respond to the therapy, and he unfortunately died 4 months after the onset of the disease.

7

Diagnostic studies used to evaluate the bones and joints

ANATOMY, PHYSIOLOGY, AND COMMON PROBLEMS OF THE BONES AND JOINTS

The skeletal system consists of a framework of bones whose main purpose is supporting the soft tissue of the body and protecting delicate internal organs. The inner soft tissue of the bone is called the bone marrow, which forms the blood cells (see Chapter 14). The outer surface of the bone is called the cortex. This cortex is rigid and capable of withstanding tremendous pressure and weight. All bones are covered externally by a strong fibrous tissue called periosteum. The ends of the long bones are called the epiphyses. The midshaft of the bone is called the metaphysis.

There are long bones (meaning that their length is greater than their breadth), short bones, flat bones, sesamoid bones, and accessory bones. Although the size and shape of the more than 200 bones in the human body vary greatly, they are all subject to the same disease processes. Fractures, infections (osteomyelitis), tumors (osteogenic sarcoma), congenital defects (ranging from complete absence to extra limbs), demineralization (osteoporosis and osteomalacia), and acquired diseases (hyperparathyroidism and vitamin D insufficiency) can involve and affect any of these bones. We will restrict our discussion to that of the long bones.

A joint exists at the connection of two or more bones to one another. Some bones articulate (join) at movable joints, such as the knee; and others join at immovable joints, such as those in the skull. The first are called synovial joints, and the latter are called fibrous joints. Synovial joints provide free movement between two bones. The opposed ends of each bone are capped with cartilage. Within each joint is a cavity lined by a synovial membrane that secretes synovial fluid into the joint. It is this membrane that becomes inflamed, granular, and eventually destroyed by ongoing arthritis. Common forms of arthritis include degenerative, which usually occurs in older age; rheumatoid, which can occur at any age; or infectious, which occurs as a result of direct bacterial contact. Likewise, the components of a joint can be involved in tumors, such as synovial cell sarcomas. Each joint is supported by a series of fibrous ligaments. When stressed, these can become partially or completely torn (minor and major sprains).

117

X-RAYS AND NUCLEAR SCANS
X-rays of the long bones
Normal values

No evidence of fracture, tumor, infection, or congenital abnormalities.

Purpose

X-rays of the long bones are usually taken when a patient has a complaint referable to a particular area of the body. Fractures (broken bones) or tumors are readily detected by x-ray. In patients who have a severe and chronic infection overlying a bone, an x-ray may be taken to detect an infection involving that bone (osteomyelitis). Growth patterns can be followed by serial x-rays of a long bone (usually the wrist). Healing of a fracture can also be documented and followed by x-ray of the long bones. X-rays of the long bones are also capable of detecting joint destruction and bone spurring as a result of persistent arthritis.

Procedure

The patient is asked to place the involved extremity in several positions and an x-ray picture is taken in each position. There is no discomfort or any complications associated with this test. The test is routinely performed in the x-ray department. No sedation or fasting is required.

Pertinent facts

- It is important to hold the extremity still while the picture is being taken. This can sometimes be difficult, especially when the patient has severe pain associated with a recent injury.
- It is appropriate to shield the ovaries, testes, or unborn child when the x-ray is being taken to avoid exposure from scattered radiation.
- The customary cost is $30 to $120, depending on the number of bones examined.

Lumbosacral spinal x-ray study (LS spine)
Normal values

Normal lumbar and sacral vertebrae.

Purpose

This is an x-ray study of the five lumbar vertebrae and the fused sacral vertebrae (see Fig. 6-2). It usually includes front-to-back (Fig. 7-1), side-to-side, and oblique views of these structures. The most common indication for this study is low back pain. Degenerative arthritic changes of the spine can frequently be seen as calcified spurs extending from the borders of the involved vertebral bodies. Traumatic fractures, spondylosis (stress fracture of the vertebrae), and spondylolisthesis (slipping of one vertebral body on the other) are also detected by x-ray films of this area.

Metastatic tumor (cancer that spreads from one area to the other) invasion of the spine may be seen as abnormal spots on the spine.

There are no complications to this study when done correctly. This test is contraindicated in the pregnant patient.

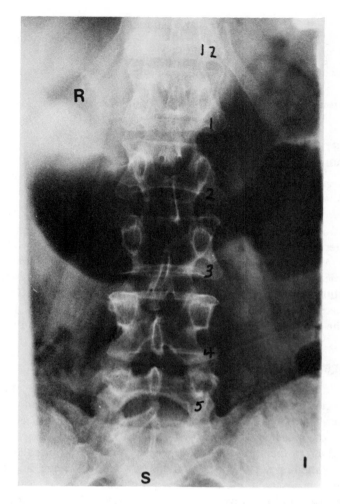

Fig. 7-1. Normal lumbosacral spine x-ray. Anteroposterior view (front to back). R, Rib; S, fused sacrum; and I, iliac bone. The lumbar vertebral bodies are numbered 1 through 5.

Procedure

The unsedated patient is taken to the x-ray department. All the patient's clothing is removed, and a long x-ray gown is placed on the patient. Metal objects (such as sanitary belts) must be removed or they will obscure visualization of the LS spinal area. The patient is then placed on an x-ray table and films are taken of the lumbar and sacral areas.

Pertinent facts

- X-ray films are taken by an x-ray technician in only a few minutes.
- The patient feels no discomfort with this study.

- If the patient is having severe back pain, the patient should be sedated with some type of medication so he or she can remain still during the x-rays.
- The menstrual status of female patients should be assessed. The patient should not be pregnant at the time of the x-ray study to prevent x-ray exposure to the fetus.
- The customary cost of the lumbosacral spine x-ray is about $50.

Bone scan
Normal values

No evidence of abnormality.

Purpose

Bone scanning is a test that permits examination of the skeleton by a scanning camera after the intravenous (IV) injection of a radioactive material. Normally a uniform concentration should be seen throughout the bones of the body. An increased concentration in a specific area is abnormal and may represent tumor, arthritis, fractures, or degenerative disorders. This test often detects abnormalities in the skeleton sooner than is possible with ordinary x-ray film. Bone scanning may also be repeated to detect the response of the body to radiation or chemotherapy.

Procedure

No fasting is required before bone scanning. For this test, the patient receives an IV injection of a radioisotope usually into a vein in the arm. The patient is then encouraged to drink several glasses of water between the injection of a radioisotope and the actual scanning. This period is approximately 1 to 3 hours. These fluids are given to facilitate renal (kidney) clearance of the circulating tracer not picked up by the bone. The patient is then instructed to urinate and subsequently is positioned on a scanning table in the x-ray department. A scanning machine then moves back and forth over the patient's body and detects radiation emitted by the skeleton. This information is then translated into an x-ray film, thus showing a two-dimensional view of the skeleton. Many x-ray pictures are taken, and the patient may have to be repositioned several times during the test.

Pertinent facts

- The only discomfort associated with this study is the IV injection of the radioisotope.
- The injection of the radioisotope takes less than 1 minute.
- Approximately 3 hours after the injection of the radioactive material, the bone scan x-rays are taken in approximately 30 minutes.
- The customary cost of this study is approximately $95.

ENDOSCOPY
Arthroscopy
Normal values

Normal joint.

Purpose

Arthroscopy is an endoscopic procedure that allows direct examination of the interior of a joint with a specially designed endoscope. Endoscopy is a very accurate test because it allows the physician to view the anatomic site directly. This technique can visualize many joints in the body. However, it is most commonly used to evaluate the knee for meniscus cartilage or ligament tears of that joint. Doctors can now perform corrective surgery on the knee through the endoscope. Arthroscopy provides a safe, convenient alternative to open surgery because the surgical instruments can be passed directly through the endoscope equipment. Endoscopy is also used to monitor the progression of disease and to monitor the effectiveness of therapy.

Procedure

For this study, the patient must fast from food and fluid (NPO) after midnight before the day of the procedure. This procedure is commonly performed using a local anesthetic (numbing of the knee area). It may also be performed with the patient under spinal or general anesthesia, especially when knee surgery is anticipated.

The patient is placed lying on his or her back on an operating table. The patient's leg is then carefully surgically scrubbed, elevated, and wrapped with an elastic bandage from the toes to the lower thigh to drain as much blood from the leg as possible. Then a tourniquet is placed on the patient's leg. If a tourniquet is not used, a fluid solution may be instilled into the patient's knee immediately before insertion of the arthroscope to distend the knee and to help reduce bleeding.

The foot of the table is then lowered so that the patient's knee is bent at about 45 degrees. The stocking is opened and a local anesthetic is administered. A small incision is then made in the skin of the knee. The arthroscope (a lighted instrument) is then inserted in and out of the joint space to visualize the inside of the knee joint. Although the entire joint can be viewed from one puncture site, it is often necessary to make additional punctures for better visualization. After the area is examined, biopsy or appropriate surgery can be performed, and the arthroscope is removed. The joint is then irrigated clean. Pressure is applied to the knee to remove the irrigating solution. After a few stitches are placed into the skin, a pressure dressing is applied over the incision site.

Pertinent facts

- Informed consent for this procedure is obtained by the physician before this study.
- The routine preoperative procedure is followed for this procedure. This means the patient must not eat or drink (NPO) after midnight on the night before the study.

- When this procedure is performed under local anesthetic (numbing of just the knee area), the patient may feel a thumping sensation as the equipment is inserted into the joint area. Patients may also feel transient pain during the insertion of the endoscope.
- This procedure is performed by an orthopedic surgeon in approximately ½ hour, depending on the number of procedures performed on the knee.
- Depending on the test results, appropriate treatment or surgery can follow arthroscopy. As mentioned before, surgery can be performed at the same time directly through the endoscopic equipment.
- After the study, the patient should be observed for any signs of infection, which would include fever, swelling, increased pain, and redness at the incision site.
- Any discomfort after this study can be usually relieved by mild analgesics such as aspirin and acetaminophen (Tylenol).
- The patient may walk on the knee as soon as the test is complete. Excessive use of the joint should not be allowed for several days.
- The patient may resume a normal diet after the study.
- Customary cost of this study is approximately $70.

BLOOD TEST
Uric acid test
Normal values

Males: 2.1-8.5 mg/dl
Females: 2-6.6 mg/dl

Purpose

Uric acid is a nitrogenous compound that is a product of purine (DNA building block) catabolism (breakdown). It is excreted in a large part by the kidney and to a smaller degree by the intestinal tract. When uric acid levels are elevated, the patient may have gout. Causes of elevated uric acid levels can be overproduction or decreased excretion of uric acid. Overproduction may occur in patients who have an enzyme deficiency or in patients with cancers. Many causes of the increased uric acid production go undefined and are therefore labeled *idiopathic*.

Decreased kidney excretion of uric acid may result from kidney failure. Dehydration caused by diuretics (water pills) can also result in a decreased kidney excretion, leading to decreased uric acid excretion.

Decreased uric acid levels are not associated with any clinical symptoms and are usually the result of poor liver function. Increased serum uric acid levels may be associated with gout, arthritis, soft tissue deposits of uric acid (tophi), and uric acid kidney stones.

Routine performance of multiphasic blood analysis studies has permitted the early detection of increased levels of uric acid in patients who have no symptoms of gout. This allows the physician to treat the disease at an early stage.

Procedure

This test is usually included in sequential multiple analysis (SMA 12) (see Chapter 15) or any other multiphasic automated systems analysis of the blood. Some hospitals require that the patient be fasting. Usually for these multiphasic analysis studies, two red-top tubes are filled with blood from a vein in the arm.

Pertinent facts

- The only discomfort associated with the study is a needle stick.
- Some hospitals require that the patient be fasting (does not eat or drink anything [NPO] from midnight before the test).
- The customary cost of the study is approximately $8.

SPECIAL STUDIES
Arthrocentesis (synovial fluid analysis)
Normal values

Synovial fluid is slightly yellow and clear with a few white blood cells, no crystals, and a good mucin clot. Chemical test values (such as glucose determinations) should approximate those found in the blood stream.

Purpose

A sterile needle is inserted into a joint space (most commonly the knee) to obtain a fluid specimen of synovial fluid for analysis. Synovial fluid is a liquid found in small amounts in the joints of the body. Joint aspiration (withdrawal of the fluid) may be obtained from the knee, shoulder, hip, elbow, wrist, and ankle.

Arthrocentesis is performed for many different reasons. These include to identify the cause of a swollen joint, to aid in the diagnosis of systemic lupus erythematosis (see p. 247), to follow the progress of joint disease, to aid in the diagnosis of arthritis, and to inject antiinflammatory medication (most commonly corticosteroids) into a joint area.

Complications of arthrocentesis include joint infection and hemorrhage (bleeding) into the joint area.

Procedure

For this procedure, the patient must fast from midnight before the test. If the patient does not fast, some of the chemical evaluations (such as glucose) may be altered from food. If glucose testing of the synovial fluid will not be performed, the patient need not restrict any food before the test.

This procedure is performed in the office or at the bedside. The patient lies on his or her back with the knee fully extended. The knee to be examined is then locally anesthetized to minimize pain. The area is meticulously cleaned. A needle is then inserted through the skin and into the joint space. A small amount of fluid is obtained for analysis. Sometimes the joint area may be wrapped with an elastic bandage to compress free fluid into a certain area to ensure a maximum collection of fluid.

If a corticosteroid is to be injected, a syringe containing the steroid preparation is attached to the needle and injected. The needle is then removed. Pressure is applied to the site, and a bandage is applied. Sometimes blood is drawn from a vein in the arm after this study to compare chemical tests on the blood with chemical studies on the synovial fluid.

Pertinent facts

- An informed consent must be signed for this procedure.
- Even though local anesthetic is used, the patient will probably feel some discomfort when the needle is inserted into the joint.
- After the test is performed, ice is generally applied to the affected joint to decrease pain and swelling.
- Often an elastic bandage is applied to the joint after fluid has been aspirated.
- After this study, the patient may usually resume his or her usual activity. However, strenuous use of the joints should be avoided for the next several days.
- Any pain, fever, or swelling at the joint site should be reported to the physician after the study.
- After the study, the patient may resume a normal diet.
- This procedure is performed by a doctor in approximately 10 minutes.
- The customary cost of this study is approximately $40.

Sample case report: herniated disc

Mr. S., a 38-year-old man, had a 3-year history of low back pain. Although the pain was intermittent and transient, he had lost many work days during the preceding year. In the 2 months before his admission to the hospital, increasing paresthesia (numbness and tingling) had developed in his toes and was associated with mild weakness of his foot. All results of his physical examination were normal except for right-sided lumbar paraspinal muscle spasm.

STUDIES	RESULTS
Routine laboratory work	Within normal limits (WNL)
Lumbosacral spinal x-ray (LS spine)	Normal (no evidence of lumbosacral arthritic degenerative joint disease)
Nerve conduction studies (see Chapter 6)	No abnormalities in the distal sacral nerve or its branches
Electromyography (EMG, see Chapter 6)	Decrease in number of muscle fibers contracting on the anterior tibial muscle
Myelography (see Chapter 6)	Narrowing of the radiographic dye column at the area of L4-5, indicating a herniated disc

The normal results of LS spinal x-ray ruled out degenerative joint disease as the cause of this patient's back pain. Nerve conduction studies and electromyography indicated nerve-root compression at L5 (the fifth lumbar area). Myelography showed that this compression was caused by a herniated intervertebral disc.

The patient underwent decompressive laminectomy of the L4 and L5 region. After the operation he had only minimal back pain that did not interrupt his normal physical activities.

8

Diagnostic studies used to evaluate the kidneys, ureters, and bladder

ANATOMY, PHYSIOLOGY, AND COMMON PROBLEMS OF THE KIDNEYS, URETERS, AND BLADDER

The urinary system consists of the kidneys, ureters, bladder, and urethra (Fig. 8-1). The kidneys are paired organs located on either side of the spinal column just above the waistline. The blood supply to each kidney comes from the renal arteries, which branch off from the abdominal aorta. The renal veins drain the kidneys and empty blood into the inferior vena cava (Fig. 8-1).

The primary function of the kidneys is to regulate the internal environment of the body. Waste products, along with excessive fluid and electrolytes (salts), are filtered out by the kidneys. The filtrate (urine) is formed within the functional units of the kidneys, called *nephrons*. Each kidney is composed of approximately 1 million nephrons. The nephron (Fig. 8-2) includes Bowman's capsule, the surrounding glomerulus, and the renal tubules. A *glomerulus* is a tuft of capillaries (tiny blood vessels). As blood flows through these glomerular capillaries, it is filtered. The filtered material is forced into Bowman's capsule. The filtrate then passes through the kidney tubules and, as it does so, the material needed by the body is reabsorbed. Also, unwanted substances are secreted into the tubules. The resulting urine is then excreted into the renal calyces (Fig. 8-2). These calyces then empty the urine into the "pelvis" (cup-shaped cavity) of the kidney. The urine passes from the kidney pelvis into the ureters and finally into the urinary bladder. The *bladder* is a saclike organ that serves as a temporary reservoir for urine. The bladder wall contains muscles that can contract, resulting in the emptying of the urine from the bladder and into the urethra. The urethra is the canal extending from the bladder and opening to the outside of the body. In the male, the urethra is also the terminal point of the reproductive tract and serves as a passageway for expelling the semen.

Diseases that affect the urinary system are similar in type to those that affect all organs. The kidneys can be the site of (1) serious infection (pyelonephritis); (2)

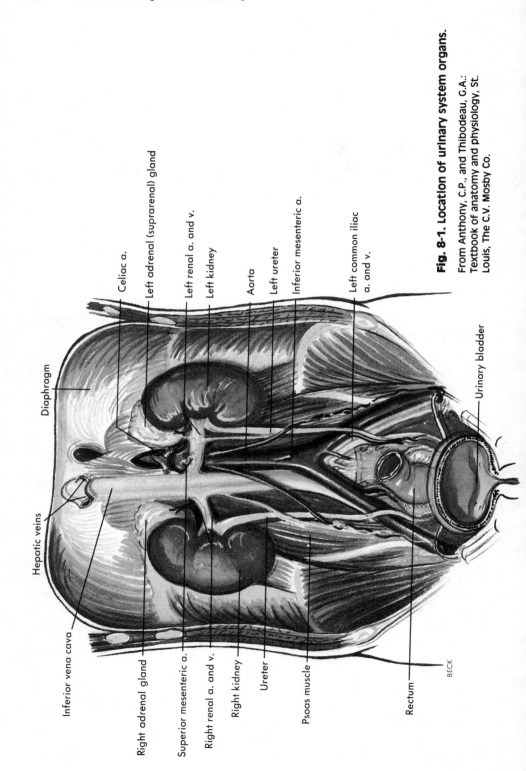

Diaphragm

Hepatic veins

Inferior vena cava

Right adrenal gland

Superior mesenteric a.

Right renal a. and v.

Right kidney

Ureter

Psoas muscle

Rectum

Celiac a.

Left adrenal (suprarenal) gland

Left renal a. and v.

Left kidney

Aorta

Left ureter

Inferior mesenteric a.

Left common iliac a. and v.

Urinary bladder

BECK

Fig. 8-1. Location of urinary system organs.

From Anthony, C.P., and Thibodeau, G.A.: Textbook of anatomy and physiology, St. Louis, The C.V. Mosby Co.

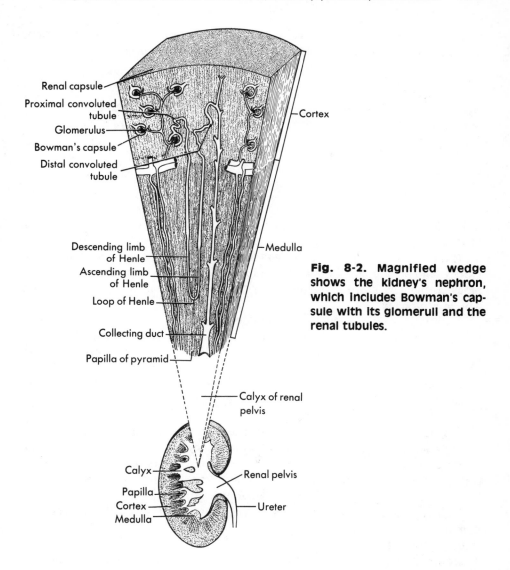

Renal capsule
Proximal convoluted tubule
Glomerulus
Bowman's capsule
Distal convoluted tubule

Cortex

Descending limb of Henle
Ascending limb of Henle
Loop of Henle
Collecting duct
Papilla of pyramid

Medulla

Fig. 8-2. Magnified wedge shows the kidney's nephron, which includes Bowman's capsule with its glomeruli and the renal tubules.

Calyx of renal pelvis

Calyx
Papilla
Cortex
Medulla

Renal pelvis

Ureter

aggressive tumors (renal cell carcinoma in adults and Wilm's tumor in children); (3) inflammation, such as poststreptococcal infection, glomerulonephritis, or drug-induced nephritis; (4) trauma, lacerations, or contusions and (5) diminished blood supply (such as, arterial occlusive disease).

The most common problem affecting the ureters is obstruction. Usually the obstructing agent is a stone (or calculus) but occasionally can be a tumor entrapping the ureter. A surgically misplaced clamp or ligature is the most common cause of sudden ureteral obstruction in the patient who has had an operation.

The bladder is the site of infection when one is said to have urinary trace infection (cystitis). Tumors also will occur, leading to painless urination of blood. The bladder outflow runs directly through the prostate gland in the male. Commonly, this gland becomes enlarged in later life as a result of benign hypertrophy or cancer. The enlargement can obstruct the free flow of urine.

X-RAYS AND NUCLEAR SCANS
Intravenous pyelography (IVP, excretory urography)
Normal values

Normal size, shape, position, and function of the kidneys, ureters, and bladder.

Purpose

In this x-ray study, dye is used to visualize the kidneys, renal pelvis, ureters, and bladder. The dye is injected intravenously and later passes through the kidney structures. X-ray films taken at various times should allow x-ray visualization of these structures.

If the artery leading to one of the kidneys is blocked, the dye cannot enter that kidney, and the kidney will not be visualized on the x-ray. If the artery is partially blocked, the length of time required for the appearance of the dye in the kidney will be prolonged.

With kidney disease (such as glomerulonephritis) there will be a reduction in the quantity of dye filtered. It will therefore take a longer period of time for enough dye to enter the kidney so that the kidneys can be visualized on x-ray films.

A tumor will distort the normal bean-shaped contour of the kidney. Also, defects in the otherwise diffusely filled kidney may be indicative of a tumor (Fig. 8-3).

IVP is used to assess the effects of trauma to the urinary system. Areas of bleeding will be detected by distortion of the kidney shape or by nonvisualization of one of the kidneys. Malposition or absence of the kidneys can also easily be detected. The exact position of the ureters is also important to the surgeon who will be doing abdominal surgery to avoid operative injury.

Kidney stones can be seen blocking the flow of dye down the ureters. Abdominal tumors or abscesses laying on the ureters can also block the flow of dye through the ureters.

Because the bladder fills with the dye, one can also detect bladder tumors and cystoceles. Enlarged prostates can be seen pushing up into the bladder. Loss of bladder muscular tone is seen as a significant amount of residual dye left in the bladder after urination. Abdominal tumors can be suspected by detecting outside compression of the ureters or bladder.

Complications of IVP include the following:

1. Allergic reaction varying from a mild flush and hives to severe life-threatening shock. If the patient has a known allergy to the iodine dye and yet requires an IVP, an allergic reaction can be avoided by medicating the patient with prednisone and diphenhydramine (Benadryl) for 3 days before and after the IVP.
2. Kidney shutdown and failure. This occurs most frequently in the elderly patient who is dehydrated before the dye injection. This can usually be prevented by assuring adequate fluids in these patients before the study.

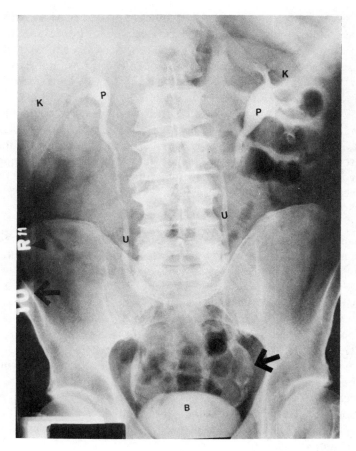

Fig. 8-3. Intravenous pyelogram (IVP). Black arrow at right indicates a tumor in the ureter. K, Kidney; P, renal pelvis; U, ureter; B, bladder.

3. Infiltration of the dye into the skin tissues. This is avoided by making certain that the needle is appropriately placed into the vein. The treatment of infiltration is to elevate the extremity and apply warm soaks.

IVP is contraindicated (not used) in the following:

1. Patients who are allergic to iodinated dyes and are not properly prepared beforehand with prednisone and diphenhydramine (Benadryl).
2. Patients who are severely dehydrated until appropriate rehydration has been achieved.

Procedure

At bedtime on the night before the examination, the patient is given two bisacodyl (Ducolax) tablets. No laxatives are required in the young child or infant. The patient is kept from having anything by mouth (NPO) after midnight. No enemas are given and no oral medications are required. The test can be done on an outpatient or an inpatient basis. On the morning of the study, the patient is taken to the x-ray department and asked to lie on his or her back. An x-ray film of the patient's abdomen is taken to ensure that there is no residual feces in the bowel that would obscure visualization of the kidney system. Skin testing for iodine allergy is sometimes done at that time. However, it is important to realize that a negative skin test does not ensure that a reaction will not occur during the IVP. Contrast dye is administered intravenously (IV). X-ray films are taken at specified times, usually at 1, 5, 10, 15, 20, and 30 minutes, and sometimes longer. The patient is then escorted to the bathroom and asked to urinate. A film is taken after urination to assess the emptying capability of the bladder. Occasionally it is necessary to put pressure on the abdomen to get better filling of the upper part of the ureters. This is done by inflating a rubber tube that is wrapped tightly around the abdomen slightly below the umbilicus.

Pertinent facts

- The patient is given cathartics (laxatives) on the evening before the test. This is because stool or gas in the bowel will obscure visualization of the kidney system. Children and infants are usually not given any cathartics.
- The patient should not eat or drink anything (NPO) after midnight before the study. Moderate dehydration is necessary for concentration of the dye within the kidney system. The oral fasting time in infants and children will vary and will be ordered specifically for each. The oral fasting time for the elderly and debilitated patients will also vary according to the patient.
- If the patient has a history of an allergy to iodine dye, the patient will be given prednisone and diphenhydramine (Benadryl) as ordered 3 days before and after the procedure.
- IVP is not uncomfortable other than for the initial IV placement. The dye injection often causes a flushing of the face, a feeling of warmth, and a salty taste in the mouth. The effects are transient.
- The IVP test is performed by a radiologist (x-ray physician) in approximately 45 minutes.
- After the procedure, the patient can resume a normal diet. The patient should be encouraged to drink a lot of fluids to counteract the fluid depletion caused by the required preparation.
- After the study the elderly and debilitated patient may be weak from the fasting required for the study. These patients should rest and should be encouraged to walk with assistance.
- The customary cost of the study is approximately $120.

Nephrotomography
Normal values

Normal kidneys.

Purpose

Nephrotomography provides a more detailed x-ray visualization of the kidney using the tomographic technique during the performance of an IVP (see previous study). Tomography is a technique by which a sequence of x-ray films, each representing a "slice" of the kidney at different depths, are taken. Tomography permits examination of a single layer or plane of the kidney tissue that would otherwise be obscured on an ordinary film by the surrounding tissue. This study permits visualization of different tissue planes in the kidney for the purpose of differentiating and diagnosing kidney masses.

Procedure

Intravenous pyelography (IVP) is performed as discussed in the previous study. Tomograms of the kidney are taken as the contrast dye is excreted through the kidneys and ureters. For tomography, the x-ray tube and the film cassette are rapidly moved in opposite directions while the x-ray film is taken. This technique effectively blurs all tissue planes except that plane, or "slice," being studied. The patient is unable to recognize these fine, synchronized movements of the tube and the x-ray film.

Pertinent facts

- See previous study for IVP.
- There is no discomfort associated with tomography.
- The duration of the study is approximately 1 hour.
- The customary cost of the study is approximately $100.

Computerized tomography of the kidney (CT of the kidney)
Normal values

No evidence of tumor, cysts, or stones within the kidneys.

Purpose

Computerized tomography of the kidney is a noninvasive yet very accurate x-ray procedure used to detect tumors, cysts, and stones in the kidneys. The technique by which CT scanning provides a cross-sectional image of abdominal organs is described on p. 59-60 in the discussion of CT of the pancreas in Chapter 4 (see Fig. 4-4).

Procedure

See p. 60. No fasting is required for this procedure. A dye may be administered intravenously to enhance the visualization of the kidney.

Pertinent facts

- See p. 60.
- No fasting is required for CT of the kidney.
- This test is performed by an x-ray technician in approximately 30 minutes.
- The customary cost of the study is approximately $200.

Cystography
Normal values

Normal structure and function of the bladder.

Purpose

Filling the bladder with an x-ray dye provides visualization for study of the bladder. Shadows within the bladder or distortion of the bladder may be caused by tumors (Fig. 8-4) or major lower abdominal trauma. Vesicoureteral reflux (abnormal backflow of the urine from the bladder to the ureters), which can cause pyelonephritis (inflammation of the kidney), may be demonstrated by cystography. Although the bladder is visualized during IVP, suspected bladder diseases are best detected by cystography.

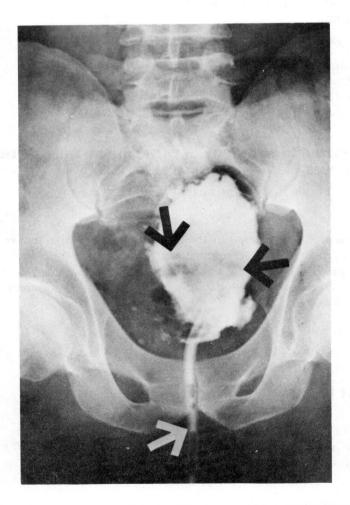

Fig. 8-4. Cystogram. Black arrows indicate large bladder cancer. White arrow indicates Foley catheter in urethra.

Procedure

The patient is given only clear liquids for breakfast on the day of the examination. No bowel cleansing agents are required. The patient is taken to the x-ray department. Unless a catheter is already present, a catheter is placed through the urethra and into the bladder (See Anatomy and physiology). Approximately 1½ cup of x-ray dye is injected through the catheter into the bladder. X-ray films are then taken while the patient lies on his or her back. If the patient is able to urinate, the catheter is removed, and the patient is asked to urinate. X-ray films are then taken to ensure complete emptying capability of the bladder.

Pertinent facts

- This test is moderately uncomfortable if bladder catheterization is required at the time of the test.
- This study is performed by an x-ray physician in approximately 15 to 30 minutes.
- After the study, the patient should watch for burning on urination or fever, which may indicate that a urinary tract infection may have been produced or exacerbated by the study.
- The customary cost of this study is approximately $60.

Retrograde pyelography
Normal values

Normal outline and size of the ureters.

Purpose

Retrograde pyelography refers to x-ray visualization of the urinary tract by placing small tubes in the ureter and injecting x-ray dye. X-ray films are then taken.

Retrograde pyelography is helpful in examining the ureters in patients in whom IVP visualization is inadequate. Retrograde pyelography is used to detect tumors, strictures, stones, and any compression that causes obstruction of the ureters.

Procedure

Ureteral catheters (Fig. 8-5) are passed into the ureters by means of cystoscopy (see p. 138-139). X-ray contrast material is injected and x-ray films are taken while the patient lies on his or her back. The entire ureter and the kidney pelvis (see Anatomy and physiology) are demonstrated. As the catheters are withdrawn, more dye is injected into the ureters and more x-ray films are taken to visualize the complete outline of the ureter.

Pertinent facts

- This study is uncomfortable because of the insertion of the cystoscope.
- See Cystoscopy, p. 139.
- This study is performed by a urologist (kidney doctor) in approximately 1 hour.
- The customary cost of this study is approximately $85.

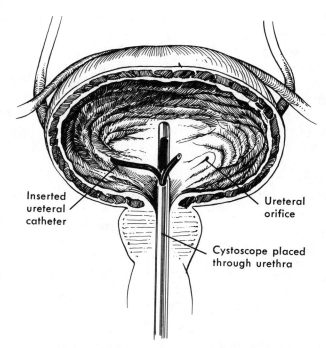

Fig. 8-5. Ureteral catheterization through cystoscope. Note ureteral catheter inserted into right orifice. Left catheter is ready to be inserted into the left ureter.

From Phipps, W.J., Long, B.C., and Woods, N.F., editors: Medical-surgical nursing: concepts and clinical practice, St. Louis, The C.V. Mosby Co.

Plain x-ray film of the kidneys, ureters, and bladder (KUB)
Normal values

No evidence of disease affecting the kidneys, ureters, or bladder.

Purpose

The KUB is a simple x-ray film of the abdomen. It is taken to demonstrate the size, shape, and location of the kidneys. It also can be used to detect tumors, malformations, and stones in the kidneys, ureters, or bladder. This study is contraindicated in a pregnant patient.

Procedure

No fasting or sedation is necessary. In the x-ray department, the patient is placed lying on his or her back. Occasionally the patient is asked to stand for the film. An x-ray film is taken of the patient's lower abdomen. This study can be performed on an outpatient basis.

Pertinent facts

- No discomfort is associated with this study.
- KUB is performed by an x-ray technician in a few minutes.
- For adequate visualization, this study should be scheduled before any barium studies (for example, upper GI, or barium enema [BE])
- The customary cost of the study is approximately $75.

Renal scanning (kidney scan, radiorenography)
Normal values

Normal kidney size, shape, and excretion.

Purpose

This nuclear medicine procedure provides visualization of the urinary tract after the IV administration of a radioisotope. Renal scanning is used to
1. Detect areas of dead renal tissue to which no blood flows
2. Detect renal arterial occlusions or tears
3. Monitor rejection of a transplanted kidney
4. Detect renal disease (such as glomerulonephritis)
5. Detect kidney disease in patients who cannot have an IVP because of allergy to the x-ray dye

Procedure

The unsedated, nonfasting patient is taken to the nuclear medicine department. A minute dose of a radioisotope (a radioactive compound) is injected into a vein in the arm. It takes only a few minutes for the radioisotope to be concentrated in the kidneys. While the patient lies on his or her back, stomach, and side, a radioactive detecting device (Geiger counter) is passed over the kidney area. The counter records the radioactive uptake on either x-ray films or Polaroid film, producing an image of the kidneys. If the artery to a kidney is blocked by atherosclerosis or torn by trauma, the affected kidney will not take up the radioactivity. There will be no radioactive visualization of the kidney on the scan film. Rejected transplanted kidneys have a delayed and abnormal uptake of the radioactive material.

The patient must lie very still during the study. Because only small doses of radioisotopes are used, no precautions need to be taken to avoid radioactive exposure to other people. The test can be performed on an inpatient or an outpatient basis.

Pertinent facts

- The patient feels no pain or discomfort during this procedure.
- The study is performed by a nuclear medicine technician in approximately 1 hour.
- The patient will not be exposed to large amounts of radioactivity because only trace doses of isotopes are used.
- The customary cost of this procedure is approximately $70.

Renal angiography
Normal values

Normal kidney vessels.

Purpose

Through the injection of an x-ray contrast material into the renal arteries (see Anatomy and physiology), renal angiography permits visualization of the large and small blood vessels of the kidney. Atherosclerotic narrowing of the renal artery is best demonstrated with this study (Fig. 8-6). The location of the stenotic (narrowed) area is helpful to the vascular surgeon considering repair of the nearly occluded artery. Complete severence of the renal artery by traumatic injury can also be detected. Tumors affecting the kidney can also be detected with the use of angiography.

As in all studies that use iodinated contrast material, anaphylaxis (allergy-induced shock) is a potential complication. Also, a fatty plaque on the inside of a blood vessel may be dislodged and travel to block the flow of blood to any abdominal organ or to the legs. This plaque would then cause death of the tissue or organ fed by the blocked artery. Another complication of this study is persistent hemorrhage (bleeding) from the "puncture site" used for the arterial needle stick.

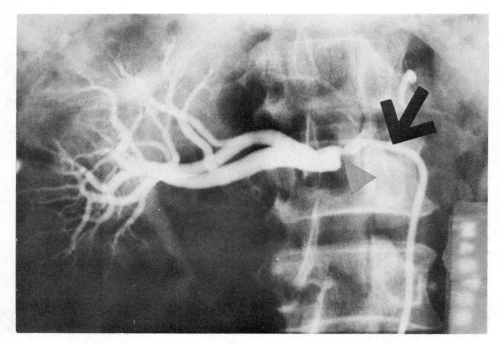

Fig. 8-6. Right renal angiogram. Black arrow indicates catheter in renal artery. Pointer indicates area of renal artery narrowing.

This study is contraindicated in
1. Patients with dye allergies
2. Patients with severe atherosclerosis

Procedure

The patient is kept from having anything by mouth (NPO) after midnight on the day of the examination. The patient is usually sedated with meperidine (Demerol) for pain and atropine to dry secretions. In the angiography room, located in the x-ray department, the patient is placed on an x-ray table. Since access to the renal artery is usually achieved through the femoral artery in the groin, this area is cleansed and draped in a sterile manner. A needle is placed into the artery after the skin is numbed. A small catheter is then passed into the femoral artery and advanced into the aorta (see Anatomy and physiology). With fluoroscopic visualization (motion picture x-ray images displayed on a television monitor), the catheter is manipulated into the renal artery. Dye is then injected and x-ray films are taken in timed sequence over several seconds. This allows all portions of the arteries to be photographed. Delayed films may be taken to visualize subsequent filling of the renal vein. After the x-ray films are taken, the catheter is removed and a pressure dressing is applied to the puncture site. The patient must be admitted to the hospital for this procedure.

Pertinent facts

- This procedure is usually performed by an angiographer (x-ray physician) in about 1 hour.
- During the dye injection, the patient may feel an intense burning flush throughout the body. This is transient and is gone in seconds. The only other discomfort associated with the study is the needle puncture into the groin, which was necessary for access to the artery.
- Written consent for this procedure is obtained before the study.
- The patient should urinate before the sedative medications are given. Bladder distention may cause the patient discomfort during the study.
- After the study, the arterial puncture site (usually in the groin) is frequently observed for bleeding or swelling. The pulse in that leg is frequently checked and the leg is assessed for any sign of decreased blood flow.
- After the study, the leg pulses and the vital signs (pulse, respirations, and blood pressure) are frequently taken to check for blood clots or bleeding, which would require immediate intervention.
- After the study, the patient is generally kept on bed rest for 12 to 24 hours to allow complete sealing of the arterial puncture site.
- Cold compresses may be applied to the puncture site to reduce any discomfort and swelling.
- After the study, fluids should be forced to prevent dehydration caused by the dye.
- The customary cost of the study is approximately $400.

ENDOSCOPY
Cystoscopy
Normal values

Normal structure and function of the urethra, bladder, prostate, and ureters.

Purpose

Cystoscopy provides direct visualization of the urethra and the bladder through the insertion of a cystoscope (a lighted telescopic tube) through the urethra and into the bladder. Cystoscopy is used diagnostically to allow

1. Direct inspection and biopsy of the prostate, bladder, and urethra to detect tumors affecting these organs
2. Collection of separate urine specimens directly from each kidney by the placement of ureteral catheters and collecting their contents
3. Measurement of bladder capacity and evidence of ureteral reflux (back-flow), which can be the cause of recurrent kidney infection.
4. Identification and removal of bladder and ureteral stones.
5. Placement of ureteral catheters for the performance of retrograde pyelography (Fig. 8-5)
6. Investigation and identification of the source of blood in the urine (hematuria)

Cystoscopy is also used to permit

1. Removal of small tumors
2. Removal of foreign bodies and stones
3. Dilatation of a narrowed urethra and ureters
4. Placement of catheters to drain urine from the renal pelvis
5. Coagulation (stopping) of bleeding points within the bladder
6. Implantation of radium seeds into a bladder tumor

After the cystoscope is placed within the bladder, the telescopic lens and lighting system of the cystoscope provide visualization of the lower genitourinary tract. Special instruments such as scissors and needles may be passed through the cystoscope and used appropriately.

Complications of cystoscopy include bleeding, perforation (making a hole), and infection of the bladder.

Procedure

Cystoscopy is usually performed in a hospital cystoscopy room or in a urologist's (kidney surgeon's) office. Fluids are forced several hours before the procedure to maintain a continuous flow of urine for urine collection and also to prevent multiplication of bacteria that may be introduced during the technique. General anesthetics can be used for children and for the uncooperative, overly anxious adult. If general anesthesia is used, the patient is kept from having anything by mouth (NPO) after midnight (or a shorter time in children). Fluids are administered by IV during the procedure.

Patients are sedated 1 hour before this test usually with diazepam (Valium) or meperidine (Demerol). The patient is placed with his or her feet in stirrups as for a female pelvic examination. The external genitalia are cleansed with an antiseptic solution. A local anesthetic (numbing agent) is instilled into the urethra. The patient is then instructed to lie very still during the entire procedure to prevent any trauma to the urinary tract. The patient will have the desire to urinate as the cystoscope passes into the bladder. When the procedure is completed, the patient stays resting in bed for a short time.

Pertinent facts

- When performed on a patient with local anesthesia, this test is uncomfortable, much more so than catheterization of the urethra.
- The cystoscope is inserted into the bladder in the same manner as a Foley catheter.
- Written consent for this procedure is obtained by the physician before the study.
- Sometimes enemas are ordered before the test to clear the bowel.
- If the procedure will be done with the patient under *local anesthesia,* the patient may be given a liquid breakfast. Fluids are encouraged to provide adequate urine samples. A good flow of urine will prevent bacteria from traveling up the urinary tract into the kidney.
- If the procedure will be performed with the patient under *general anesthesia,* general hospital procedures for anesthesia are followed. These include keeping the patient from having anything by mouth (NPO) after midnight. The patient will be given fluids by vein to provide urine samples.
- Medications (diazepam or meperidine) are usually given 1 hour before the test. In addition to reducing the patient's anxiety, the sedatives also decrease any spasm of the bladder and therefore decrease the patient's discomfort. Deep-breathing exercises can also minimize bladder spasms.
- The patient should not be allowed to stand or walk alone immediately after his or her legs are removed from the stirrups. The sudden change in the blood volume may cause dizziness and fainting.
- After the study, the patient's ability to urinate should be evaluated over the next 24 hours. If the patient cannot void, a Foley catheter will need to be inserted. After the test, the urine is checked for color and for the presence of blood. Pink-tinged urine is common. The presence of bright red blood and clots should be reported to the physician.
- The patient may complain of back pain, bladder spasms, urinary frequency, and burning on urination. Warm sitz baths and mild pain pills may be ordered and given. Sometimes belladonna and opium (B & O) suppositories are given to relieve bladder spasms.
- The fluid intake should be encouraged after the study. A dilute urine decreases burning on urination. Fluids also maintain a constant flow of urine to prevent the accumulation of bacteria in the bladder.
- After the test, the patient's vital signs (temperature, pulse, blood pressure, and respiration) are evaluated to detect bleeding or infection.
- Occasionally antibiotics are ordered 1 day before and 3 days following this procedure to reduce the incidence of bacterial infection.
- This procedure is performed by a urologist in about 25 minutes.
- The customary cost of this study is approximately $75.

BLOOD TESTS
Blood urea nitrogen (BUN) test
Normal values

5-20 mg/dl.

Purpose

The tests most commonly used to assess kidney function include the blood urea nitrogen (BUN) test, the serum creatinine test, and the creatinine clearance test (see next several studies). These tests are referred to as "renal function studies." Each will be discussed separately after the BUN study.

Urea is formed in the liver as an end product of protein breakdown and is excreted entirely by the kidney. Therefore the blood concentration of urea is directly related to the excretory function of the kidney and serves as an index of kidney function.

Within the gastrointestinal tract, protein is digested to amino acids, which are absorbed into the bloodstream. In the liver, these amino acids are broken down, and free ammonia is formed as the end product. This ammonia molecule is combined to form urea. The urea is deposited into the blood and transported to the kidneys, through which it is excreted.

Nearly all severe kidney diseases cause inadequate excretion of urea, and the blood concentration (BUN) then rises above the normal value. These kidney diseases include glomerulonephritis, pyelonephritis, acute tubular necrosis, and prolonged urinary obstruction from tumor or stones.

Medications such as gentamycin and tobramycin will decrease BUN excretion. In dehydration there is a physiologic decrease in BUN excretion in the urine, causing the blood level to rise above normal.

BUN may also be elevated in circumstances other than kidney disease. For example, when excessive amounts of protein are available and broken down, larger amounts of urea are made. The normal kidneys are overwhelmed and unable to excrete the sudden increased load of urea, causing the BUN level to rise. Urea levels may also be increased in gastrointestinal bleeding disorders where intestinal blood is broken down and acts as an excessive protein load. Finally, one must be aware that the synthesis of urea depends on the liver. With combined liver and renal disease, the BUN level may be normal not because the renal excretory function is good but rather because liver function is so poor that the liver cannot make BUN.

Procedure

One or two red-top tubes of blood are drawn from a vein in the arm and sent to the chemistry laboratory. A multifunctional analysis machine is usually used to determine the level of BUN.

Pertinent facts

- The only discomfort associated with this study is the needle stick.
- The customary cost of the study is approximately $13.

Creatinine test
Normal values

0.7-1.5 mg/dl.

Purpose

Creatinine, like BUN (see previous study), is excreted entirely by the kidneys and is therefore directly proportional to the kidney excretory function. Unlike BUN, however, it is affected very little by dehydration, malnutrition, or liver function. Creatinine is the breakdown product of creatine, which is used for skeletal muscle contraction. The daily production of creatine, and subsequently creatinine, depends on muscle mass, which fluctuates very little. It is evident with normal kidney excretory function, the serum creatinine level should remain constant and normal. Therefore only kidney disorders (as mentioned in the previous study) will cause an abnormal elevation of creatinine. The normal BUN/creatinine ratio is about 20:1.

Procedure

One or two red-top tubes of blood are drawn from a vein in the arm and sent to the chemistry laboratory. A multifunctional analysis machine determines the level of the creatinine.

Pertinent facts

- The only discomfort associated with this study is the needle stick.
- Creatinine and BUN are usually always done together.
- The customary cost of this study is approximately $11.

URINE TESTS
Urinalysis
Normal values

pH: 4.6-8.0 (6.0 average).
Color: Amber to yellow.
Specific gravity: 1.005-1.030 (usually 1.010-1.025).
Protein (albumin): Up to 8 mg/dl.
Glucose: None.
Ketones: None.
Blood: Up to two red blood cells (RBCs).

Purpose

The urinalysis is a very informative, inexpensive, and easily performed test for kidney disease. The routine urinalysis includes the following: measurement of pH, color, specific gravity; determination of the presence of protein, glucose, ketones, and blood; and finally a microscopic examination of the urine for cells, casts, bacteria, and crystals. Each is discussed separately.

pH. The analysis of the pH of a freshly voided urine specimen is an indication of the acid-base balance of the patient. However, some kidney diseases cause the kidney to inappropriately excrete too much or too little acid. Also certain types of kidney stones are formed in acid urine, while other types are formed in alkaline urine.

Color. The color of urine ranges from pale yellow to amber. The color indicates the concentration of the urine and varies with the specific gravity. Diluted urine is straw-colored and concentrated urine is deep amber.

Abnormally colored urine can result from disease conditions or from the ingestion of certain medications or foods. For example, bleeding from the kidney produces a dark red urine. Dark yellow urine may indicate the presence of bilirubin (see Chapter 4). Beets can cause a red urine. Phenazopyridine (Pyridium) and phenytoin (Dilantin) produce a pink or red to red-brown urine specimen.

Specific gravity. Specific gravity is a measure of the concentration of particles (including water and electrolytes) in the urine and indirectly is a measurement of hydration. A high specific gravity indicates a concentrated urine; a low specific gravity indicates a dilute urine.

Protein (albumin). Normally protein is not present in the urine because the spaces in the normal kidney filter are too small to allow its passage (see Anatomy and physiology). If the filter is injured (as in glomerulonephritis), the spaces become much larger and protein is allowed to seep out of the filtrate and into the urine. If this persists at a significant rate, the patient can lose a lot of protein. Because protein keeps the "water" within the blood vessels, this loss of protein will then cause severe edema in the skin. This is known as the *nephrotic syndrome.*

Glucose. Normally no glucose is detected in the urine. In diabetic patients who are not well controlled with sugar-lowering agents, blood glucose levels can become very high. High glucose levels can also be produced artificially by intravenous (IV) administration of dextrose (sugar)-containing fluids.

In most patients, when the blood glucose level exceeds 180 mg/dl (the renal threshold), glucose begins to spill over into the urine. As the blood glucose level further increases, the amount of glucose in the urine also increases. The amount of glucose is measured as trace to 4 + .

Ketones. In poorly controlled diabetic persons (most often young diabetic persons), there is a massive amount of fatty acid breakdown. The purpose of this breakdown (catabolism) is to maintain an energy source at a time when glucose cannot be used by the cells because of the lack of insulin, which transports glucose into the cells. Ketones are the end products of that fatty acid breakdown. Like glucose, when ketones become increased in the blood, they will spill over into the urine. Ketones in the urine can also be seen in nondiabetic patients suffering from dehydration, starvation, or excessive aspirin ingestion.

Blood. Any destruction in the blood-urine barrier, whether at the glomerular or tubular level (see Anatomy and physiology), will cause blood cells to enter the urine. This is seen with glomerulonephritis, interstitial nephritis, acute tubular necrosis, pyelonephritis, and renal trauma or tumor. Disease conditions affecting the lining of the collecting system (for example, scraping caused by kidney stones) will also cause hematuria (blood in the urine).

Cells. Normally only one or two red blood cells or white blood cells are microscopically found in the urine sediment on microscopic examination. The presence of more than five white blood cells indicates a urinary tract infection. The findings of more than five red blood cells indicates hematuria, the causes of which are previously discussed.

Casts. Casts are clumps of materials or cells. They are found in the renal collecting tubule (see Anatomy and physiology) and have the shape of the tubule, hence the name *cast*. On microscopic examination of urine sediment, white blood cell casts (clumps of white blood cells) may indicate pyelonephritis and red blood cell casts may indicate glomerulonephritis. Hyaline casts are conglomerations of protein and indicate the presence of protein in the urine. It is important that a fresh urine specimen be examined for casts because after the specimen sits for awhile, the casts will break up.

Bacteria. Demonstration of bacteria under microscopic examination indicates a urinary tract infection.

Crystals. Crystals found in the urine sediment on microscopic examination indicate that renal stones are forming, if they are not already formed. The type of crystal found varies with the urine pH (for example, urate crystals occur with an acid urine, and calcium crystals occur in alkaline urine).

Procedure

Urine collection. A reliable urinalysis depends on the proper collection of the urine specimen and the immediate performance of the analysis. The first-voided morning specimen is the ideal urine specimen for analysis because of its concentration and characteristic acidity. However, a fresh urine specimen collected at any other time is usually reliable. For a *routine urinalysis,* usually no special preparation of the patient is needed. The patient urinates (voids) into a clean bedpan, urinal, or preferably a urine container. This specimen cannot be used for a culture and sensitivity (C & S) test. If a C & S test is also required, a *clean-catch,* or *midstream specimen,* is collected. This requires meticulous cleansing of the perineal area or penis with a cleansing preparation to reduce contamination of the specimen by external organisms. The midstream collection is then obtained by having the patient begin to urinate into a bedpan, urinal, or toilet and then stop. (This washes the urine out of the distal urethra, which is the canal extending from the bladder and opening to the outside of the body.) Then a sterile urine container is correctly positioned, and the patient urinates several ounces of urine into the container. The container is then capped. The patient then finishes urinating. For patients unable to urinate, urinary catheterization may be needed. However, this procedure is not commonly performed because of the risk of introducing organisms during the procedure and also because of patient discomfort. In patients with a urinary catheter already in place, the specimen can be obtained by attaching a small needle and syringe into the catheter and withdrawing a sterile urine specimen.

Suprapubic aspiration of urine is a safe and well-tolerated method of collecting urine in newborns and infants. For this technique, the abdomen is cleansed with an antiseptic and a small needle attached to a syringe is introduced into the suprapubic area, which is the area above the pubis. Urine is aspirated into the syringe and then transferred to a sterile urine container.

Routine examination. The pH and the presence of protein, glucose, ketones, or blood can easily be detected by using Multistix reagent strips for urinalysis.

Multistix is a plastic stick to which several separate reagent strips are fixed for testing various substances. The reagent strip is completely immersed in the well-mixed urine and removed immediately to avoid dissolving the reagents. The strip is held in a horizontal position to prevent possible mixing of the chemicals and is then compared with a test chart at the specified times.

Specific gravity. Specific gravity is measured in several easy steps by the use of a urinometer. A weighted instrument (urinometer) is suspended or floated in a cylinder of urine. The concentration of the urine determines the depth at which the urinometer will float. This depth is measured by a calibrated scale on the urinometer and is called the specific gravity.

Microscopic examination. A small amount of urine is placed in a test tube and spun around for several minutes. A drop of the sediment is then placed on a glass slide and examined under a microscope. Another drop of the sediment is smeared on a slide for staining. Cells, casts, crystals, and bacteria are then identified.

Pertinent facts

- The patient should understand the purpose and the specific method of urine collection desired by the physician. The patient should have the proper specimen jars and cleaning agents necessary. Most hospitals use commercial kits for the clean-catch specimen. These contain all the necessary equipment and provide directions for obtaining the specimen.
- If possible, the first-voided specimen of the day should be obtained, because it is usually more concentrated than later specimens.
- If the specimen cannot be tested immediately, it should be covered and refrigerated. Refrigeration may reduce bacterial cell growth and also retard deterioration of the casts and the cells. The pH of uncovered specimens is also altered because carbon dioxide will diffuse into the air and the specimen will become alkaline (basic).
- If the patient is menstruating, this must be indicated on the lab slip.
- Toilet paper or feces should not be placed in the urine container. This would contaminate the specimen.
- The customary cost of a routine urinalysis is $6.00. The C & S takes 48 to 72 hours and adds approximately $20 to the price.

Creatinine clearance test
Normal values

Men: 95-104 ml/min.
Women: 95-125 ml/min.

Purpose

Creatinine clearance is a measure of the glomerular filtration rate, that is, the amount of filtrate made by the kidney per minute. Urine and blood creatinine levels are assessed and the clearance rate is then calculated.

The amount of filtrate made in the kidney depends on the amount of blood present to be filtered and on the ability of the glomeruli of the kidney to act as a filter. The amount of blood present for filtration is decreased in renal artery stenosis (narrowing), dehydration, or shock. The ability of the glomeruli to act as a filter is decreased in certain kidney diseases such as glomerulonephritis.

One must be aware that when one kidney alone becomes diseased, the opposite kidney, if normal, has the ability to compensate by increasing its filtration rate. Therefore with kidney disease affecting only one kidney, one would not expect a decrease in the creatinine clearance.

Procedure

The patient's urine is collected in the appropriate specimen container over a 24-hour period. It is then sent to the chemistry laboratory for measurement of volume and the quantity of creatinine. No special diet is necessary. During the 24-hour collection, a blood creatinine level test is drawn and sent to the chemistry laboratory.

Pertinent facts

- The patient should be shown where to store the urine specimen. The 24-hour urine specimen for creatinine does not need refrigeration. (Some hospitals, however, prefer that all urine specimens be refrigerated.)
- The 24-hour collection begins after the patient urinates. The first urine specimen is then discarded. All urine passed by the patient during the next 24 hours is then collected. Test results are calculated on the basis of a 24-hour output, and results will be inaccurate if any specimens are missed. If one voided specimen is accidentally discarded, the 24-hour collection should begin again.
- The hours for urine collection should be posted somewhere where the patient can be aware of the collection times.
- It is not necessary to measure each urine specimen.
- The patient should urinate before having a bowel movement so that the urine is not contaminated by feces.
- The patient should be encouraged to drink fluids during the 24-hour period, unless this is contraindicated for medical purposes (such as congestive heart failure).
- The last specimen should be collected as close as possible to the end of the 24-hour period.
- A blood sample is drawn from a vein in the arm sometime during the 24-hour period. The only discomfort associated with this study is this needle stick.
- The customary cost for a creatinine clearance test is approximately $15.

SPECIAL STUDIES
Kidney biopsy (renal biopsy)
Normal values

No disease found.

Purpose

Biopsy of the kidney affords microscopic examination of renal tissue. Renal biopsy is performed for the following purposes:
1. To diagnose the cause of glomerulonephritis (an inflammation of the glomeruli of the kidney)

2. To detect cancer of the kidney
3. To evaluate the amount of rejection that occurs after kidney transplantation (information that enables the physician to determine the appropriate dose of certain drugs designed to impede rejection)

Renal biopsy specimens are most often obtained percutaneously (through the skin). During this procedure, a needle is inserted through the skin and into the kidney to obtain a sample of tissue. The most common complication of this procedure is hemorrhage (bleeding) from the kidney. This procedure can also be complicated by inadvertent puncture of the liver, lung, bowel, and blood vessels, which would require surgical repair. Occasionally an open renal biopsy is performed. This involves making a cut through the abdominal wall to expose the kidney and then obtain the specimen. Renal biopsy is contraindicated in uncooperative patients and in patients with

1. Bleeding disorders, because of the risk of extensive bleeding
2. Known kidney tumors, because tumor cells may be spread during the procedure
3. Infections, because the needle insertion may spread the infection

Procedure

The patient is kept from having anything by mouth (NPO) after midnight on the day of the procedure. No sedatives are required. The needle stick can be done at the bedside. This study can also be performed in the x-ray or ultrasonography department, if x-ray or sound wave guidance is used to determine exact placement of the needle stick. The patient is placed lying on his or her stomach with a sandbag or pillow under the abdomen to straighten the spine. Under sterile conditions, the skin overlying the kidney is locally anesthetized (numbed). While the patient holds his or her breath, a physician inserts the biopsy needle into the kidney and takes a specimen. After the procedure is completed, the needle is removed and pressure is applied to the site. A pressure dressing is then applied and the patient is turned on his or her back and instructed to remain on bed rest for about 24 hours. The vital signs (pulse, blood pressure, and respiration), puncture site, and blood values are assessed frequently during the period after the biopsy.

Pertinent facts

• This procedure is uncomfortable, but only minimally if enough local anesthetic is used.
• The procedure is performed by a physician in approximately 10 minutes.
• The physician obtains written consent for this procedure.
• Before the study, the patient's blood clotting ability is assessed. The patient's hemoglobin and hematocrit values (see Chapter 14) should be checked also. The patient may also be typed and cross matched for blood (Chapter 14) in the event of serious bleeding requiring transfusions.
• After the removal of the biopsy specimen, pressure is applied to the site of the needle stick. The patient is usually kept lying on his or her stomach for 20 to 30 minutes after the needle stick to minimize bleeding. The patient is then kept on bed rest for approximately 24 hours.

- After the study, the vital signs and puncture site are checked frequently. The patient is assessed for signs of bleeding, for backache, for shoulder pain, and for lightheadedness. The stomach is evaluated for signs of pain or tenderness.
- All urine specimens should be inspected for bleeding. Usually the patient's urine will contain blood initially. This will usually not continue after the first 24 hours. The urine specimens are placed in consecutive chronologic order to facilitate comparison for evaluation of hematuria (blood in the urine).
- The patient should be encouraged to drink large amounts of fluids to prevent clot formation and urine retention.
- Frequently the patient will have blood drawn for a hemoglobin and hematocrit determination (see p. 226) after the study to check for bleeding.
- For at least 2 weeks, the patient should avoid strenuous activities, such as heavy lifting, contact sports, horseback riding, or any other activity that will cause jolting of the kidney and subsequent bleeding.
- The customary cost of this study is approximately $70.

Renal vein assay for renin
Normal values

Renin ratio of involved kidney to uninvolved kidney less than 1.4

Purpose

This test is used to diagnose hypertension caused by kidney disease. Overproduction of renin is caused by a decreased blood flow to the kidney. Renin, in turn, causes blood vessels to contract. This leads to severe hypertension. For this study, a catheter is placed into each renal vein, and blood is drawn from each vein. A special laboratory technique called radioimmunoassay is used to determine the renin quantity in each. If hypertension is caused by renal artery stenosis (narrowing), the renal vein renin level of the affected kidney should be 1.4 or more times greater that that of the unaffected kidney. If the levels are the same, the hypertension is not caused by kidney artery stenosis. Another cause for the patient's elevated blood pressure must be investigated.

Procedure

To obtain maximum renin stimulation, the patient is placed on a "no added salt" diet and diuretics (water pills) for 3 days before the examination. With a "no added salt" diet, the patient is not allowed to add any salt to a prepared meal. The patient is asked to stay in the upright position for at least 2 hours before the test. The fasting patient is then premedicated with meperidine (Demerol) and atropine and taken to the x-ray department. There the patient is placed on a fluoroscopy table lying on his or her back. The patient's groin area is cleansed and anesthetized. The femoral vein is then punctured, and a thin catheter is placed into the vein and advanced into the inferior vena cava (Fig. 8-1). Fluoroscopy (moving picture x-ray study) is used to monitor the catheter placement. Dye is injected, and the renal veins are identified. The catheter is then placed into one renal vein at a time, and separate blood specimens are withdrawn.

The blood is usually sent to a commercial laboratory for analysis. This test is contraindicated in patients with allergies to iodine dye.

Pertinent facts

- This procedure is not done on patients with allergies to iodine dye.
- Written consent for this procedure is obtained by the physician before the study.
- The patient is kept in the upright sitting or standing position for at least 2 hours before the test, because the renin level is at its maximum when the patient is in this position.
- A "no added salt" diet and diuretics are taken for 3 days before the examination to obtain maximum renin stimulation.
- Medications are given usually 1 hour before the procedure to relax the patient.
- After the test, the patient should check his or her urine for blood.
- The patient should report any back pain or bloody urine to the physician.
- This procedure is performed by a physician in approximately 45 minutes.
- The customary cost of this study is approximately $75.

Split renal function study
Normal values

Equal values for sodium and creatinine in both kidneys.

Purpose

Renal function studies are used to diagnose renal artery stenosis (narrowing). In normal persons and in patients with essential hypertension, there is very little difference between the two kidneys in their ability to absorb and excrete water, sodium, creatinine, and other products. In patients with renal artery narrowing, the affected kidney will absorb excessive amounts of sodium and water. As a result, the urine made by that affected kidney will decrease in volume and have a decreased sodium concentration. The concentration of creatinine will be increased in the urine of the affected kidney because of the increased water reabsorption causing a concentrated urine. The major complication of this study is a urinary tract infection, which is caused by the actual procedure.

Procedure

Cystoscopy (see p. 138-139) is performed, and catheters are placed into both ureters (see Anatomy and physiology). The cystoscope is removed and the two catheters are brought out through the urethra. Urine from each catheter is collected separately for a specified period of time, usually 1 to 24 hours. Both urine specimens are correctly labeled and sent to the chemistry laboratory for analysis and comparison.

Pertinent facts

- The test itself is not uncomfortable, but cystoscopy is moderately uncomfortable. For cystoscopy, a cystoscope (a lighted instrument) is inserted into the bladder in the same manner as is a Foley catheter (see Cystoscopy, p. 138-139).

- It is important that the urine catheters and specimens be correctly labeled.
- No special diet is required.
- This test is performed by a physician in 1 to 24 hours.
- The customary cost of the study is approximately $100.

Sample case report: glomerulonephritis

Bobby G., a 7-year-old boy, was brought to his pediatrician because he had developed bloody urine. About 6 weeks before his admission, he had had a severe sore throat but had received no treatment for it. Subsequently, he had done well except for complaints of mild tiredness and a decrease in appetite. For the 10 days before admission he had had a temperature of 101° daily. He complained of slight back pain. Physical examination revealed a well-developed young boy with moderate back tenderness. The remainder of his physical examination results were negative. His blood pressure was slightly elevated.

STUDIES	RESULTS
Urinalysis	Blood, +4; protein, +1; red blood cell casts, positive; specific gravity, 1.025; red-tinged urine (normal: negative for blood, protein, and red blood cell casts; specific gravity, 1.010-1.025; amber to yellow urine)
Blood urea nitrogen (BUN)	42 mg/dl (normal: 7-20 mg/dl)
Creatinine	1.8 mg/dl (normal: 0.7-1.5 mg/dl)
Creatinine clearance test	64 ml/min (normal: approximately 120 ml/min)
Intravenous pyelography (IVP)	Delayed visualization of both kidneys; enlarged kidneys; no tumors; no obstruction seen.
Renal biopsies	Findings compatible with glomerulonephritis

The blood, protein, and red blood cell casts in this child's urine indicated a kidney problem. The elevated creatinine and BUN levels indicated that the problem was severe and that it was markedly affecting his kidney function. IVP was helpful only in ruling out a tumor. The kidney biopsy was most helpful in suggesting glomerulonephritis. The history of recent sore throat and the renal biopsy findings suggested glomerulonephritis as a result of streptococcal infection.

The patient was placed on a 10-day course of penicillin. He was given antihypertensive medication to lower his blood pressure, and his fluid balance was closely monitored. At no time did the creatinine or BUN level rise to a point requiring dialysis. After 6 weeks, the child's renal function returned to normal (creatinine, 0.7 mg/dl; BUN, 7 mg/dl). His blood pressure medications were discontinued, and he returned to normal activity.

9

Diagnostic studies used to evaluate the thyroid and parathyroid glands

ANATOMY, PHYSIOLOGY, AND COMMON PROBLEMS OF THE THYROID AND PARATHYROID GLANDS
Thyroid gland

The thyroid gland lies in the neck (Fig. 9-1). It has two lobes with a narrow strip of tissue connecting them, thus giving the gland an H-shaped appearance. Within the thyroid gland, thyroid hormones (T_3 and T_4) are produced. Iodine (the basic building block of T_3 and T_4) must be eaten in adequate quantities for thyroid hormone synthesis. Once in the thyroid, iodine is transformed to its inorganic form, which is bound to thyroglobulin. By a complicated coupling mechanism, T_3 (triiodothyronine) and T_4 (thyroxine) are formed. T_4 contains four iodine atoms in each molecule, whereas T_3 contains only three atoms. The hormones, still bound to thyroglobulin, are stored in their inactive states. When secretion is required, the thyroglobulin is broken off, and the free hormone is secreted from the thyroid into the bloodstream. Thyroid hormone regulates the rate of metabolism by increasing the physical and chemical reactions within each cell.

Thyroid disorders

Hyperthyroidism, or thyrotoxicosis, is the hypermetabolic state that occurs with excess production of thyroid hormone. A common cause of hyperthyroidism is Graves' disease. In this disease, the patient will show an enlargement of the thyroid gland, causing swelling in the front part of the neck (goiter). These patients may also have protruding eyeballs (exophthalmos). Another form of hyperthyroidism is Plummer's disease. Benign tumors (adenomas) also can cause hyperthyroidism.

Hypothyroidism results when the thyroid gland produces too little of either or both of its hormones (T_3 and T_4). Major causes of hypothyroidism include
   1. Cretinism (a disorder of infancy and childhood caused by insufficient thyroid hormone during fetal or newborn life)

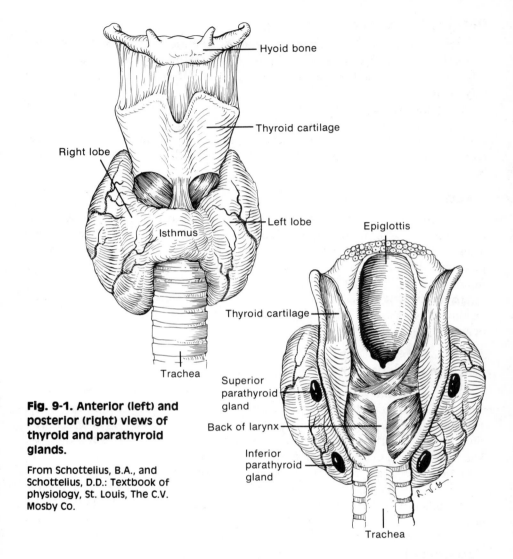

Fig. 9-1. Anterior (left) and posterior (right) views of thyroid and parathyroid glands.

From Schottelius, B.A., and Schottelius, D.D.: Textbook of physiology, St. Louis, The C.V. Mosby Co.

2. Myxedema (the deficient synthesis of thyroid hormone in the adult)
3. Surgical removal of all of the thyroid tissue
4. Radioactive iodine destruction of the thyroid

Both benign tumors (adenomas) and malignant tumors (adenocarcinomas) affect the thyroid gland. Cysts also frequently occur in the thyroid. Usually patients who have tumors or cysts of the thyroid have neither hyperthyroidism or hypothyroidism. They have euthyroidism (normal thyroid function). These patients do not have symptoms of increased or decreased thyroid function but rather have an enlarged "lumpy" gland in their neck.

Inflammation and infection can involve the thyroid gland. Hashimoto's thyroiditis is the most common form of inflamed thyroid. Here again the thyroid is large yet mildly tender to touch. More acute bacterial infections also occur.

Parathyroid glands

Most people have four parathyroid glands; a pair is located behind each lobe of the thyroid gland (Fig. 9-1). The position of the parathyroid gland varies in different patients, and therefore it is often difficult for the surgeon to locate these tiny glands.

The parathyroid glands secrete parathormone (PTH). This hormone is one of the major factors in the control of calcium metabolism. The most potent stimulus to PTH secretion is a low blood calcium level. When the blood calcium level decreases, the parathyroids are stimulated to secrete PTH. This in turn will raise the blood calcium level.

Parathyroid disorders

Hyperparathyroidism (abnormally increased activity of the parathyroid gland) can be the result of overgrowth or tumor of the parathyroid gland. In these diseases both the blood calcium and the blood PTH levels are high. Hyperparathyroidism can also be the result of many other problems, such as kidney failure or PTH-secreting tumors of the lung.

The most common cause of hypoparathyroidism (a disorder caused by underproduction of PTH) is destruction or removal of the parathyroid during thyroid or parathyroid surgery.

Calcium metabolism

Because calcium is the main mineral most affected by PTH, it is important to understand its metabolism. Ingested calcium is actively absorbed in the intestines. The absorption of calcium is facilitated by the action of vitamin D and PTH. Calcium is used in nerve conduction and in skeletal and cardiac muscle contractility. There are large stores of calcium in the bone. PTH can mobilize these stores from the bone and thereby raise the blood calcium level whenever necessary.

Hypercalcemia (high level of calcium in the blood) can be caused by many disorders other than hyperparathyroidism, including tumors of the bone, PTH-producing tumors, vitamin D intoxication, and overingestion of calcium. Hypercalcemia is considered to be a contributing factor in pancreatitis, peptic ulcers, kidney stone formation, and fractures.

Hypocalcemia (low level of calcium in the blood) is most frequently caused by kidney disease, hypoparathyroidism, or low blood albumin levels.

X-RAYS and NUCLEAR SCANS
Thyroid scanning
Normal values

Normal size, shape, position, and function of the thyroid gland; no areas of decreased or increased uptake.

Purpose

This study allows one to determine the size, shape, position, and anatomic function of the thyroid gland with the use of radionuclear scanning (Fig. 9-2). A

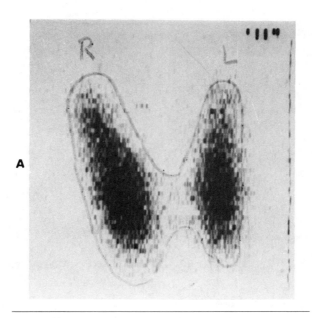

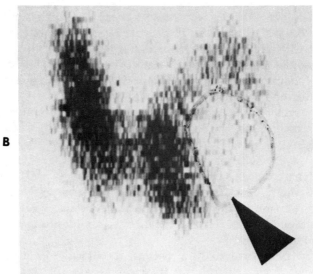

Fig. 9-2. A, Normal thyroid scan. **B,** "Cold" area (pointer) on thyroid scan.

Continued.

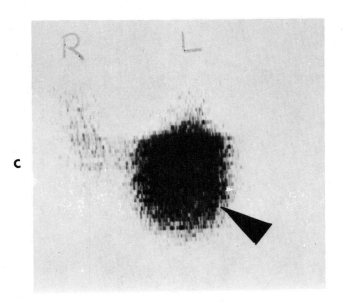

Fig. 9-2, cont'd. C, "Hot" area (pointer) on thyroid scan.

radioactive substance (such as iodine or technetium) is given to the patient to demonstrate the ability or inability of the thyroid gland to take up the radioactive substance. A scanner is placed over the neck area. The scanner makes a graphic record (a photograph or an x-ray film) of the radiation emitted. Areas of increased or decreased uptake are demonstrated.

Thyroid nodules (lumps) are easily detected by this technique. Nodules are classified as functioning (hot) or nonfunctioning (cold), depending on the amount of radiation taken up by the nodule (Fig. 9-2, **B** and **C**). A functioning nodule could represent a benign tumor. A nonfunctioning nodule, on the other hand, may represent a cancer or cyst.

Scanning is useful in

1. Patients with a neck mass, because it can determine whether the mass is arising from within or outside of the thyroid.
2. Patients who have a known thyroid nodule, because it will indicate the nodule's function (that is, whether the nodule is hot or cold) and therefore assist in the diagnosis. Thyroid cancers are almost always nonfunctioning (cold) nodules.
3. Patients with hyperthyroidism, because it will assist in differentiating the exact type of hyperthyroidism (Graves' disease, Plummer's disease, or adenoma). Scanning is also used in evaluating the success of medical therapy for these forms of hyperthyroidism. With successful treatment, one would expect the gland to get smaller.
4. Patients with evidence of metastatic tumor (spreading cancer) without a known origin of the cancer. Scanning may demonstrate that the thyroid was the original site.

5. Patients who have a well-differentiated form of thyroid cancer. Areas of metastasis (spread) will show up on a subsequent nuclear scan of the body because the metastatic thyroid tumor retains its ability to trap radioactive iodine or technetium.

Radiation-induced cancer is the only complication associated with this study. This complication is eliminated if technetium is used instead of iodine. This study is contraindicated in the following:

1. Patients who are taking thyroid or antithyroid drugs, because the drug will affect thyroid uptake of the radioactive agent.
2. Patients who have had recent x-ray dye studies.
3. Pregnant patients, because the radioactive agent administered may adversely affect the fetus.
4. Patients who have recently had radioactive studies.

Procedure

No patient preparation is required. The patient is taken to the nuclear medicine department as an inpatient or an outpatient. A history concerning previous x-ray studies, nuclear scanning, or intake of any thyroid-suppressive or antithyroid drugs is taken. A standard dose of radioactive iodine or technetium is given by mouth. The capsule is tasteless. Scanning is performed 24 hours later. If technetium is used, scanning is performed 2 hours later. A gamma-ray detector is passed over the thyroid area, and the radioactive counts are recorded and displayed in the image of the thyroid gland (Fig. 9-2). The image appears as a photograph or an x-ray film, depending on the technique used.

Pertinent facts

- The study is performed by a technician, and the results are interpreted by a physician.
- No discomfort is associated with this study.
- The duration of the study is approximately 30 minutes.
- The customary cost of this study is approximately $45.

Radioactive iodine uptake test
Normal values

2 hours: 4%-12% absorbed by the thyroid.
6 hours: 6%-15% absorbed by the thyroid.
24 hours: 8%-30% absorbed by the thyroid.

Purpose

The radioactive iodine uptake (RAIU) test is a useful guide to thyroid function. It is based on the ability of the thyroid gland to trap and retain iodine. In this procedure, a known quantity of radioactive iodine is given orally to the patient. A gamma-ray detector determines the quantity or percentage of radioactive iodine taken up by the gland over a specific period of time.

Performing the measurement at different times after the iodine is given allows one to evaluate several aspects of thyroid function. Routinely, the RAIU test is performed 24 hours after the iodine is given. Increased thyroid uptake of radioactive iodine is seen in hyperthyroid states (as mentioned on p. 150), and decreased uptake occurs in hypothyroid conditions (see p. 150-151).

Radioactive exposure to the thyroid is the only complication of this procedure. This is minimized when ^{123}I or ^{125}I is used instead of ^{131}I. (The exposure to radiation is increased as the number is increased.)

The RAIU test is contraindicated in the following:
1. Patients who have taken thyroid or antithyroid drugs
2. Patients who have had a recent x-ray dye study
3. Pregnant patients
4. Patients taking iodine preparations
5. Patients who have recently had radioactive studies

Procedure

The patient is asked to eat only a light breakfast and to report to the nuclear medicine laboratory. Some laboratories prefer that the patient fast overnight. A short history, including dietary habits, recent medication, and previous x-ray dye studies, is obtained. A tasteless standard dose of radioactive iodine (usually ^{123}I) is given by mouth. If RAIU is to be determined at 2 hours, the iodine must be administered intravenously. The patient is then asked to return to the laboratory anywhere from 2 to 24 hours later (usually 24 hours). When the patient returns, a counter is placed over the patient while he or she lies on the back. The amount of radioactive iodine accumulation in the thyroid is then calculated.

Pertinent facts

- The test is not uncomfortable and takes only 30 minutes to perform. A technician performs the study and computes the uptake. A physician interprets the results.
- Before the study, the patient's intake of iodine or thyroid hormone is determined.
- The patient should be informed of any dietary restrictions necessary before the study. Some hospitals prefer that the patient be in a fasting state before taking the tracer dose of radioactive iodine. The patient is allowed to eat 45 minutes later.
- The dose of radioactive iodine used in the study is minute and therefore harmless. No isolation is necessary.
- The customary cost of this study is approximately $45.

BLOOD TESTS
Serum thyroxine (T$_4$) test
Normal values

Murphy-Pattee: 4-11 ug/dl.
Radioimmunoassay: 5-10 ug/dl.

Purpose

This study is a direct measurement of the total amount of thyroxine (T_4) present in the patient's blood. Greater-than-normal levels would indicate hyperthyroid states as seen in Graves' disease, Plummer's disease, or thyroid adenomas. Subnormal values are seen in hypothyroid states such as cretinism or myxedema.

This is a very reliable test of thyroid function. However, it is affected by thyroid-binding globulin (TBG). Because T_4 is bound by serum proteins (that is, TBG), any increase in these proteins (as seen in pregnancy and patients taking oral contraceptives) will cause elevated levels of T_4 and to some extent T_3. This must be considered in interpreting T_4 test results. There are no complications associated with this test.

Procedure

No special preparation is required. Blood is drawn from a vein in the arm and sent to the chemistry laboratory for analysis. There are two commonly used methods of determining T_4 concentrations in the blood. The first is the Murphy-Pattee technique, which measures the ability of T_4 to displace radioactive thyroxine from the thyroxine-binding globulin (TBG). The second more accurate method of determining the quantity of T_4 in the blood is by radioimmunoassay. For this test antibodies tagged with a radioactive tracer are added to the blood sample for binding. All T_4-bound antibodies are then separated out and measured, thus allowing for accurate estimation of the quantity of T_4.

Pertinent facts

- The only discomfort associated with this study is the needle stick.
- If the patient is pregnant or taking any oral contraceptives, this should be reported to the physician, since these conditions will alter the blood levels of T_4. Thyroid medications also will affect the results of the test.
- The approximate cost of the study is $50.

Serum triiodothyronine (T_3) test
Normal values

110-130 ng/dl.

Purpose

Like the T_4 test (see previous study), the serum triiodothyronine (T_3) test is an accurate measure of thyroid function. Generally when the T_3 level is below normal, the patient is in a hypothyroid state. The T_3 determination is clinically important in the patient who has a normal T_4 level but has all the symptoms of hyperthyroidism. This test may incriminate T_3 as the cause of the patient's hyperthyroidism.

Procedure

No special patient preparation is required. A blood sample is drawn from a vein in the arm. There are no complications associated with this study.

Pertinent facts

• The only discomfort associated with this test is the needle stick.
• The customary cost of this study is approximately $40.

Serum calcium test
Normal values

9.0-10.5 mg/dl.

Purpose

This test is used to evaluate parathyroid function and calcium metabolism by directly measuring the total amount of calcium in the blood. Total calcium exists in the blood in its free (ionized) form and in its protein-bound form (with albumin). The serum calcium level is a measure of both. As a result, when the serum albumin level is low, the serum calcium level will also be low, and vice versa.

When the serum calcium level is elevated on three separate determinations, the patient is said to have hypercalcemia (high level of calcium in the blood). Some of the causes of hypercalcemia include tumor of the bone, hyperparathyroidism, vitamin D intoxication, and excessive ingestion of concentrated milk or calcium-containing antacids. Certain diuretics (water pills) may cause hypercalcemia by impairing the urinary excretion of calcium. Hyperparathyroidism can be confirmed by obtaining a serum parathormone blood level determination (see next study).

Hypocalcemia (low level of calcium in the blood) is seen in patients who have hypoparathyroidism (usually following parathyroid surgery) and in patients with kidney failure. Rickets and vitamin D insufficiency also lead to hypocalcemia. There are no complications associated with this study.

Procedure

No fasting is required. Blood is drawn from a vein in the arm. Usually the serum calcium determinations are part of a multiple chemical analysis done automatically by a machine. The patient may be kept fasting for these multichannel examinations.

Pertinent facts

• The only discomfort associated with this test is the needle stick.
• The customary cost of this study is approximately $13.

Serum parathormone test (PTH)
Normal values

Less than 2000 pg/ml.

Purpose

This test is used to measure the quantity of parathormone (PTH) (see Anatomy and physiology) within the blood. Increased levels are seen in patients with hyperparathyroidism and in patients with PTH-producing lung tumors or as a normal compensatory response to low calcium levels in patients with kidney failure or vitamin D deficiency. Decreased levels are seen in patients with hypoparathyroidism (mostly resulting from surgery) or as an appropriate response to high blood levels of calcium in patients with conditions such as bone tumors or vitamin D intoxication. There are no complications associated with this study.

Procedure

The procedure of acquiring blood for this study varies according to the laboratory performing the study. Most laboratories will require that the patient be fasting (that is, not have anything to eat or drink [NPO] since midnight before the test). The serum calcium level determination should be obtained at the same time that the PTH specimen is drawn.

Pertinent facts

- The only discomfort associated with this study is the needle stick.
- The patient should not have anything to eat or drink (NPO) from midnight on the day of the test.
- The customary cost of the study is approximately $80.

SPECIAL STUDIES
Ultrasound examination of the thyroid (thyroid echogram)
Normal values

Normal size, shape, and position of the thyroid.

Purpose

As with other ultrasound studies, a thyroid nodule (lump) can be evaluated with the use of reflected sound waves. In diagnostic ultrasound, a harmless high-frequency sound wave is emitted and penetrates the thyroid. The sound waves are bounced back from the thyroid to a sensor and by electrical conversion are arranged into a pictorial image of the thyroid gland. A realistic Polaroid picture of the thyroid is then obtained. Ultrasound examination of the thyroid is valuable in distinguishing different types of nodules. Solid nodules are tumors. Cystic nodules are abscesses or cysts.

This study also may be repeated at intervals to determine if a thyroid mass is responding to medical therapy. There are no complications associated with this study.

Procedure

The nonfasting, unsedated patient is taken to the ultrasonography department (usually in the x-ray department) and placed lying on his or her back. Gel is applied to the patient's neck area. An ultrasound technician passes a sound transducer over the nodule (lump) in the neck. Photographs are taken of the image displayed, and these are evaluated by the ultrasound physician.

Pertinent facts

- No discomfort is associated with this study. Breathing and swallowing will not be affected by the placement of the transducer on the neck.
- A liberal amount of lubricant will be applied to the neck to ensure effective transmission and reception of the sound waves.
- After the study, the patient can remove the lubricant from his or her neck.
- The test is usually performed by a technician in approximately 15 minutes.
- The customary cost of the study is approximately $100.

Sample case report: thyroid nodule

Mrs. H, a 43-year-old woman, went to her doctor complaining of a lump in her neck. She had no abnormal symptoms. Physical examination revealed a mass on the left side of her thyroid gland.

STUDIES	RESULTS
Routine laboratory work	Within normal limits (WNL)
T_4 test	8 ug/dl (normal: 4-11 ug/dl)
T_3 test	115 ng/dl (normal: 110-130 ng/dl)
Radioactive iodine uptake (RAIU) test	20% (normal: 8-30%)
Thyroid scanning	Cold nodule in the lower lobe of thyroid (normal: no nodules)
Ultrasound examination of the thyroid	Mixed pattern of solid and cystic components (normal: normal size, shape, and position of the thyroid)

The normal values of T_3, T_4, and RAIU testing indicated that the patient was euthyroid (that is, had normal thyroid function). The thyroid scan detected a non-functioning nodule in the thyroid, which could have been caused by a cancer, cyst, or goiter. Ultrasonography eliminated the possibility that this was merely a cyst. Surgery was required to exclude cancer as the cause.

A left-sided thyroid lobectomy was performed with the patient under general anesthesia. Microscopic examination of the tissue indicated that the mass was a goiter. The patient was given medication after the operation to suppress her thyroid gland, and she had no further problems.

10

Diagnostic studies used to evaluate the adrenal glands

ANATOMY, PHYSIOLOGY, AND COMMON PROBLEMS OF THE ADRENAL GLANDS

The adrenal glands (see Fig. 8-1) lie immediately above the kidneys. Because of this anatomic relationship, any significant enlargement in the adrenal glands will displace the kidneys. The adrenal glands have the ability to secrete many hormones that regulate metabolism, growth, development, reproduction, and the stress response. Excess or deficiency of hormones causes various types of abnormalities. The adrenal cortex (outer layer of the adrenal gland) secretes glucocorticoids, mineralocorticoids, androgens, and estrogens. The adrenal medulla (inner layer of the adrenal gland) is responsible for production of epinephrine and norepinephrine.

Glucocorticoid secretion

Cortisol is the primary and physiologically the most important glucocorticoid. The functions of cortisol include the following: control of glucose metabolism, reduction of inflammation, control of protein metabolism, mobilization and redistribution of body fat, regulation of body water distribution by directing the excretion of sodium and potassium, and maintenance of integrity of personality.

Mineralocorticoid secretion

Aldosterone is the primary mineralocorticoid whose functions include increasing water reabsorption, increasing sodium reabsorption, and increasing potassium excretion. Regulation of this hormone is influenced by the pituitary gland and the kidney.

Androgen and estrogen secretion

The quantity of these hormones produced by the adrenals (in contrast to the amount produced by the reproductive glands) is the subject of ongoing debate. However, it is sufficient to say that adrenal production of these hormones is secondary to that produced by the reproductive organs. Androgen is associated with

161

secondary male sex characteristics. Estrogen is associated with secondary female sex characteristics. Either sex has both hormones, although men have more testosterone (an androgen), and women have more estrogen. In men the adrenal gland is the primary source of estrogen; and in women the adrenal gland is the primary source of androgens. After menopause, the adrenals become the only source of estrogen production in women.

Epinephrine secretion

Epinephrine is secreted by the adrenal medulla. This hormone affects smooth muscle and cardiac muscle along with many other tissues. Increased secretion of epinephrine is one of the body's first responses to physical and emotional stress by stimulating the heart to beat fast and stimulating the blood vessels to shunt blood to the muscles and heart.

Diseases affecting the adrenal glands

Many diseases affect the adrenal glands. Cushing's syndrome is the result of an adrenal gland oversecretion of cortisol. This results in diabetes, hypertension, edema, low potassium levels, increased susceptibility to infection, and emotional lability. Cushing's syndrome can be caused by adrenal tumors, adrenal hyperplasia, or nonadrenal ACTH-secreting tumors. One must also be aware that ingestion of steroid medication can also produce the signs and symptoms of cortisol excess.

Addison's disease is the result of decreased cortisol function. Signs and symptoms of this may include low blood sugar, weakness, hypotension, and irritability. Addison's disease is most commonly found in patients who have had their adrenal gland surgically removed and are taking inadequate cortisol drug replacement.

Oversecretion of epinephrine is usually caused by pheochromocytoma (that is, tumor of the adrenal medulla). These patients have persistent severe high blood pressure, rapid heart rate, weight loss, and other symptoms.

X-RAYS AND NUCLEAR SCANS
X-ray study of the sella turcica
Normal values

No abnormalities.

Purpose

This study involves taking an x-ray film of the sella turcica (see Fig. 6-3), which contains the pituitary gland (where adrenocorticotropic hormone [ACTH] is made). ACTH pituitary tumors can cause Cushing's syndrome. One can diagnose these tumors easily by detecting erosion and destruction of the normal sella turcica. This study is usually performed on all patients with Cushing's syndrome.

Procedure

See the procedure for skull x-ray (p. 99).

Pertinent facts

- See the pertinent facts for skull x-ray (p. 99).
- Customary cost for this study is approximately $40.

Adrenal angiography (adrenal arteriography)
Normal values

Normal adrenal artery vessels.

Purpose

In this study, the adrenal gland and its arterial system are visualized by the injection of a radiopaque dye (dye that is visible on x-ray film) into the adrenal artery. Tumors of the adrenals can be easily detected by this technique. Also, adrenal hyperplasia (enlargement) can be diagnosed.

The major complication of this study is anaphylaxis (shock) caused by an allergy to the iodinated dye. In patients with pheochromocytoma (epinephrine-producing tumor of the adrenal medulla), a fatal episode of severe hypertension (high blood pressure) can be precipitated simply by the stress caused by arteriography. Precautionary measures are necessary to prevent this complication. Other complications from this study include hemorrhage (bleeding) from the puncture site used for arterial access and extremity ischemia (decreased blood flow) from dislodgement of a fatty plaque within the artery. Occasionally arteriography can induce serious bleeding within the adrenals. This may lead to destruction of the gland and cause Addison's disease.

Procedure

The procedure used in adrenal angiography is similar to that of renal (kidney) angiography (see p. 137). The only difference is that in adrenal angiography, a tube is inserted (cannulation) for dye injection into the inferior adrenal artery, a branch of the renal artery.

Pertinent facts

- See the pertinent facts associated with renal angiography (p. 137).
- If the patient is suspected of having a pheochromocytoma, propranolol and phenoxybenzamine are ordered before the study to prevent the precipitation of an episode of hypertension.
- The customary cost of this study is approximately $400.

Computerized tomography of the adrenal gland (CT scan of the adrenals)
Normal values

No evidence of abnormality.

Purpose

Computerized tomography (CT) of the adrenal gland is a noninvasive and yet a very accurate method of detecting even very small tumors of the adrenal gland.

Some x-ray physicians feel capable of diagnosing even the type of adrenal tumor on the basis of the density coefficient shown on the CT scan (see p. 59-60). The density coefficients of a normal adrenal gland can also be used to detect adrenal hyperplasia (enlargement).

Adrenal hemorrhage causing Addison's disease can also be detected with this highly refined, recent advance in radiographic tomography.

Procedure

See the procedure for CT of the pancreas (p. 60). No fasting is required. A contrast agent may be administered orally to outline the stomach or intravenously to enhance visualization of the kidney.

Pertinent facts

- See the pertinent facts for CT of the pancreas (p. 60).
- There is no discomfort associated with this study.
- No fasting is required for this study.
- The customary cost of computerized tomography of the adrenal gland is approximately $200.

BLOOD TESTS
Cortisol test
Normal values

AM specimen: 6-28 ug/dl.
PM specimen: 2-12 ug/dl.

Purpose

The best method of evaluating adrenal activity is by direct measurement of the blood cortisol levels. Normally, cortisol levels rise and fall during the day. This is called the diurnal variation. Cortisol levels are highest around 6 to 8 AM and gradually fall during the day to their lowest point around midnight. When an individual's regular working hours are changed (as by working nights and sleeping days), the cortisol secretion rates are usually reversed. Thus it is important for this test to know the patient's activity and sleep times. Sometimes the earliest sign of adrenal hyperfunction is the loss of this diurnal variation, even though the cortisol levels are not yet elevated. For example, individuals with Cushing's syndrome (adrenal gland hyperactivity) often have high plasma cortisol levels in the morning and do not exhibit a decline as the day proceeds. Low levels of plasma cortisol or blood cortisol are suggestive of Addison's disease (adrenal gland hypofunction).

Cortisol can be detected and measured in either the blood or the urine. This study has no complications. Physical and emotional stress can artificially elevate the cortisol level.

Procedure

At 8 AM, after the patient has had adequate sleep, one red-top tube of blood is drawn from a vein in the arm. It is then sent to the chemistry lab for analysis. A second specimen is usually taken later in the day to identify the normal diurnal variation of the plasma cortisol levels. Although the level is at its nadir at midnight, this is a very inconvenient time for the staff, patient, and laboratory. Therefore the blood is collected in a manner similar to the 8 AM collection at around 4 PM. One would expect the 4 PM value to be one third to two thirds of the 8 AM value. Normal values may be transposed in individuals who have worked during the night and slept during the day for long periods of time.

Pertinent facts

- The only discomfort associated with the study is a needle stick.
- Stress (emotional or physical) will cause elevated cortisol levels and complicate test interpretation. Any signs of infection or illness should be reported to the physician.
- The customary cost of this study is approximately $25.

Adrenocorticotropic hormone (ACTH) test
Normal values

AM specimen: 15-100 pg/ml.

Purpose

This is a test of anterior pituitary function that affords the greatest insight into the cause of either Cushing's syndrome or Addison's disease (see Anatomy and physiology). Elevated levels of adrenocorticotropic hormone (ACTH) in patients with Cushing's syndrome eliminate adrenal tumor as the cause of the disease. Whereas low ACTH levels in the patient with Cushing's syndrome point to either a benign or malignant adrenal tumor, likewise, low ACTH levels in the patient with Addison's disease points to primary pituitary failure rather than adrenal disease. High ACTH levels in the patient with Addison's disease is caused by compensatory diseased adrenals. The pituitary ACTH secretion is dependent on the blood cortisol levels. That is, as the blood cortisol levels increase, ACTH secretion should fall; as cortisol levels decrease, ACTH secretion is stimulated (should rise). This important feedback mechanism provides an adequate level of cortisol within the blood.

One must be aware that, like cortisol, there is a diurnal variation in ACTH levels. The levels vary less than cortisol levels (see previous study) and in a way, opposite to them (that is, ACTH levels are lowest at 8 AM and highest in the evening). Normal values are given for the 8 AM specimen.

Procedure

A sample of blood is drawn from the fasting patient usually between 8 and 10 AM. A chilled, plastic heparinized syringe is used to collect 20 ml (approximately 5 teaspoons) of blood from a vein in the arm. The blood is placed on ice and sent immediately to the chemistry laboratory for analysis. As with cortisol (see previous test), stress of any kind can artificially increase the ACTH level.

Pertinent facts

- The only discomfort associated with this study is a needle stick.
- Stress (either physical or emotional) will cause elevated levels and complicate the test interpretation. Any sign of physical stress (such as infection or illness) or emotional stress should be reported to the physician.
- The customary cost of this study is approximately $90.

Adrenocorticotropic hormone (ACTH) stimulation test
Normal values

Greater than 40 ug/dl after 24-hour infusion.

Purpose

In this test, ACTH medication (cosyntropin) is given to the patient and the ability of the adrenals to respond to ACTH stimulation is measured by blood cortisol levels. As mentioned earlier, ACTH is the pituitary hormone that causes the adrenals to secrete cortisol. In normal patients, after a 24-hour ACTH intravenous infusion, the plasma cortisol level should increase and exceed 40 ug/dl. Patients with Cushing's disease and bilateral adrenal hyperplasia will have an exaggerated response to ACTH stimulation. However, there is little or no cortisol increase above the baseline in patients who have adrenal tumors (because the tumor is unresponsive to ACTH stimulation).

This test is even more valuable in a patient suspected of having Addison's disease (adrenal insufficiency). If blood cortisol levels are between 10 and 40 ug/dl after a 24-hour infusion of ACTH, this shows that the adrenal gland is capable of function if stimulated. The cause of the adrenal insufficiency then lies within the pituitary gland. The patient thus has a "secondary" adrenal insufficiency. If there is little or no rise in cortisol levels, the adrenal gland is incapable of secreting cortisol because of destruction, tumor, surgical removal, enzyme deficiency, or other causes.

Procedure

After obtaining a baseline blood cortisol level (see p. 164-165), an intravenous (IV) infusion of ACTH is administered in an IV bottle over a 24-hour period. Blood is then drawn from a vein in the arm at the end of the 24-hour period and sent to the chemistry laboratory for a blood cortisol level analysis. This test can also be performed by comparing the baseline urine hydroxycorticosteroid secretion (see p. 170-171) with the stimulated hydroxycorticosteroid excretion. In normal patients, stimulated hydroxysteroid excretion should exceed 25 mg per day.

The ACTH stimulation test can also be performed by administering ACTH (cosyntropin) intravenously over an 8-hour period on 2 or 3 consecutive days. The response seen at the end of the second and third 8-hour period should approximate that seen after the continuous 24-hour infusion.

For the sake of convenience, a rapid ACTH stimulation test can be done by giving an intramuscular (IM) injection of cosyntropin and measuring the blood cortisol levels before and at 30- and 60-minute intervals after drug administration. Normal patients have an increase in cortisol of more than 7 ug/dl above baseline values.

Pertinent facts

- The discomfort associated with the study is a needle stick to withdraw blood for the blood cortisol levels and for the intravenous or intramuscular injection of ACTH.
- This test takes approximately 24 hours to complete. As described above, the test can also be done alternate ways over a 3-day period or over a several hour period.
- The approximate cost of this study is $90.

Dexamathasone suppression test (adrenal suppression test, cortisol suppression test)
Normal values

Greater than 50% reduction of plasma cortisol and 17-hydroxycorticosteroid (17-OCHS) levels.

Purpose

This is the most important test for diagnosing adrenal hyperfunction (Cushing's syndrome). This test also enables one to distinguish the different causes of adrenal hyperfunction.

As described in the discussion of the physiology of the adrenals (see Anatomy and physiology), pituitary ACTH is dependent on the blood cortisol levels. That is, as the blood cortisol levels increase, ACTH secretion is suppressed; as cortisol levels decrease, ACTH secretion is stimulated. This important feedback system does not function properly in patients with Cushing's syndrome.

Dexamethasone is a potent synthetic glucocorticoid, much like cortisol. In normal patients, even low doses of dexamethasone will inhibit ACTH secretion. This will result in reduced stimulation to the adrenals and ultimately a drop of 50% or more in blood cortisol and urinary 17-OCHS levels.

Patients with adrenal hyperplasia will not suppress cortisol production with low-dosage dexamethasone administration but will do so on high-dosage administration. Patients with adrenal tumors will not suppress even with high dosages of dexamethasone.

Procedure

In this test, urinary 17-OCHS levels are usually measured (see p. 170-171). However, with the increased ease in obtaining blood cortisol levels, this measurement is gradually replacing the urine determination. Nevertheless, we will describe the commonly performed classic dexamethasone suppression test.

Day 1 A baseline, 24-hour urine test for corticosteroids (urinary 17-OCHS or urinary cortisol) is done.

Day 2 Same as day 1.

Day 3 A small dose of dexamethasone is given by mouth every 6 hours. A 24-hour urine test for corticosteroids is done (as on day 1 and day 2).

Day 4 Same as day 3.

Day 5 A large dose of dexamethasone is given by mouth every 6 hours. A 24-hour urine test for corticosteroids is done.

Day 6 Same as day 5.

The creatinine content (see p. 141) should be measured in all 24-hour urine collections to demonstrate the accuracy and adequacy of the collection. The urine sample for cortisol and 17-OCHS should not contain a preservative. Specimens can be refrigerated or kept on ice during the collection. They are sent to the chemistry laboratory at the end of each 24-hour period.

Pertinent facts

- The patient should be certain that he or she completely understands this study. Patient anxiety or stress can cause ACTH release and obscure the interpretation of test results.
- The dexamethasone medication is administered orally usually with milk or an antacid to prevent any stomach irritation. Sometimes a sleeping pill is ordered at night to assure adequate sleep.
- The 24-hour urine collection begins *after* the patient urinates. The starting time is then indicated on a special laboratory slip. The first sample of urine is discarded. All urine passed by the patient during the next 24 hours is collected. Test results are calculated on the basis of a 24-hour output, and results will be inaccurate if any specimens are omitted. If one voided specimen is accidentally discarded, the 24-hour collection usually must begin again.
- It is not necessary to measure each urine specimen. The last specimen is collected as close as possible to the end of the 24-hour period. The 24-hour collection should then be sent to the laboratory.
- In studies such as the dexamethasone suppression test, when six continuous 24-hour urine collections are needed, no urine specimens are discarded except the first one, after which the collection begins.
- Fluids are to be encouraged over the 24-hour period, unless this is contraindicated for medical purposes.
- Since dexamethasone is a steroid preparation, steroid-induced side effects should be monitored by evaluating the patient's weight daily, checking the urine for sugar and acetone (see Chapter 11), checking blood potassium levels, and evaluating the patient for evidence of any stomach irritations.
- If blood cortisol level determinations will be needed, the procedure on p. 164-165 will be used.
- This test takes 6 days and requires hospitalization during this period.
- The customary cost of this study is approximately $180.

Rapid dexamethasone suppression test
Normal values

Cortisol levels nearly zero.

Purpose

See preceding Dexamethasone suppression test.

This is an easily and rapidly performed test that is mostly done as a screening test to diagnose Cushing's syndrome. It is less accurate and less informative than the *overnight* dexamethasone suppression test, but when its results are normal, the diagnosis of Cushing's syndrome can safely be excluded. The ease with which this test can be performed in comparison to the overnight dexamethasone suppression test makes it very useful in clinical medicine.

Cortisol levels are determined in the morning after dexamethasone administration on the previous night. In normal patients, the plasma (blood) cortisol level will fall to nearly zero. Cortisol levels in patients with Cushing's syndrome (despite the cause) will be greater than 10 ug/dl. If this test is positive, it should be followed by a more extensive, overnight dexamethasone suppression test. There are no complications associated with this study.

Procedure

For this test, dexamethasone is given to the patient by mouth at around 11 PM. The patient is also sedated to assure adequate sleep. At 8 AM the next morning, the patient's blood cortisol level is determined as described on p. 164-165.

Pertinent facts

- See Pertinent facts for the plasma cortisol test, p. 165.
- See Pertinent facts for the overnight dexamethasone suppression test (previous study).
- The customary cost of this study is approximately $30.

Metyrapone test
Normal values

Baseline excretion of urinary 17-OCHS should be more than doubled.

Purpose

Metyrapone (Metopirone) is a blocker of an enzyme involved in cortisol productino. When this drug is administered, the resulting fall in cortisol production should then stimulate the pituitary secretion of ACTH by way of the feedback mechanism. However, since cortisol itself cannot be synthesized because of metyrapone inhibition, there will be an abundance of cortisol precursors formed. These can be detected in the urine when urinary 17-hydroxycorticosteroid (17-OCHS) is measured. This test is similar to the ACTH stimulation test.

This test is useful in differentiating adrenal hyperplasia from adrenal tumor. In patients with adrenal hyperplasia, the urinary levels of 17-OCHS are markedly increased even more so than in normal patients. There is no response (no increase in urinary 17-OCHS levels) to metyrapone in patients who have Cushing's syndrome as a result of tumor.

This test has no significant advantage over the ACTH stimulation test in the differential diagnosis of Cushing's syndrome. Chlorpromazine (Thorazine) interferes with the response to metyrapone and therefore should not be administered during the testing. Because metyrapone inhibits cortisol production, Addison's disease (cortisol insufficiency) and addisonian crisis are potential complications of this study.

Procedure

Before this study is performed, a baseline 24-hour urine specimen for 17-OCHS (see next study) should be collected. A 24-hour urine collection for 17-OCHS is also obtained during and again 1 day after the oral administration of metyrapone, which is given every 4 hours over a 24-hour period. The 24-hour excretion of 17-OCHS on the last day of the collection should at least double the baseline excretion.

Pertinent facts

- See next study for 24-hour collection procedure of urinary 17-OCHS.
- The patient should be aware that he or she will be responsible for collecting three 24-hour urine specimens.
- Because metyrapone inhibits cortisol production, the patient will be carefully evaluated for impending signs of addisonian crisis (muscle weakness, mental and emotional changes, nausea, vomiting, anorexia, hypotension, high potassium level in the blood, and vascular collapse). Addisonian crisis is a medical emergency that must be treated vigorously. Basically the immediate treatment includes replenishing steroids, reversing shock, and restoring blood circulation.
- There is no discomfort associated with this study. The patient only has the inconvenience of collecting three 24-hour urine specimens.
- Customary cost of this study is approximately $90.

URINE TESTS
Urine test for 17-hydroxycorticosteroids (17-OCHS) and 17-ketosteroids (17-KS)
Normal values

17-Hydroxycorticosteroids (17-OCHS)
      Men: 5.5-15 mg/24 hr.
      Women: 5-13.5 mg/24 hr.
      Children: Lower than adult values.
17-Ketosteroids (17-KS)
      Men: 8-15 mg/24 hr.
      Women: 6-12 mg/24 hr.
      Children: 12-15 yr: 5-12 mg/24 hr.
                  Under 12 yr: Less than 5 mg/24 hr.

Purpose

This study is used to assess adrenal cortical function by measuring the cortisol (17-OCHS) and testosterone or estrogen (17-KS) precursors in a 24-hour urine collection. Elevated levels of 17-OCHS are seen in patients with hyperfunction of the adrenal gland (Cushing's syndrome). Low values of 17-OCHS are seen in patients who have a hypofunctioning adrenal gland (Addison's disease).

Elevated 17-KS levels are frequently seen in patients who have congenital (occurring at birth) adrenal hyperplasia (enlargement) and testosterone or estrogen-secreting tumors of the adrenals, ovaries, or testes. Low levels of 17-KS occur in patients with Addison's disease and in patients who have undergone removal of the ovaries or testes.

Testing the urine for these hormone precursors is only an indirect measurement of adrenal function. It is far more accurate to measure urine and plasma levels of cortisol, testosterone, or estrogen.

This study is without complications. Many drugs, however, can effect the test results. Aspirin, acetaminophen, morphine, barbiturates, reserpine, furosemide, and thiazides artificially decrease measurements. Paraldehyde, monoamine oxidase inhibitors, spironolactone, cloxacillin, and licorice artificially raise them.

Procedure

Urine is collected over a 24-hour period in a 1-gallon urine container. A preservative is necessary for the 17-KS test. The urine specimen is refrigerated or kept on ice during the collection period. At the end of the collection period, the urine specimen is sent to the chemistry laboratory.

Pertinent facts

- Valid interpretation of adrenal function depends on a complete 24-hour urine collection. The 24-hour urine collection begins *after* the patient urinates. The first sample is discarded. All urine passed by the patient during the next 24 hours is collected. Test results are calculated on the basis of a 24-hour output, and results will be inaccurate if any specimens are missed. If one voided specimen is accidentally discarded, the 24-hour collection must begin again. It is not necessary to measure each urine specimen.
- The patient should urinate before having a bowel movement so that urine is not contaminated by feces.
- The patient should be encouraged to eat and drink fluids during the 24-hour period, unless this is contraindicated for medical purposes (for example, congestive heart failure).
- The last specimen is collected as close as possible to the end of the 24-hour period.
- None of the drugs just mentioned in the discussion of purpose should be administered during the collection.
- Emotional stress and physical stress (such as infection) may cause increased adrenal activity. These complications will alter test results.
- There is no discomfort associated with this study.
- The customary cost of this study is approximately $30.

24-Hour urine test for vanillylmandelic acid (VMA) and catecholamines
Normal values

Vanillylmandelic acid (VMA): 1-9 mg/24 hr.

Catecholamines
    Epinephrine: 5-40 ug/24 hr.
    Norepinephrine: 10-80 ug/24 hr.
    Metanephrine: 24-96 ug/24 hr.
    Normetanephrine: 75-375 ug/24 hr.

Purpose

A 24-hour urine test for VMA and catecholamines is primarily performed to diagnose hypertension caused by pheochromocytoma. A pheochromocytoma is an adrenal tumor that frequently secretes abnormally high levels of epinephrine and norepinephrine. These hormones in turn cause episodic or persistent hypertension (high blood pressure) by causing arterial vasoconstriction. Metanephrine and normetanephrine are breakdown products of epinephrine and norepinephrine respectively. VMA is the breakdown product of metabolism of both metanephrine and normetanephrine. In patients with pheochromocytoma, one or all of the above substances will be present in excessive quantities in a 24-hour urine collection.

Procedure

VMA. For 2 or 3 days before the 24-hour urine collection and throughout the entire collection period, the patient is placed on a special VMA-restricted diet. Generally the foods restricted include coffee, tea, bananas, chocolate, citrus fruits, all foods and fluids containing vanilla, and aspirin. Blood pressure medications (and sometimes all medications) are also prohibited during this period. A 24-hour urine specimen is collected and a preservative is required.

Catecholamines. A 24-hour urine specimen is collected and sent to the chemistry laboratory. No special diet is required.

Pertinent facts

- See the previous study for the method of collecting a 24-hour urine specimen. A 24-hour urine specimen for VMA does require a preservative.
- After the 24-hour collection for VMA is completed, the patient is then permitted to have all the foods and drugs that were restricted (as described in the procedure).
- Excessive physical exercise and emotion can alter catecholamine test results by causing an increased secretion of epinephrine and norepinephrine. Therefore any factors contributing to the patient's stress and anxiety should be identified and minimized.
- Customary cost for the 24-hour VMA is approximately $40 and for the 24-hour urine for catecholamines is approximately $30.

Sample case report: Cushing's syndrome

Miss D., a 22-year-old nurse, complained of weakness, tiredness, easy bruising, leg edema, recent acne, and hirsutism (excess hair on the body). Her menstruation cycle became irregular. Her family commented that she was emotionally labile. They also believed that her face had become fuller. On physical examination, she was found to be a mildly hypertensive with moon (rounded) face, "buffalo hump" in the neck and chest area, a heavy trunk, diffuse skin striae (lines), and edema. The results of a recent chest x-ray performed at work were reported as normal.

STUDIES	RESULTS
Routine laboratory work	Normal except for glucose: 240 mg/dl (normal: 60-120 mg/dl)
Urine test for 17-hydroxycorticosteroid (17-OCHS)	28 mg/24 hr (normal: 5-13.5 mg/24 hr)
Urine test for 17-ketosteroids (17-KS)	14 mg/24 hr (normal: 6-12 mg/24 hr)
Plasma (blood) cortisol test	
8 AM	88 ug/dl (normal: 6-28 ug/dl)
4 PM	78 ug/dl (normal: 2-12 ug/dl)
Dexamethasone suppression test	
Plasma cortisol level after 2 mg/day	60 ug/dl (normal: less than 10 ug/dl)
Plasma cortisol level after 8 mg/day	8 ug/dl (normal: less than 10 ug/dl)
Plasma ACTH test	140 pg/ml (normal: 15-100 pg/ml)
Plasma cortisol level after ACTH stimulation test	140 ug/dl (normal: greater than 40 ug/dl, less than 60 ug/dl)
Urine 17-OCHS level after metyrapone stimulation test	Baseline excretion of 17-OCHS tripled (normal: double excretion)
X-ray study of the sella turcica	Normal
Adrenal angiography	Enlarged adrenal gland, no tumor seen (normal: no enlargement or tumor)

The patient had the classic signs and symptoms of Cushing's syndrome (adrenal gland hyperactivity). Her elevated urinary 17-OCHS level and the elevation and loss of the normal diurnal variation of plasma cortisol level substantiated the diagnosis. The underlying pathologic condition causing the adrenal gland to hyperfunction ahd to be determined to permit appropriate therapy. The causes could have been adrenal hyperplasia, adrenal tumor, pituitary tumor, or an ACTH-secreting tumor. Lack of adrenal gland suppression with 2 mg dexamethasone, combined with complete suppression with 8 mg dexamethasone, strongly indicated that adrenal hyperplasia, rather than an adrenal tumor, was causing Cushing's syndrome. The patient's elevated levels on the plasma ACTH, metyrapone suppression, and ACTH stimulation tests were all consistent with adrenal hyperplasia. The x-ray study of the sella turcica and adrenal angiography eliminated the possibility of pituitary or adrenal tumors. The patient underwent bilateral adrenalectomy (removal of both adrenal glands) and had no further symptoms. She was given steroid replacement medications and had no further difficulties.

11

Diagnostic studies used to evaluate diabetes mellitus

ANATOMY, PHYSIOLOGY, AND MAJOR PROBLEMS OF THE ENDOCRINE PANCREAS

The pancreas, which is located in the abdomen (see Fig. 4-1), secretes both digestive enzymes and hormones. The islets of Langerhans are clusters of cells embedded in the pancreatic tissue that secrete insulin (and many other hormones). The major action of insulin is to lower the blood glucose (sugar) level by facilitating the movement of glucose out of the bloodstream into the cells, liver, muscles, and other tissue. In these cells, glucose is either used for immediate energy or stored as glycogen for later energy requirements. Insulin also promotes the storage of ingested fat in adipose tissue and aids in the synthesis (buildup) of body protein.

In the absence of insulin, the blood glucose level rises because it cannot move into the cells. When the level of glucose in the bloodstream reaches about 180 to 240 mg/dl (renal threshold), glucose spills over into the urine. This explains why diabetic patients have a high sugar level in their bloodstream and sugar in their urine. Diabetes mellitus is a chronic disorder characterized by inadequate levels of insulin, leading to a disturbance in the processing of glucose, fat, and protein.

BLOOD TESTS
Serum glucose test (blood sugar, fasting blood sugar [FBS])
Normal values

60-120 mg/dl.

Purpose

This test is helpful in diagnosing many metabolic diseases. In general true glucose (sugar) elevations indicate diabetes mellitus. However, one must be aware of other possible causes of hyperglycemia (high levels of sugar in the blood). These include

1. An acute stress response, such as to surgery
2. Overfunctioning of the adrenal gland
3. Pheochromocytoma
4. Overfunctioning of the thyroid gland
5. Cancer of the pancreas
6. Pancreatitis
7. Administration of diuretics (water pills) such as furosemide (Lasix) and hydrochlorothiazides
8. Administration of steroids

Likewise, hypoglycemia (low blood sugar level) has many causes. However, the most common cause is insulin overdose. As a result, glucose determinations are usually performed frequently in new diabetic patients to constantly monitor the dose of insulin and avoid overdosage. Other causes of hypoglycemia include

1. Insulin-producing tumors of the pancreatic islet cells (insulinoma)
2. Low-functioning thyroid gland
3. Low-functioning pituitary gland
4. Low-functioning adrenal gland
5. Extensive liver disease inhibiting the normal destruction of excess insulin

Serum glucose levels must be evaluated according to the time of the day at which they are obtained. A glucose level of 135 mg/dl may be abnormal if the patient is in a fasting state. However, it would be within normal limits if the patient had eaten a meal within the last hour.

There are no complications associated with this study.

Procedure

For a fasting blood sugar (FBS), the patient is kept fasting for at least 8 hours, usually from the midnight before the test. Water is permitted. The patient should not fast longer than 16 hours before the study is performed to prevent starvation effects, which may artificially raise the glucose level. A needle is inserted into a vein and approximately 2 teaspoons of blood is obtained and taken to the chemistry laboratory.

Blood should always be obtained before insulin or any hypoglycemic (blood glucose-lowering) agents are administered. Diabetic patients who are being regulated with different types of insulin require blood glucose tests after fasting (before breakfast) and at 3 or 4 PM. Late afternoon glucose levels are obtained to make sure that the patient is getting the appropriate dose of insulin and to make sure that the blood glucose is not too low when the insulin peaks or reaches its highest point in the bloodstream (around 4 PM). Serum glucose levels should be obtained on any diabetic patient suspected of having an insulin reaction. An insulin reaction is caused by administration of too much insulin. This causes the blood sugar level to drop dangerously low.

Glucose determinations are now part of most multichannel specimen machine analysis. This means that blood drawn for multiple analysis will also be tested for glucose, because the glucose is also determined on that machine. For this reason, the time that the blood is obtained is very important.

Pertinent facts

- The patient must understand the timing of a blood test in relationship to meals. If fasting is required, the patient must understand that breakfast will be withheld until the blood is obtained. If breakfast were eaten before the blood were obtained, the fasting blood sugar would be erroneously high.
- Insulin or oral hypoglycemic agents (such as Diabinese) will be withheld until the blood is obtained, because these drugs will lower the glucose level.
- The only discomfort associated with this study is a needle stick. Many patients complain about the need for frequent blood glucose studies. These studies are important to regulate the amount of insulin required by the patient.
- The customary cost of this study is approximately $12.

Two-hour postprandial glucose test (2-hour PPG, 2-hour postprandial blood sugar [2-hour PPBS])
Normal values

60-120 mg/dl.

Purpose

This is a measurement of the amount of glucose in the patient's blood 2 hours after a meal is ingested (postprandial). For this study, the meal acts as a glucose challenge to the body's metabolism. In normal patients, insulin is secreted immediately after a meal in response to the elevated sugar level, thus causing a return within 2 hours to the patient's range before a meal. However, in diabetic patients, the glucose level is usually still elevated 2 hours after the meal because of inadequate amounts of insulin.

This is an easily performed screening test for diabetes mellitus. If the results of this test are abnormal, a glucose tolerance test (see next study) should be performed to confirm the diagnosis. There are no complications associated with this study.

Procedure

The patient is given a routine meal. Two hours after the meal, approximately 2 teaspoons of venous blood is obtained in a gray- or red-top tube and taken to the chemistry laboratory for glucose determinations.

Pertinent facts

- The only discomfort associated with this study is a needle stick.
- The patient must be sure to eat the entire meal and then not to eat anything else until the blood is obtained.
- Customary cost for this study is approximately $32.

Glucose tolerance test (GTT, oral glucose tolerance test [OGTT])
Normal values

Fasting: 80 mg/dl.
30 minutes: 145 mg/dl.

1 hour: 135 mg/dl.
2 hours: 100 mg/dl.
3 hours: 80 mg/dl.
4 hours: 80 mg/dl.

Purpose

The oral glucose tolerance test is the most specific and sensitive test for diabetes mellitus. In this study, one evaluates the patient's ability to tolerate a standard oral glucose load by obtaining blood and urine specimens for glucose levels *before* glucose administration and then at 30 minutes, 1 hour, 2 hours, 3 hours, and 4 hours *after* glucose administration. Normal patients with appropriate insulin response are able to tolerate the dose quite easily with only a minimal and transient rise in the serum glucose level within 1 hour after the ingestion. Also, normal patients will not spill glucose into the urine.

Patients with diabetes who have a deficiency of active insulin (glucose-lowering hormone) will not be able to tolerate this sugar load. As a result their blood glucose levels will be markedly elevated from 1 to 5 hours (Fig. 11-1). Also glucose can usually be detected in their urine.

High glucose levels after glucose load can also be seen in nondiabetic patients with hyperthyroidism, infection, or ongoing chronic illness (such as cancer). Pregnant or obese patients may also show elevations. Drugs such as nicotine, aspirin, steroids, thiazide diuretics, and oral contraceptives may also cause glucose intolerance in nondiabetic patients.

Procedure

After at least 3 days of consuming a high carbohydrate diet (at least 300 g), the patient is kept from having anything by mouth (NPO) after midnight on the day of the test. A specimen for fasting blood sugar is obtained, and the patient's urine is tested for glucose and acetone. The patient is then given a 100 g carbohydrate (glucose) load, usually in the form of a carbonated sugar beverage (Glucola) or a cherry-flavored gelatin (Gel-a-dex). If these commercial preparations are unavailable, 100 g glucose is dissolved in water and flavored with lemon

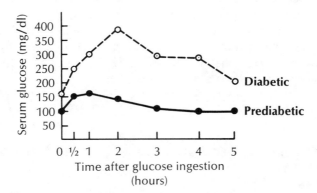

Fig. 11-1. Glucose tolerance test (GTT) curve for a patient who has diabetes and a patient before the onset of diabetes.

juice to increase its palatability. The entire glucose load must be ingested by the patient, since the GTT normal values are based on consumption of the 100 g glucose. For children, smaller quantities of glucose are given.

Blood and urine specimens for glucose level determinates are obtained at 30 minutes, 1 hour, 2 hours, 3 hours, and 4 hours after the patient ingests the carbohydrate load. Sometimes a specimen is also obtained in 5 hours. All specimens must be clearly marked with the time at which they were obtained. During the testing, the patient is not permitted to eat or smoke. The patient is encouraged to drink water, however, so that urine specimens can be obtained more easily. Coffee and tea are not permitted. The patient should rest during the entire procedure. Any exercise (including walking) can affect the glucose levels.

During the testing, especially between the second and third hours, the patient should be carefully observed for reactions such as dizziness, sweating, weakness, and giddiness. These reactions are usually transient. The time of these reactions is noted.

The patient should not take insulin or oral hypoglycemics (drugs that lower the blood sugar level) before or during the testing. The study can be performed in the outpatient department or in the patient's hospital room. The serum glucose specimens are drawn by a nurse or by a technician. The patient is responsible for providing the urine specimens, unless nursing assistance is needed.

Pertinent facts

- The glucose tolerance test is uncomfortable because of the number of blood tests required for blood sugar determinations. Other than that, patients may complain only of boredom. It is recommended that the patients bring reading material with them for this study.
- An appropriate diet must be followed very carefully before the test is obtained. If the patient has not received a high carbohydrate for 3 days before the test, his or her tolerance of carbohydrates may be low, thus simulating diabetes mellitus.
- Water is permitted during the testing time and should be encouraged because it will help in obtaining the urine specimens.
- Tobacco, coffee, and tea are not allowed during the test since they cause physiologic stimulation, which can alter the test results.
- No drugs should be taken before the test without the physician's approval.
- After the study is performed, the patient can eat or drink normally. Insulin or oral hypoglycemic agents may be administered if ordered after the study.
- The duration of this study is approximately 5 hours.
- The customary cost of this study is about $70.

URINE TEST
Urine test for glucose and acetone (urine S and A, fractional urines)
Normal values

Negative for glucose and acetone (no sugar or acetone).

Purpose

Glucose. Glucose is filtered into the urine when the blood glucose level exceeds 180 mg/dl (renal threshold). As the blood glucose level increases, the amount of glucose in the urine likewise increases.

Acetone (ketone). Poorly controlled diabetic patients frequently have excessive fat breakdown. The purpose of this breakdown, or catabolism, is to provide an energy source from fat when glucose cannot be transferred into the cell because of the insufficiency of insulin. Ketones are the end product of this fat breakdown. As with glucose, ketones spill over into the urine when their levels are elevated in the blood.

Because urine glucose and acetone determinations are easily performed, painlessly obtained, and accurately reflective of serum glucose levels, they are used to monitor insulin therapy in diabetic patients. It is important to know that the negative results for glucose and acetone are not necessarily indicative of well-controlled diabetes. Although these results would rule out hyperglycemia (high sugar levels), the patient could be dangerously hypoglycemic (low blood sugar levels). Because of this, many physicians prefer that young diabetic patients show a trace of glucose in the urine. This is because glucose levels in young diabetic patients are very difficult to regulate and often swing rapidly from hyperglycemia to hypoglycemia.

Procedure

Fractional urine tests for glucose and acetone are performed at specified times during the day, generally before meals and at bedtime. Test results are used to determine the patient's insulin requirement. Because accuracy is necessary, the urine specimen for testing should contain "fresh voided" urine only. Stagnant urine that has been sitting in the bladder for several hours will not accurately reflect the amount of glucose and acetone in the blood at the time of testing. For this reason a "double-voided" specimen is required. This is obtained by collecting a urine specimen 30 to 45 minutes before the time at which the test specimen is actually needed. This first specimen is discarded and the patient is given a glass of water (approximately 8 ounces) to drink. A second specimen is then obtained at the required time and tested for both glucose and acetone. The result obtained from this double-voided or second specimen accurately reflects the amount of glucose in the blood.

Urine glucose and acetone are usually detected by using a reagent strip (Keto-diastix or Multistix). The reagent strip is completely immersed in a well-mixed urine specimen and removed immediately to avoid diluting the reagents. The strip is held in a horizontal position to prevent possible mixing of chemicals. At the time indicated, the strip is compared with the test chart located on the jar of reagent strips. The ketone reading is made in exactly 15 seconds, and the glucose reading is made in exactly 30 seconds. The ketone results range from negative to 3 + (large). The glucose results range from negative to 4 + , or 2%.

Urine testing for glucose can also be performed quickly and easily by the Clinitest method. For this study, a test tube, medicine dropper, Clinitest tablet, and color chart are required. Five drops of well-mixed urine are placed in the test tube containing 10 drops of water. After the Clinitest table is placed into the test tube, boiling ensues for a few seconds. The resultant color change (pea green to yellow-green to yellow or brown) permits estimation of the approximate content of sugar up to 2%. This test can be modified to allow estimation of sugar concentrations up to 5% by using 2 (instead of 5) drops of urine and 10 drops of water. A special color chart is used with a scale ranging up to 5%. This modification is particularly useful in children in whom markedly high blood sugar levels may escape recognition by the standard 5-drop procedure.

Acetone in the urine can be detected by Acetest tablets. For this test, a drop of urine is placed on the Acetest tablet. If acetone is present, varying shades of lavender will occur, and these can be compared with a color chart after the time indicated in the instructions.

Urine tests for glucose and acetone are performed by the nurse or by the patient. Patients with diabetes *must* be taught to accurately test their own urine.

Pertinent facts

- Diabetic patients should understand how to accurately perform urine testing, using a double-voided specimen. However, if a double-voided specimen cannot be obtained, a single specimen could be used.
- The directions on the bottle or container of the reagent strip must be carefully read. The color reactions must be compared with the manufacturer's color chart at the *exact* time specified. The expiration date on the bottle must be checked before use. The bottle should be tightly closed after the reagent strips are removed to prevent them from absorbing moisture and altering future results.
- The directions on the Acetest and Clinitest bottles must be carefully read before use. The physician will determine whether the Clinitest should be performed using 2 or 5 drops of urine. The expiration date on the bottle should be checked before use. The reagent bottle should be tightly closed after a Clinitest or Acetest tablet is removed, because the tablets attract moisture and lose their potency.
- If the patient is receiving cephalothin (Keflin or Keflex), Clinitest tablets cannot be used because false positive (indicates positive when it is really negative) results can occur. Vitamin C and probenecid also cause false positive results. Therefore for patients taking these medications reagent *strips* should be used instead of Clinitest tablets.
- The customary cost of this procedure is approximately $4.

Sample case report: adolescent with diabetes mellitus

Mike F., a 16-year-old high school football player, was brought to the emergency room in a coma. His mother said that during the past month he had had a 12 lb weight loss. He also has had excessive thirst associated with a large amount of urination that often required voiding several times during the night. There was a strong family history of diabetes mellitus. The results of his physical examination were essentially normal except for increased heart rate and deep respirations.

STUDIES	RESULTS
Serum glucose test (on admission)	1100 mg/dl (normal: 60-120 mg/dl)
Arterial blood gas (on admission) (see Chapter 5)	
pH	7.23 (normal: 7.35-7.45)
P_{CO_2}	35 mm Hg (normal: 35-45 mm Hg.)
HCO_3	12 mEq/liter (normal 22-26 mEq/liter)
Urine test for glucose (sugar) and acetone	4+ and large (normal: negative/ negative)
Serum glucose test (fasting blood sugar)	250 mg/dl (normal: 60-120 mg/dl)
Two-hour postprandial glucose	500 mg/dl (normal: 60-120 mg/dl)
Glucose tolerance test (GTT)	
Fasting blood sugar	150 mg/dl (normal: 80 mg/dl)
30 minutes	300 mg/dl (normal: 145 mg/dl)
1 hour	325 mg/dl (normal: 135 mg/dl)
2 hours	390 mg/dl (normal: 100 mg/dl)
3 hours	300 mg/dl (normal: 80 mg/dl)
4 hours	260 mg/dl (normal: 80 mg/dl)

The patient's symptoms and diagnostic studies were classic for high blood sugar and acidosis associated with diabetes mellitus. The results of his blood gas test drawn on admission indicated metabolic acidosis caused by excessive fatty acid breakdown. The patient was treated in the emergency room with intravenous (IV) regular insulin and IV fluids.

During the first 72 hours of hospitalization, the patient was monitored by frequent blood and urine glucose determinations and urine acetone determinations. The insulin was administered according to the results of these studies. The patient was eventually stabilized on 40 units insulin (NPH iletin) daily. Comprehensive patient instructions regarding urine testing, insulin administration, diet, exercise, foot care, and recognition of the signs and symptoms of high and low blood sugar levels were given. He was discharged from the hospital and able to return to his normal activity.

12

Diagnostic studies used to evaluate pregnancy and the reproductive system

ANATOMY, PHYSIOLOGY, AND COMMON PROBLEMS OF THE REPRODUCTIVE SYSTEM

This disccusion of anatomy and physiology of the reproductive system deals only with materials relevant to the diagnostic studies included in this chapter and the next. A detailed discussion of this complex system can be found in many other books.

Male reproductive organs

The testes (Fig. 12-1) are located in the scrotum, which is ideally suited to provide the appropriate temperature required for sperm production. Special cells within the testes produce the spermatozoa, or sperm cells. Sperm production is a major function of the testes. The genital ducts, which include the epididymis, the vas deferens, the ejaculatory duct, the seminal vesicles, and the urethra (Fig. 12-1), provide a conduit for the transport of sperm cells.

A second function of the testes is the secretion of testosterone (the major male hormone). Testosterone induces the development of the external genital organs as well as the secondary male sexual characteristics (such as dermal hair, musculoskeletal development, and beard).

Female reproductive organs

The ovaries are the internal sex organs in the female reproductive system (Fig. 12-2). Like the testes, the ovaries are multifunctional. They are responsible for ovulation (production of ova, or eggs) and for the secretion of the female hormone (estrogen and progesterone). The fallopian tube arises from the uterus and terminates adjacent to the ovary (Fig. 12-2). The egg is made in the ovary and

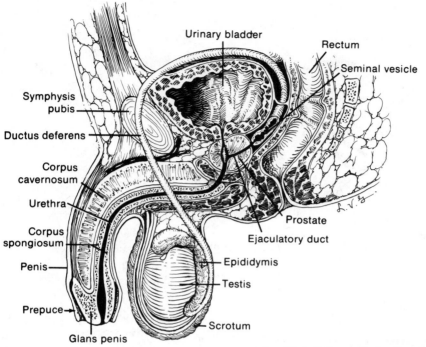

Fig. 12-1. Male reproductive organs.

From Schottelius, B.A., and Schottelius, D.D.: Textbook of physiology, St. Louis, The C.V. Mosby Co.

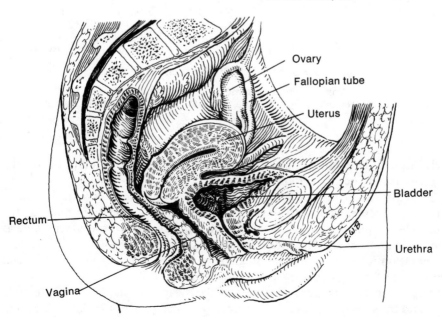

Fig. 12-2. Female reproductive organs.

From Schottelius, B.A., and Schottelius, D.D.: Textbook of physiology, St. Louis, The C.V. Mosby Co.

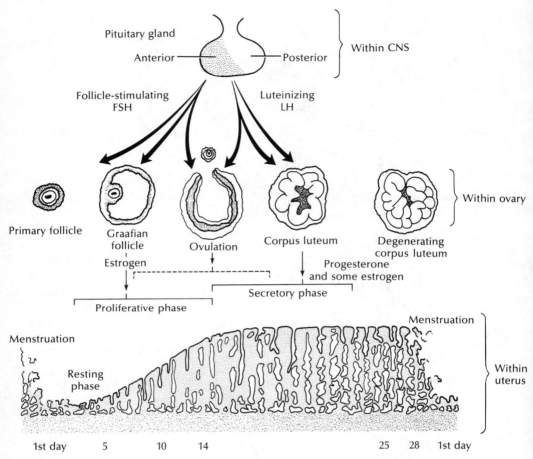

Fig. 12-3. Hormonal control of menstrual cycle.

From Jensen, M.D., Benson, R.C., and Bobak, I.M.:
Maternity care: the nurse and the family, St. Louis, The C.V. Mosby Co.

travels through the fallopian tube and into the uterus. Fertilization of the ova by the sperm usually occurs within these fallopian tubes.

The uterus can be divided into the cervix and corpus. The cervix is the cap of the uterus, which extends into the vagina. The corpus is the main body of the uterus. The corpus uteri (Fig. 12-2) is a muscular organ whose inner lining is called the endometrium. The endometrium undergoes cyclic (menstrual) changes in preparation for conception and pregnancy. Events occurring in the ovary and uterus during the menstrual cycle are shown in Fig. 12-3.

There are three phases of a menstrual cycle: the menstrual phase, proliferative phase, and the secretory phase. The average menstrual cycle is 28 days. The menstrual cycle begins with the menstrual phase (menses, or vaginal blood flow). During menses the endometrium undergoes degenerative changes so that the superficial layer of the endometrium is discharged into the menstrual flow. After the blood flow ceases, there is a gradual estrogen-stimulated growth of the endometrium (proliferative phase). At approximately the fourteenth day of the cycle (Fig. 12-3), the graafian follicle within the ovary ruptures, and the ovum (egg) is expelled into the fallopian tubes (ovulation). The ruptured follicle is then called a corpus luteum. Large amounts of progesterone and some estrogen are secreted by the corpus luteum and cause the endometrial glands of the uterus to thicken and mature. This is called the endometrial secretory phase (Fig. 12-3). The uterine lining then becomes extremely vascular (has a large blood supply) and edematous (swollen). The purpose of this secretory phase is to prepare the uterine lining to receive and nourish a fertilized egg. If fertilization does not take place, the corpus luteum degenerates (breaks down), and the endometrium is discarded from the body in the vaginal blood flow (menses), which occurs on approximately the twenty-eighth day of the cycle (Fig. 12-3).

When feritilization does occur, the fertilized egg moves through the fallopian tube and into the prepared uterine cavity. The fertilized egg absorbs nutrition from the uterine glands until a placenta forms. The placenta produces human chorionic gonadotropin (HCG), which maintains the corpus luteum's existence. The corpus luteum continues to secrete the progesterone required to maintain the pregnancy. Through continued growth, the embryo becomes surrounded by two membranes. The space between the embryo and the inner layer of the fetal membrane is called the amniotic cavity and is filled with amniotic fluid.

At approximately 8 weeks, the embryo is completely developed and is called a fetus. For the remaining 32 weeks, the fetus grows, using the nutritional support provided by the mother through the placenta. Toward the end of pregnancy, HCG and progesterone levels decrease, and the placenta degenerates and separates. Uterine contractions (labor) begin in an effort to expel the fetus vaginally.

Many disease states can jeopardize the normal events associated with pregnancy, labor, and delivery. When such threats are recognized beforehand, pregnancy is considered "at high risk" and is monitored more closely than normal. A few examples of situations that are responsible for high-risk pregnancy include the following factors in the patient's history or current status:

1. Advanced maternal age
2. Eclampsia
3. Previous stillbirth or abortion
4. Previous premature deliveries
5. Previous infant with Rh factor problems
6. Previous infant with genetic disorders
7. Previous infant with birth deformity
8. Previous small-for-status infant or present small-for-status fetus (caused by growth retardation)
9. Previous or present multiple pregnancy (twins, triplets)
10. Abnormalities in the genital tract
11. Medical condition (such as high blood pressure, diabetes mellitus, heart disease, or kidney disease)

X-RAYS
X-ray of the pelvis (x-ray pelvimetry)
Normal values

Width of the midpelvis greater than 10.5 cm.

Purpose

Although most abnormalities of the pelvis can be suspected by clinical measurement, x-ray pelvimetry (x-ray of the pelvis) is the most accurate means of determining adequacy of the pelvic bony structures for a normal vaginal delivery. With an x-ray of the pelvis, one can compare the capacity of the mother's pelvis to the size of the infant's head to detect any cephalopelvic disproportion, which means that the head (cephalic) of the baby is larger than the width of the maternal pelvis, thus making a vaginal delivery impossible.

X-ray pelvimetry is an outmoded procedure that is used only rarely in modern obstetrics. This study is currently indicated in

1. Patients suspected of having fetuses in abnormal positions (such as breech) who desire a vaginal delivery.
2. Patients who have had injury or disease of the pelvis or hips that may have caused pelvic distortion.
3. Patients with a pelvis that appears to be abnormal by a routine pelvic examination.
4. Patients who have a debilitating illness complicating their pregnancy and a clinically small or unfavorable pelvis, because an elective cesarean section may then be recommended if a difficult or hazardous delivery is predicted.
5. Patients who have had a history of difficult delivery.
6. Women pregnant for the first time and in labor with the head unengaged (not descended into the birth canal) to rule out cephalopelvic disproportion.
7. Patients having dysfunctional labor, especially when the physician is considering administering oxytocin, which will increase the strength of contractions.

Although measuring the pelvis by pelvic examination is less accurate than x-ray determination, it is adequate for most patients. X-ray of the pelvis is only important late in pregnancy or during labor. If x-ray pelvimetry indicates a difficult or dangerous vaginal delivery, cesarean section is recommended. Cesarean section is now more frequently performed in cases where vaginal delivery is *clinically* suspected to be difficult. As a result, x-ray pelvimetry rarely affects the physician's decision concerning the type of delivery. In those rare situations in which vaginal delivery is attempted despite an anticipated difficult delivery, x-ray pelvimetry is performed more for legal purposes than for medical benefits.

Procedure

The patient is taken to the x-ray department. She removes her clothes and dons a long x-ray gown. An x-ray film is taken from the side with the patient standing to detect the effect of gravity on engagement of the fetal head in the pelvis and to indicate the position of the fetal head when it reaches the lower level of the birth canal. The patient may then be placed lying on her back, side, or stomach. During the x-ray exposure, the patient is asked to stop breathing. Generally the patient is instructed to hyperventilate (breathe very quickly) and then stop breathing while the film is taken.

This study is contraindicated in early pregnancy because x-rays at this time may injure the fetus.

Pertinent facts

- There is no discomfort associated with this study.
- An x-ray technician performs this study in approximately 15 minutes. Results are interpreted by the radiologist.
- The approximate cost of this study is $35.

Mammography
Normal values

Negative, no tumor seen.

Purpose

This is an x-ray examination of the breast. Careful interpretation of these x-ray films by a skilled x-ray physician can
1. Detect breast cancer (Fig. 12-4) that cannot be palpated (felt), especially in patients with large, pendulous breasts
2. Detect cancer 1 to 2 years before it may have become clinically palpable, thus providing an excellent opportunity for care
3. Provide a reliable means of following patients at high risk for breast cancer
Although mammography is not a substitute for a biopsy (removal of tissue and examination under the microscope), it is reliable and accurate when interpreted by a skilled x-ray physician.

Mammography cannot replace complete and careful physical examination, yet it frequently can substantiate questionable findings or detect unrecognized lesions. There is some controversy concerning the role of mammography in the routine evaluation of patients. Because x-ray study of the breast is costly and may possibly induce cancer, there has been some resistance to the routine performance of mammography. However, with recent advance in technique, as little as 0.4 rad of radiation is delivered per examination. With this minimal exposure, the chance of x-ray–induced cancer is minimal. Thus in light of the fact that more and more early, easily curable breast cancers are being detected by routine mammography, few physicians will now dispute the importance of mammography in certain patients who are at risk for breast cancer. At present, the American Cancer Society recommends that a baseline mammogram be taken when a woman is between 35 and 45 years old. Women over 50 years old should have mammography performed yearly. Women who have had cancer surgically removed from one breast should have mammography of the opposite breast performed yearly regardless of age.

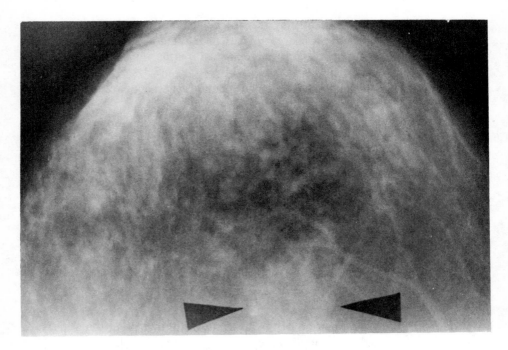

Fig. 12-4. Mammogram. Pointers indicate breast cancer.

Procedure

The unfasting, unsedated patient is taken to the x-ray department and placed in front of the mammographic x-ray machine (Fig. 12-5). One breast is placed on an x-ray plate and the x-ray cone is brought down on top of the breast to gently compress it between the broadened cone and the plate. An x-ray film is taken. Next, the x-ray plate is turned perpendicular to the floor and placed on the other side of the outer aspect of the breast. The broadened cone is brought in at the center and again gently compresses the breast. Occasionally other views are taken from different angles.

Xeromammography provides the same information as mammography and has equal risks. The final picture is a "positive" print rather than the normal x-ray "negative" picture. The form of mammography used depends on the preference of the radiologist who must interpret the mammogram.

Pertinent facts

- Very little discomfort is associated with mammography. Some pain may be caused by the pressure that is required to flatten the breast tissue while the x-ray films are being taken.
- Mammography is performed by an x-ray technician in approximately 10 minutes.
- Some patients may be embarrassed by this procedure because clothing from above the waist must be removed.
- The customary cost for this procedure is approximately $35.

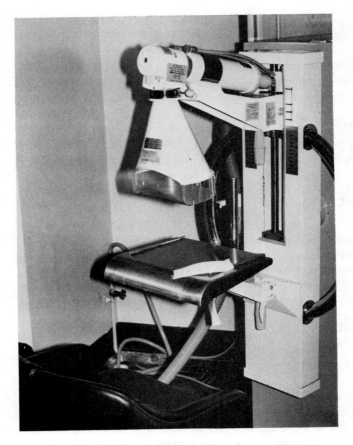

Fig. 12-5. X-ray machine used in mammography.

ENDOSCOPY
Amnioscopy
Normal values

Normal color of the amniotic fluid; no meconium staining.

Purpose

This study allows direct visualization of the amniotic fluid (in which the fetus floats within the pregnant uterus) through the cervix to detect meconium staining of the fluid. Meconium constitutes the first feces passed by the newborn infant. If the fetus is not receiving adequate oxygen supply, this will result in passage of meconium through the rectum of the fetus. This meconium, which can be detected through the intact membranes with a vaginal speculum, may indicate fetal distress or death. However, meconium is also present in some normal pregnancies. Therefore results must be evaluated within the overall clinical situation.

The major risk associated with amnioscopy is rupture of the uterine membrane. A disadvantage of the study is that although the color of the fluid can be evaluated, no fluid is obtained for laboratory analysis.

This study is contraindiated in patients with

1. Active labor
2. Premature membrane rupture
3. Active cervical infection (such as gonorrhea)

Procedure

The patient is placed with her feet in stirrups. The cervix is dilated, and an endoscope (amnioscope) is introduced into the cervical canal. The color of the amniotic fluid is evaluated.

Pertinent facts

• This study is performed by a physician in approximately 10 to 15 minutes.
• The patient will be uncomfortable during the dilation of the cervix.
• After the study, the patient may have vaginal discomfort and menstrual-type cramping. A sanitary pad may be worn.
• The customary cost of this study is approximately $75.

COLPOSCOPY
Normal values

Normal vagina and cervix.

Purpose

Colposcopy provides an examination of the vagina and cervix wtih a colposcope, which is a special microscope with a light source and magnifying lens. With this procedure tiny areas of abnormal cells (such as cancer), which may be missed by the naked eye, can be visualized, and biopsy specimens can be removed. This study is performed on patients with abnormal vaginal cell patterns, cervical lesions, or suspicious Pap smear results. It may be a sufficient substitute to cone biopsy (removal and examination of a cone tissue from the cervix) in evaluating the cause of abnormal cervical cell findings.

It is important that one realizes that colposcopy is useful only in identifying a suspicious lesion. Definitive diagnosis, however, requires biopsy of the tissue (surgical removal and examination under a high-powered microscope). One of the major advantages of this procedure is that of directing the biopsy to the area most likely to be truly representative of the lesion. A biopsy performed without colposcopy may not necessarily be representative of the lesion's true disease condition, resulting in a significant risk of missing a serious problem.

Procedure

The patient is placed with her feet in stirrups, and a vaginal speculum is used to expose the vagina and cervix. After the cervix is sampled for cell findings, it is cleansed with a solution to remove any excess mucus and cellular debris. The colposcope is then focused on the cervix, which is turn is carefully examined. Usually the entire lesion can be outlined, and the most abnormal areas selected for biopsy.

A more extensive cone biopsy is needed if

1. Colposcopy did not explain the problem or correlate with the cell findings of the Pap smear.
2. The entire area was not clearly visualized.
3. The lesion extended up the cervical canal beyond the visualization of the colposcope.

The need for up to 90% of cone biopsies is eliminated by an experienced colposcopist. Cervical curettage (cleansing of a diseased surface with a spoon-shaped instrument or curet) may accompany colposcopy to detect unknown lesions in the cervical canal.

Pertinent facts

- Colposcopy is performed by a physician in approximately 15 minutes.
- Some patients complain of pressure pains from the vaginal speculum. Momentary discomfort may be felt when the biopsy specimens are obtained.
- After the study, the patient may have some vaginal bleeding if biopsy specimens were removed. The patient should wear a sanitary pad.
- The results of this study are usually available within 2 or 3 days.
- The customary cost of the study is approximately $75.

BLOOD TEST
Pregnancy test
Normal values

Negative, unless the patient is pregnant.

Purpose

All pregnancy tests are based on the detection of human chorionic gonadotropin (HCG), which is secreted after the egg is fertilized (see Anatomy and physiology). HCG will appear in the blood or urine of pregnant women as early as 10 days after conception (union of sperm and ova).

False negative pregnancy tests may occur especially when performed early in the pregnancy, before there are sufficient HCG levels. Urine diluted by diuretics (water pills) and also laboratory technical errors are less common causes of false negative results. False positive results (incorrectly indicates the patient is pregnant) occur in some women with hormone deficiencies, which can cause HCG-like positive reactions. Tranquilizers may also produce false positive results.

It is important to know that all the different types of pregnancy tests demonstrate the presence of HCG and do not necessarily indicate a normal pregnancy. Hydatidiform mole (benign tumor of the uterus), along with cancer of the uterus, testes, or ovaries can produce HCG. Because HCG can also be produced by tumors, determination of HCG is also used to determine progression or regression of these tumor types. When HCG levels are elevated in these patients, tumor extension must be suspected. Decreasing HCG levels indicate effective antitumor treatment.

Procedure

Blood tests for pregnancy are examined by radioimmunoassay (RIA). This is a highly sensitive and reliable method of examining the blood for the detection of HCG. Blood samples are obtained according to the requirements of the laboratory. There is a similar, less accurate urine test for HCG. The urine test is more frequently and easily performed.

Pertinent facts

- Blood is drawn from a vein in the arm. The only discomfort associated with this test is the needle stick.
- The customary cost of this test is approximately $18.

URINE TESTS
Pregnancy test
Normal values

Negative, unless the patient is pregnant.

Purpose

See previous study.

Procedure

The urine specimen should be collected in a standard container and taken to the laboratory. A first-voided morning specimen is preferred. Urine tests for pregnancy are usually recommended 2 weeks after the first missed menstrual period.

Pertinent facts

- The patient should be given the urine container on the evening before the test so she can provide a first morning specimen. This specimen generally contains the greatest concentration of HCG.
- The customary cost of this study is approximately $18.

Estriol excretion study
Normal values

Greater than 12 mg/24 hours; rising urinary estriol values indicate normal fetal growth.

Purpose

Serial 24-hour urine studies for estriol excretion provide an objective means for assessing the function of the placenta and also the fetus in high-risk pregnancies. Excretion of estriol (the type of estrogen present in the blood and urine in the largest amounts) increases around the eighth week of pregnancy and continues to rise until shortly before delivery. A rise in urinary values greater than 12 mg in 24 hours indicates that the fetus and the placenta are functioning adequately. Decreasing values suggest either fetal or placental deterioration. If the estriol levels fall, early delivery of the fetus may be indicated.

Procedure

Serial studies are usually begun around the twenty-eight to thirtieth week of pregnancy and repeated at weekly intervals. The frequency of these estriol determinations can be increased as needed to evaluate a high-risk pregnancy. Collection may even be done daily. Although the first collection is a baseline value, all collection results are compared with previous ones because decreasing values suggest deterioration of the fetal-placental unit.

A 24-hour urine specimen is collected using a special preservative. The urine specimen must be refrigerated or kept on ice during the entire collection period. It is taken to the laboratory at the end of 24 hours.

Pertinent facts

- The 24-hour collection begins after the patient urinates. The first urine specimen is discarded. All urine passed by the patient during the next 24 hours is to be collected. Test results are calculated on the basis of the 24-hour output, and the results will be inaccurate if any specimens are missed. If one voided specimen is accidentally discarded, the 24-hour collection must usually begin again. (The last specimen is collected as close as possible to the end of the 24-hour period.)
- The patient should void before having a bowel movement so that the urine is not contaminated by feces.
- The patient can drink fluids during the 24-hour period, unless this is contraindicated by her physician.
- The urine is collected in a container with a preservative. The urine should be kept refrigerated or in a bucket of ice.
- There is no discomfort associated with this study. Collection of the urine and delivery to the laboratory can be inconvenient and stressful to the patient and her family, especially when done frequently.
- The laboratory will usually provide the containers for collection.
- The customary cost of the study is approximately $35.

SPECIAL STUDIES
Papanicolaou's smear (Pap smear, Pap test, cytologic or cell test for cancer)
Normal values

No abnormal or atypical cells found.

Purpose

A Pap smear is taken to detect cancer cells in the cervical and vaginal secretions. This test is based on the fact that normal and abnormal cervical and uterine cancer cells are shed into the cervical and vaginal secretions. By examining these secretions under a microscope, one can detect early cellular changes compatible with precancer or cancerous conditions. The Pap smear is 95% accurate in detecting cervical cancer. Its accuracy and detection of uterine cancer approaches 40%. The cells are classified as follows:

Class 1 Absence of atypical or abnormal cells (normal)

Class 2 Atypical cells but no evidence of cancer (worrisome but most frequently caused by inflammation of the cervix)

Class 3 Cell findings suggestive of but not conclusive of cancer (should be evaluated more extensively)

Class 4 Cell findings strongly suggestive of cancer (requires more extensive evaluation)

Class 5 Cell findings conclusive of cancer (requires treatment)

Abnormal smears in classes 2 through 4 do not necessarily indicate that the patient has a cancer. For these patients, additional procedures such as D & C (dilatation and curettage) (see p. 217), cone biopsy, or colposcopy with cervical biopsy (see p. 190-191) are indicated.

A general movement has occurred over the last 5 years to reclassify Pap smear/cervical biopsies to report in terms of cervical intraepithelial neoplasia (CIN). This is a simple designation of the spectrum of abnormal cell development, which usually occurs before invasive cervical cancer. In contrast to the older, rigid classification, CIN reporting recognizes the continuum of abnormally developed cervical cells and allows for some overlap. The subclasses of CIN are classified as follows:

CIN 1 Mild and mild to moderate dysplasia (abnormal development)

CIN 2 Moderate and moderate to severe dysplasia

CIN 3 Severe dysplasia and cancer

Roughly, CIN includes classes 2 and 3, CIN 2 includes class 3, and CIN 3 comprises classes 4 and 5.

A Pap smear may also be performed to follow some abnormalities such as infertility. An estrogen/progesterone hormonal imbalance can be detected by the Pap smear.

A Pap smear should be part of the routine pelvic examination. Usually a routine cervical culture for gonococcus is obtained during the Pap smear examination.

Procedure

The patient should refrain from douching and tub bathing for 24 to 48 hours before her Pap smear. She should not be menstruating. If abnormal bleeding is present, however, the Pap smear and examination should be performed because of the significant possibility that serious cervical or uterine lesions may be present. A common error is to delay Pap testing for 2 to 3 months because of intermittent bleeding or continuous bleeding.

For this test, the patient is placed with her legs in stirrups, and a nonlubricated vaginal speculum is inserted to expose the cervix. Material is collected from the cervical canal using a moist saline cotton swab or spatula. The cells are immediately wiped across a clean glass slide and fixed either by immersing the slide in equal parts of 95% alcohol and ether or by using a commercial spray. The secretions must be fixed before drying occurs, because drying will distort the cells and make interpretation difficult. The slide is labeled.

Pertinent facts

- No discomfort other than that of the insertion of the speculum is associated with this procedure.
- A Pap smear is obtained in about 5 minutes by a physician or a nurse.
- The patient will be appropriately draped to prevent unnecessary embarrassment and exposure.
- The patient should not have douched or have taken a tub bath within the past 24 hours because this may wash away cell deposits that are desired in the specimen.
- Usually the patient will be notified by the physician's office only if further evaluation is necessary. If the smears were abnormal, this does not necessarily mean that the patient has cancer. Many patients associate a suspicious test with malignancy and become very frightened.
- The customary cost for the study is approximately $15.

Ultrasonography (obstetric echogram)
Normal values

Normal fetal and placental size and position.

Purpose

Ultrasound evaluation of the obstetric patient has proven to be a harmless, noninvasive method of evaluating the female reproductive system and the fetus. In diagnostic ultrasound, harmless, high-frequency sound waves are emitted from a transducer (Fig. 12-6) and penetrate the structure (uterus, placenta, and fetus) to be studied. These sound waves are bounced back to a sensor within the transducer and by electrical conversion are arranged into a pictorial image of the desired organ (Fig. 12-6). A realistic Polaroid- or x-ray-type picture is taken of the pattern.

Obstetric ultrasonography may be useful in

1. Making an early diagnosis of normal pregnancy and abnormal pregnancy (such as tubal pregnancy). Pregnancy may be diagnosed as early as 5 weeks after the last menstrual period (LMP).
2. Identifying multiple pregnancies. Multiple pregnancies can be detected by 13 to 14 weeks by demonstrating the presence of more than one fetal head.
3. Differentiating a tumor (such as hydatidiform mole) from a normal pregnancy.
4. Determining the age of the fetus by the diameter of its head. A single scan is not completely reliable in determining fetal age. Ultrasonography is more accurate if an earlier reference scan is available for later comparison.
5. Measuring the rate of fetal growth. Intrauterine growth retardation of the fetus can be indicated by sequential measurements of the fetus' head. Growth retardation should be confirmed by other studies, such as estriol level determinations, nonstress testing, or oxytocin stress testing. Fetal death can be determined by sequential scans showing lack of growth, loss of fetal outline, and an increased number of echoes coming from within the fetal body.

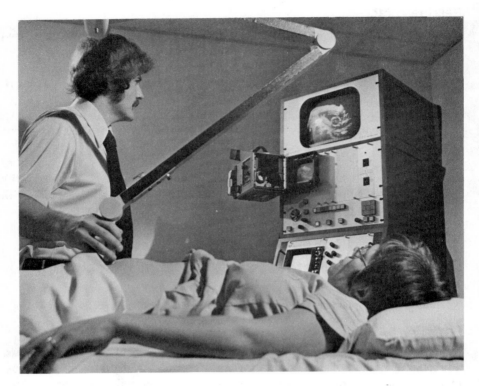

Fig. 12-6. Ultrasonography is a safe, painless method of scanning mother's abdomen with sound waves to follow fetal growth and development.

Courtesy March of Dimes, White Plains, New York.

6. Identifying placental abnormalities, such as abruptio placentae (partial or complete premature separation of the placenta) and placenta previa (abnormally implanted placenta in the thin, lower part of the uterus). Ultrasound localization of the placenta is often done before amniocentesis (see next study) to avoid puncture of the placenta and before cesarean section so that the placenta can be avoided when the uterus is opened.
7. Making the diagnosis of various uterine and ovarian enlargement (such as neoplasms, cysts, and abscess).
8. Determining fetal position. This information is helpful when a normal vaginal delivery may not be possible because the fetus is in a transverse or breech position.

There are no known complications for the mother or the fetus associated with this study. This study is safe even when used repeatedly. The patient is not exposed to any radiation.

Procedure

No fasting or sedation is required. The patient is given 3 to 8 glasses of water 1 hour before the study and instructed *not* to void. The patient will be uncomfortable with a full bladder. The full bladder provides better transmission of the sound waves and better visualization of the uterus by pushing the uterus into a better position for visualization. The patient is then taken to the ultrasound room (usually in the radiology department) and examined lying on her back on an examining table. The ultrasonographer (usually an x-ray physician) applies a greasy conductive paste to the abdomen. This paste is used to enhance sound transmission and reception. A transducer is then moved vertically and horizontally over the skin, and pictures are taken of the reflection (Fig. 12-6).

Pertinent facts

- There are no adverse effects to the mother or the fetus, even when the study is repeated several times.
- The patient must drink several glasses of water before the study and not void until the entire study is completed. This will permit better transmission of the sound waves and enhance visualization of the uterus.
- The study is not associated with any pain. The patient may have some discomfort because she will have a full bladder and the urge to void. Some patients may be uncomfortable lying on the hard x-ray table.
- A gel is applied to the skin to enhance the transmission and the reception of the sound waves. The gel will feel cold. After the study the gel will be removed from the skin.
- After the study the patient will be given the opportunity to urinate.
- The duration of the study is approximately 20 minutes.
- The customary cost of the study is approximately $45.

Amniocentesis
Normal values

Normal fetus.

Purpose

Amniocentesis involves the placement of a needle through the patient's abdominal and uterine walls and into the amniotic cavity to withdraw fluid from the pregnant uterus for analysis (Fig. 12-7). The study of amniotic fluid has been vitally important in assessing
1. Fetal maturity status (in cases where early delivery is preferred)
2. Sex of the fetus
3. Genetic and chromosomal abnormalities (such as hemophilia and Down's syndrome)
4. Status of the fetus affected by Rh blood incompatibilities
5. Hereditary disorders (such as cystic fibrosis)
6. Anatomic abnormalities (such as spina bifida)
Fetal maturity is determined by analysis of the amniotic fluid for
1. Lecithin/sphingomyelin (L/S) ratio. The L/S ratio is a measure of fetal lung maturity. Lecithin is the major constituent of surfactant, which is an important substance required for ventilation of the lung. In the immature fetal lung, the sphingomyelin concentration in the amniotic fluid is higher

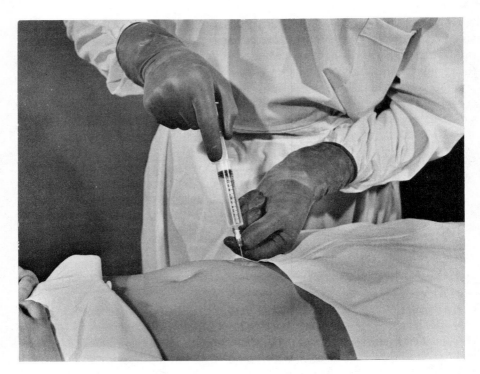

Fig. 12-7. Amniocentesis is performed to remove and examine a sample of amniotic fluid.

Courtesy March of Dimes, White Plains, New York.

than the lecithin concentration. At 35 weeks of gestation, the concentration of lecithin rapidly increases, whereas sphingomyelin concentration decreases. An L/S ratio of 2:1 or more is a highly reliable indication that the fetal lung, and therefore the total fetus, is mature. In such a case, the infant would be unlikely to develop any respiration distress syndrome after birth.

2. Creatinine clearance. Creatinine is excreted in the fetal urine and is used to assess fetal kidney function and fetal muscle mass. Creatinine concentrations can be used to indicate fetal maturity.

3. Bilirubin levels. The amount of bilirubin in the amniotic fluid is a measure of liver maturity and should decrease near term in a normal fetus.

4. Cell findings. Cells shed by the fetus can be stained with a dye to estimate the age of the fetus.

The L/S ratio is the single most accurate indicator of fetal maturity. Although the accuracy of the other studies is only between 50% and 60%, they are used for comparative purposes.

Timing of the amniocentesis varies according to the clinical circumstances. With advanced maternal age and if chromosomal or genetic abnormalities are suspected, the test should be done early enough (14 to 16 weeks) to easily allow safe abortion. If knowledge of fetal maturity is sought, it is best to perform the study during or after the thirty-fifth week of pregnancy. The exact position of the placenta can be determined by ultrasonography (see previous study) to avoid inserting the needle into the placenta and possibly interrupting the placenta and inducing bleeding or abortion.

Procedure

Amniocentesis is usually performed on an outpatient basis under sterile conditions. The patient is instructed to empty her bladder, unless ultrasound guidance is used. The fetal heart rate is auscultated with a special stethoscope. The placental site is determined by ultrasound before the study to permit selection of a puncture site that will avoid placental interruption.

The patient is then placed lying on her back and the skin overlying the chosen site is cleansed and numbed. A 5-inch needle is then inserted through the abdominal wall and directed at an angle toward the middle of the uterus. About 3 to 5 teaspoons of amniotic fluid is then withdrawn into a syringe. The needle is removed, and the site is covered with an adhesive bandage.

The amniotic fluid is placed in a sterile glass container and transported to the special chemistry laboratory for analysis. Sometimes the specimen may be sent by airmail to another commercial laboratory.

After the procedure, the fetal heart rate is again assessed. The patient is instructed to report any fluid loss, bleeding, cramping, dizziness, or fever following the study. The mother's blood type should be determined if not known. Women with Rh-negative blood should receive Rho (D) immune globulin (RhoGAM) because of the risk of immunization from the fetal blood and subsequent injury to the fetal blood.

Amniocentesis should be performed by an experienced obstetrician who is able to provide counseling and treatment based on the results of the study.

This study is contraindicated in patients with
1. Abruptio placentae (partial or complete premature separation of the placenta)
2. Placenta previa (abnormally implanted placenta in the thin, lower portion of the uterus)
3. A history of premature labor (before 34 weeks), unless the patient is receiving antilabor medication at this time
4. Incompetent cervix

Pertinent facts

- The discomfort associated with this study is that of mild uterine cramping, which occurs when the needle hits the uterus. Some women may complain of a "pulling" sensation as the amniotic fluid is withdrawn. Many women are extremely anxious during this procedure.
- The duration of this procedure is approximately 20 to 30 minutes.
- The physician will obtain a signed consent from the father and the mother before the study.

- The fetal heart rate will be determined before and after the study to detect any ill effects related to the procedure. With any ill effects, the patient would be placed on bed rest with continuous fetal heart monitoring. An immediate cesarean section may be performed if the age of the fetus is older than 35 weeks and there are any signs of fetal distress.
- If the woman felt dizzy or nauseated during the procedure, usually lying on her right side for several minutes after the study will alleviate these problems.
- The patient will be instructed to call her physician if she has any fluid loss or temperature elevation after the study.
- The duration of this procedure is approximately 20 to 30 minutes.
- The customary cost of this study is approximately $75.

Oxytocin challenge test
Normal values

Negative (no evidence of fetal distress).

Purpose

The oxytocin challenge test (OCT) is a test used to determine the adequacy of the fetus and the placenta in the assessment of high-risk pregnancy (see Anatomy and physiology). For this study a temporary stress in the form of uterine contractions is applied to the fetus. Uterine contractions cause a transient blockage of placental blood flow. If the fetal heart rate (FHR) remains normal during the contraction, the test is considered normal (or a negative test). The placental and fetal unit can then be considered adequate for the next 7 days. On the other hand, if the placental and fetal unit is inadequate, the fetus will not receive enough oxygen during the contraction. This will result in a marked decrease of the fetal heart rate. This result is then considered positive. A positive test result warrants a complete review of other studies (such as amniocentesis, which was discussed previously) before the pregnancy is terminated by delivery.

Two advantages of the OCT are that it can be done at any time of the day and that its results are available immediately. Although this test can be performed reliably at 32 weeks of pregnancy, it is usually done after 34 weeks. OCT can induce labor, and a 34-week fetus is more likely to survive an unexpectedly induced delivery than is a 32-week fetus. Nonstress testing of the fetus (see next study) is the preferred test in most every instance and can be performed more safely at 32 weeks and then followed 2 weeks later by OCT if necessary. The OCT may be performed weekly until the pregnancy is ended by delivery.

The OCT can be used clinically in a high-risk pregnancy where fetal well being is suspected to be threatened. These include pregnancies marked by diabetes, high blood pressure, intrauterine growth retardation, Rh factor incompatibilities, and history of stillbirth.

Procedure

The OCT is safely performed on an outpatient basis in the labor and delivery unit, where qualified nurses and necessary equipment are accessible. If the OCT is performed on an elective basis, the patient should be kept from having anything by mouth (NPO), in case labor occurs as a result of the testing. Performance of this test should not be delayed if the patient is not fasting and fetal trouble is suspected. The test is performed by a nurse with a physician available.

After emptying her bladder, the patient is placed lying on her side. Her blood pressure is checked frequently to avoid a blood pressure drop, which could reduce the placental blood flow and cause a false positive test result. Blood pressure is then checked routinely every 15 minutes throughout the test. An external fetal monitor is placed over the abdomen to record the fetal heart tones, and an external "tocodynamometer" is attached to the abdomen to monitor the uterine contractions. The tones and the uterine contractions are recorded on a strip paper recorder. Baseline fetal heart rate and uterine activity are monitored for 15 minutes. If uterine contractions are detected during this pretest period, oxytocin is withheld, and the response of the fetal heart tone to spontaneous uterine contractions is monitored.

If there are no spontaneous uterine contractions, oxytocin (Pitocin) is administered by an IV infusion to induce uterine contractions. Oxytocin is administered until the patient is having good contractions for 10 minutes. The fetal heart rate is recorded.

The oxytocin infusion is then discontinued while the fetal monitoring is continued for another 30 minutes, until the uterine activity has returned to the pre-oxytocin intensity. The patient should be informed of the test results at this time.

The OCT is contraindicated in
1. Multiple pregnancy, because the uterus is under greater tension and more likely to be stimulated to premature labor.
2. Premature ruptured membrane, because labor may be stimulated by the OCT.
3. Placenta previa, because vaginal delivery may be induced, leading to life-threatening bleeding from the mother and the child.
4. Abruptio placentae, because the placenta may separate from the uterus as a result of the oxytocin-induced uterine contractions.
5. Previous cesarean section, again because the strong contractions may cause uterine rupture. (However, if necessary the OCT may be performed if it is carefully monitored and controlled.)
6. Pregnancies of less than 33 weeks, because early delivery may be induced before the fetus is mature enough to sustain life outside the uterus.

Pertinent facts

- The discomfort associated with this procedure may consist of mild labor contractions. Usually breathing exercises will be enough to control any discomfort. Pain medication may be given if needed.
- The oxytocin medication is usually administered by an infusion pump to precisely deliver the appropriate dose. After the oxytocin is discontinued, the IV is removed. A bandage is applied to the site.
- Many patients will have the study repeated at weekly intervals until delivery. This regimen is very tiring and anxiety-producing for the parents. The duration of the study is approximately 2 hours.
- The customary cost of the study is approximately $50.

Nonstress test
Normal values

"Reactive" fetus (heart rate speeds up with fetal movement).

Purpose

The nonstress test (NST) is a noninvasive study in which fetal heart rate (FHR) acceleration in response to fetal movement is monitored. Fetal activity may be spontaneous, induced by uterine contractions, or induced by external manipulation. Oxytocin medication is not used. Fetal response is categorized as "reactive" or "nonreactive." The NST is said to indicate a reactive fetus when with fetal movement fetal heart rate (FHR) accelerations are detected. The test is 99% reliable in indicating fetal viability and negates the need for the OCT (see previous study). If the test detects a nonreactive fetus (no FHR acceleration with fetal movement), the patient is then a candidate for the OCT.

The NST is useful in screening high-risk pregnancies (see Anatomy and physiology) and in selecting those patients who may require the OCT. An NST is now routinely performed before the OCT to avoid the complications associated with oxytocin administration. There are no complications associated with NST.

Procedure

The NST is performed by a nurse in the physician's office or in the hospital ward. After emptying her bladder, the patient is placed lying on her side. An external fetal monitor is placed on the abdomen to record the fetal heart rate (FHR). The mother can indicate the occurrence of fetal movement by pressing a button on the fetal monitor whenever she feels the fetus move. FHR and the uterine contractions are concomitantly recorded on a 2-channel strip graft. The fetal monitor is then observed for fetal heart rate acceleration associated with fetal movement. If the baby is quiet for 20 minutes, fetal activity is stimulated by external methods, such as rubbing the mother's abdomen, pressing on the abdomen, ringing a bell near the abdomen, or placing a pan on the abdomen and banging on the pan.

This study should be performed after a recent meal because the fetus frequently is more active when the mother's blood sugar level is increased.

Pertinent facts

- There is no discomfort or adverse effects associated with this study.
- If the patient is hungry, it may be helpful to send her to the cafeteria before initiating the NST. Fetal activity is enhanced after the mother has eaten a meal.
- The duration of the study is approximately 20 to 40 minutes.
- The customary cost of the study is $40.

Sample case report: high-risk pregnancy

Mrs. P., a 22-year-old patient, had a known history of diabetes mellitus. She had been well regulated on insulin in the past few years. She had been trying to get pregnant. She went to her obstetrician 4 weeks after missing her expected menstrual period. Her physical examination results were essentially normal. Positive findings on the pelvic examination indicated mild enlargement of the uterus compatible with early pregnancy.

STUDIES	RESULTS
Routine laboratory studies.	Blood and urine test within normal limits (WNL) except the fasting blood sugar: 160 mg/dl (normal: 60-120 mg/dl; see Chapter 11); 2-hour postprandial glucose: 200 mg/dl (normal value: 60-120 mg/dl; see Chapter 11)
Pap smear	Class I cell findings (normal)
Pregnancy test	Positive
Ultrasonography (at 24 weeks)	Diameter of the fetal skull 5 cm (baseline value)

The routine Pap smear did not indicate any cancer cells. The pregnancy test confirmed the clinical diagnosis of pregnancy with 80% accuracy. With close monitoring of her diabetes, the patient was doing well at her thirty-sixth week of pregnancy. The following studies were then performed:

STUDIES	RESULTS
Ultrasonography	Normal placenta located high in the uterus; diameter of the fetal skull 8.7 cm
Amniocentesis	
L/S ratio	3:1 (normal: greater than 2:1)
Creatinine level	2.3 mg/dl (normal: greater than or equal to 2 mg/dl)
Cell findings	30% of the cells stained orange (normal: greater than 20%)
	Male child with no genetic or chromosomal abnormalities

In the patient's thirty-sixth week of pregnancy, ultrasonography indicated the fetal size was compatible with the week of pregnancy and that there were no abnormalities in the location of the placenta. Amniocentesis indicated that the fetus was mature and able to sustain life outside of the womb.

In the patient's thirty-eighth week of pregnancy, spontaneous fetal movements ceased. The following studies were then performed:

STUDIES	RESULTS
Serial 24-hour urine test for estriol	12 mg/24 hr; 11.2 mg/24 hr; 10 mg/24 hr (normal: greater than 12 mg/24 hr)
Nonstress test (NST)	No heart rate acceleration with fetal movement (normal: heart rate increased with movement)

STUDIES	RESULTS
Oxytocin challenge test (OCT)	Positive; falling heart rate with uterine contraction (normal: negative)
X-ray pelvimetry	Birth canal size inadequate for vaginal delivery
Amnioscopy	No meconium staining (normal: no meconium staining)

In the patient's thirty-eighth week of pregnancy, although amnioscopy ruled out fetal distress, the urine test for estriol and the OCT indicated deterioration of the fetal-placental unit. X-ray pelvimetry implied that the size of the baby's head would not pass through the pelvis (cephalopelvic disproportion, or CPD).

A cesarean section was performed, and a healthy 7-pound 8-ounce boy was delivered. Both mother and child were discharged 1 week after delivery.

13

Diagnostic studies used to evaluate infertility

INFERTILITY

Infertility may be diagnosed whenever a woman is unable to conceive during at least 1 year of regular unprotected intercourse. Ninety percent of couples will be able to achieve a pregnancy within a 1-year period. Normal fertility is dependent on many factors in both the man and the woman (see Anatomy and physiology, Chapter 12). The man must able to produce a sufficient number of normal, motile sperm that can be ejaculated through a patent pathway (vas deferens) into the vagina. The sperm then must be able to survive in the female cervical environment and ascend through the cervix, the uterus, and the fallopian tubes (see Fig. 12-2). The woman must be able to produce an egg that remains in the fallopian tubes until it is fertilized by the sperm. To begin normal development, the products of conception must move into the uterus and become implanted there. Any defect in these essential processes will result in infertility.

Male infertility

Problems in male fertility are the sole factor or an important contributing factor in 30% to 40% of infertile marriages. These problems usually involve defects in sperm production or transmission. Male infertility may be caused by one or more of the following:

1. Abnormalities of the sperm. These include reduced number of sperm, reduction in the ejaculatory volume, abnormal sperm quality (such as too dilute), and abnormally shaped sperm.
2. Testicular abnormalities (such as complete absence or inappropriate development of the testes). Infections, particularly mumps, can destroy the testicles.
3. Abnormalities of the penis. If the penis is abnormally short, buried in fat, or malformed, the sperm emission may take place outside the vagina.

4. Faulty sperm transmission. The sperm may not be able to enter the female reproductive tract because of scarring that obstructs the epididymis, the vas deferens, or the urethra. The most common cause of this scarring is from gonorrhea.
5. Advanced nutritional deficiency. This condition alters the function of all organ systems including the gonads (sex organs).
6. Emotional factors. These may induce impotence or premature ejaculation.

Female infertility

Ovulation occurs between the twelfth and sixteenth days of most menstrual cycles. Unprotected intercourse must take place within 12 to 24 hours of ovulation. Often failure to conceive is the result of incorrect timing of ovulation. Other causes of female infertility include the following:

1. Cervical abnormalities. Alterations in the cervical membrane or mucus may interfere with sperm passage.
2. Vaginal disorders. Absence or incomplete formation of the vagina prevents vaginal penetration by the penis and the sperm. Inflammation (redness and swelling) of the vagina alters the pH and may destroy or inactivate sperm.
3. Endocrine (hormone) abnormalities. Abnormal function of any of the hormones of the body can prevent ovulation.
4. Uterine disorder. Scarring, malformation, malposition, or tumors of the uterus may prevent implantation of the fertilized egg into the uterus or may cause early abortion.
5. Tubal disorders. Partial or complete occlusion of the fallopian tubes occurs in a large number of women who fail to conceive. The most common cause of tubal obstruction is scarring. Appendicitis and other pelvic infections (for example, gonorrhea) may result in adhesions that subsequently can partially or completely obstruct the fallopian tubes.
6. Ovarian disorders. Incomplete development of the ovaries may prevent the patient from ovulating. Tumors or infections may also disrupt ovarian function transiently or permanently.
7. Severe nutritional deficiencies and chronic disease states. These conditions reduce or inhibit ovulation.
8. Advancing age. Fertility in women is maximum about 20 to 25 years of age. This slowly declines until menopause.
9. Emotional factors. Painful spasm of the vagina that prevents intercourse and pain during intercourse may be the result of psychologic disturbance. Stress may also affect ovulation.
10. Immunologic reactions to sperm. Unexplained infertility may be caused by female production of antibodies that perceive the sperm as foreign and destroy it.
11. Drugs. Nearly all women cease to ovulate while on chemotherapy medications for cancer. Other drugs can affect ovulation.
12. Radiation. Ovulation is usually permanently obliterated by exposure of the ovaries to high radiation levels.

Since one factor or a multiplicity of factors may be the cause of infertility, the man and the woman both must be evaluated. A systematic investigation of infertility is described in the case study at the end of this chapter. Therapy for infertility may require correction of faulty intercourse techniques, attention to proper timing, surgery to correct a malfunction or anatomic problem, or recognition and correction of emotional factors. If the infertility persists, the condition is then referred to as *sterility*. Approximately 1 out of 10 American couples is truly "barren."

X-RAYS AND NUCLEAR SCANS
Hysterosalpingography (uterotubography, uterosalpingography)
Normal values

Patent (open) fallopian tubes; no defects in the uterine cavity.

Purpose

In this procedure, the uterus and fallopian tubes are visualized with x-ray after the insertion of dye into the cervix. Uterine tumors, adhesions, and developmental abnormalities can be detected. Postinflammatory scarring, tumor, or kinking of the tubes (from pelvic adhesions) can also be seen. This study is more accurate than the uterotubal insufflation test (also discussed in this chapter). Unlike hysterosalpingography, the insufflation test may be normal even when one tube is completely blocked.

This test may also be used to document the adequacy of surgical tubal ligation. Potential complications of this study include allergy to the iodinated contrast material and infection of the uterus or fallopian tubes caused by using contaminated dye.

Procedure

It is best for this test to be performed 4 to 5 days after the patient completes menstruation. At this time, one avoids the risk of aborting an unknown pregnancy.

This test is usually performed on an outpatient basis in the x-ray department by a gynecologist. The x-ray films are interpreted by the radiologist. A laxative is given on the night before the test. An enema or suppository is administered on the morning of the test. Immediately before the test is performed, an x-ray film of the abdomen is taken to ensure that the stomach and intestines are free of gas and feces.

After urinating, the patient is placed on an x-ray table with her legs in stirrups (as for a pelvic exam). A speculum is inserted into the vagina, and the cervix is visualized and cleansed. A sterile cannula is inserted into the cervix. A 2-minute rest period is necessary to allow for the relaxation of tubal spasm associated with cervical dilatation. Dye is injected through the cannula, and x-ray films are taken. More dye is then injected to fill the entire genital tracts (the uterus and tubes). This study can only be considered satisfactorily performed if the uterus and the tubes are distended to maximum capacity or dye flows out of the fallopian tubes.

Pertinent facts

- It is important for the patient to take the enema and suppository as ordered to prevent gas shadows from obscuring the x-ray film.
- If the patient is allergic to iodine, this should be reported to the physician.
- The duration of this procedure is about 15 minutes.
- The patient may feel occasional transient menstrual-type cramping. A mild sedative or antispasmodic is sometimes used.
- Cramping and dizziness may occur following this study.
- A vaginal discharge (sometimes blood) may be present 1 to 2 days after the test.
- After this study, the patient should wear a vaginal pad, because the x-ray dye material can stain her underclothing.
- The customary cost of this study is approximately $65.

ENDOSCOPY
Laparoscopy (pelvic endoscopy)
Normal values

Normal appearing reproductive organs.

Purpose

During this procedure, the abdominal organs can be visualized by inserting a special instrument through the abdominal wall and into the abdominal cavity. This study is particularly helpful in diagnosing pelvic adhesions, ovarian tumors and cysts, and other tubal and uterine causes of infertility. Ectopic pregnancy, ruptured ovarian cyst, and inflammation of the fallopian tubes also can be detected during an evaluation for pelvic pain. Surgical procedures (such as biopsy of the liver and tubal ligation) can easily be performed with the laparoscope. Laparoscopy is much more informative than culdoscopy (see next study) in that one is able to more accurately examine the entire abdominal cavity.

Although laparoscopy is relatively safe, general anesthesia is usually required. The recovery period from the effects of anesthesia is usually short. Because bleeding may occur after this study, some physicians may prefer to perform this study on an inpatient basis. However, in certain instances laparoscopy can be safely performed on an outpatient basis.

Procedure

The routine preoperative procedure of the hospital is carried out. The patient is kept from having anything by mouth (NPO) after midnight on the day of the procedure. In the morning, she empties her bladder and is premedicated before going to the operating room.

In the operating room, after the abdominal skin is cleansed, a blunt-tip needle is inserted through a small incision in the area of the umbilicus (belly button). The abdominal cavity is then filled with approximately 2 to 4 liters of carbon dioxide (pneumoperitoneum) to separate the abdominal wall from the organs inside the abdomen (Fig. 13-1). This enhances visualization of the pelvic structures and allows the laparoscope to be safely inserted into the abdominal cavity. The pelvic

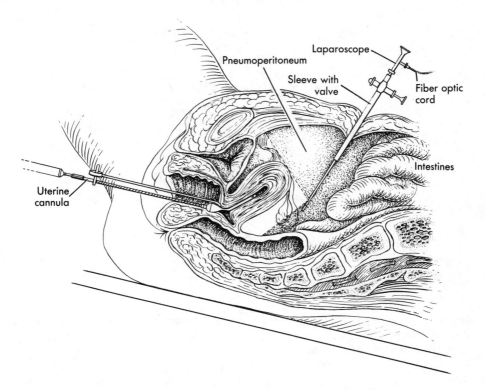

Fig. 13-1. Laparoscopy. Note the lighted laparoscope examining the uterus.

and abdominal organs are then carefully examined with the scope. After the desired procedure (such as inspection, tubal ligation, or biopsy) is completed, the carbon dioxide gas is allowed to escape, and the laparoscope is removed. The small incision is closed with a few skin stitches and covered with an adhesive strip (Band-Aid).

Pertinent facts

- The patient should not eat or drink anything (NPO) after midnight before the test. Food or fluid in the stomach may cause vomiting during the procedure.
- A written consent should be obtained from the patient before the study.
- Before this procedure, the abdomen may be shaved because hair is a source of bacteria.
- The patient should urinate before going to the operating room. It is very easy to penetrate a distended bladder during the procedure.
- The duration of the procedure is approximately 20 to 40 minutes.
- After the procedure, most patients will have mild incisional pain. Some patients may complain of pain in their shoulders caused by the carbon dioxide gas.
- If this procedure is being done on an outpatient basis, the patient is usually discharged within 2 to 3 hours.

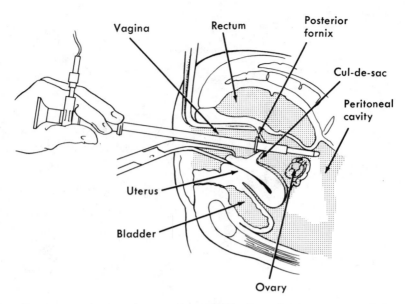

Fig. 13-2. Culdoscopy. With the patient in the knee-chest position, the culdoscope is inserted through the back wall of the vagina into the cul-de-sac of Douglas. Note that ovaries can be seen.

From Cinkota, E., and Woods, N.F.: Assessment of the reproductive and sexual systems. In Phipps, W.J., Long, B.C., and Woods, N.F., editors: Medical-surgical nursing: concepts and clinical practice, St. Louis, The C.V. Mosby Co.

- After the procedure, the patient's pulse, blood pressure, and respirations are monitored frequently to detect any signs of internal bleeding.
- The customary cost of this study is approximately $500.

Culdoscopy
Normal values

Normal appearing reproductive organs.

Purpose

The pelvic organs can be directly visualized by placing a culdoscope (a lighted instrument similar to a cystoscope) through a small incision in the vaginal area and into the space between the rectum and the uterus (cul-de-sac of Douglas) (Fig. 13-2). This procedure affords direct visualization of the uterus, the fallopian tubes, the broad ligaments, the rectal wall, and the colon.

Culdoscopy is used in the evaluation of infertility because it can determine abnormalities of the fallopian tubes. It is also used in the detection of suspected ectopic pregnancy and also in the study of unexplained pelvic pain or masses. Culdoscopy has fallen out of favor since the introduction of laparoscopy (see previous study). Laparoscopy has largely replaced culdoscopy because

1. Laparoscopy provides better visualization of the pelvic organs.
2. A lower infection rate is associated with laparoscopy.

Culdoscopy is accurate and relatively safe if performed by an experienced gynecologist. Possible complications include infection or hemorrhage and penetration of the rectum, bladder, or small intestines.

Procedure

The patient is prepared for culdoscopy in the same manner as for any type of minor vaginal surgery. The patient is kept from having anything by mouth (NPO) after midnight. This procedure is performed in the operating room with the patient placed in stirrups or in the knee-chest position. Spinal or local anesthesia is used. A small incision is made in the vagina and a culdoscope is passed into the desired area. The pelvic and abdominal organs are then visualized and examined (Fig 13-2).

After the study, the scope is removed. No sutures are used to close the incision in the vaginal area. No douching or intercourse is permitted until the healing is complete (usually 1 to 2 weeks).

Pertinent facts

- This procedure is performed by a physician in approximately 1 hour.
- Patients are usually very uncomfortable from the required knee-chest position.
- Written consent for this procedure is obtained before the study.
- After the study, douching and intercourse are not permitted until the vaginal wall has healed. This healing takes approximately 1 to 2 weeks. The patient may take sitz baths 4 days after the procedure.
- Mild oral analgesics (pain pills) may be ordered for any discomfort.
- The customary cost for this study is approximately $75.

URINE TEST
Hormone assay for urinary pregnanediol
Normal values

Increased excretion after ovulation to greater than 1 mg/24 hr.

Purpose

Urinary pregnanediol is measured to evaluate progesterone production by the ovaries and the placenta. The main effect of progesterone is on the endometrium (the specialized lining on the inside of the uterus). Progesterone initiates the secretory phase of the uterus in anticipation of implantation of a fertilized ovum (see Fig. 12-3). Normally, progesterone is secreted following ovulation. Both the blood progesterone level and the urine concentration of progesterone breakdown products (pregnanediol and others) are significantly increased during the latter half of the ovulation cycle.

Pregnanediol is the most easily measured breakdown product of progesterone. The urinary level of pregnanediol excretion increases after ovulation for approximately 10 days to greater than 1 mg/24 hr (compared to the 0.4 plus or minus 0.1 mg/24 hr before ovulation). Since the pregnanediol level rises rapidly after ovulation, this study is useful in documenting whether ovulation has occurred and the exact time of ovulation.

During pregnancy, the pregnanediol level normally rises because of placental production of progesterone. Repeated studies can be used to monitor the status of the placenta. A decrease in the pregnanediol level may precede a spontaneous abortion. The urine test for pregnanediol is being replaced by newer and quicker blood studies.

Procedure

Progesterone determinations begin 4 to 6 days after a change in the biphasic curve (according to basal body temperature measurements, p. 218-219). A 24-hour urine specimen is collected in a standard specimen container and sent to the chemistry laboratory. During the entire collection time, the specimen should be kept refrigerated. No food or fluid restrictions are necessary during this collection period.

Pertinent facts

- The 24-hour collection period begins after the first urine specimen is discarded. All urine passed by the patient during the next 24 hours is collected. Test results are calculated on the basis of 24 hours. Results will be inaccurate if any of the specimens are not collected. If one voided specimen is accidentally thrown out, the 24-hour collection must begin again.
- The patient should urinate before having a bowel movement so that the urine is not contaminated by feces.
- No food or fluid restrictions are necessary during the 24-hour collection.
- The 24-hour urine collection must be kept refrigerated or in an ice bucket during the entire 24 hours.
- The customary cost for this procedure is approximately $40.

SPECIAL STUDIES
Semen analysis
Normal values

Volume: 2-6 ml.
Sperm count (density): 20-200 million/ml.
Sperm motility: 60%-80% actively motile.
Sperm morphology: 70%-90% normally shaped.

Purpose

The semen analysis is one of the most important aspects of the infertility workup, since the cause of the woman's inability to conceive often lies within her male partner. After 3 to 5 days of sexual abstinence, sperm is collected and examined for voume, sperm count, motility, and morphology.

The freshly collected semen is first measured for volume. Then a sperm count is performed. Men with very low or very high sperm counts are likely to be infertile. The motility (movement) of the sperm is then evaluated. At least 60% of the sperm should show progressive motility. Cell structure or morphology is then studied by staining a semen preparation and calculating the number of normal versus abnormal sperm forms.

A simple sperm analysis, especially if it indicates infertility, is inconclusive, because the sperm count varies from day to day. A semen analysis should be done at least twice. Men with no sperm or with less than 20 million sperm should be evaluated for endocrine problems (such as pituitary, thyroid, adrenal, or testicular abnormalities).

A normal semen analysis does not accurately assess the male factor unless the effect of the female's vaginal secretion on sperm survival is also determined (see Sims-Huhner test, also in this chapter). In addition to its value in infertility workups, semen analysis is also helpful in documenting adequate sterilization after a vasectomy. It is usually performed 6 weeks after the surgery. If any sperm are seen at that time, the adequacy of the vasectomy must be questioned.

Procedure

After 3 to 5 days of sexual abstinence, a semen specimen is collected by ejaculation into a clean container. For best results, this specimen should be collected by masturbation in a physician's office or laboratory. Less satisfactory specimens may be obtained in the patient's home by coitus interruptus or masturbation. These home specimens must be delivered to the laboratory within 1 hour after collection. Excessive heat and cold should be avoided during transportation of the specimen.

If the couple cannot obtain a specimen by masturbation or coitus interruptus for religious reasons, a plastic condom may be used. Rubber condoms should not be used because the powder and lubricants used in their manufacture may kill the sperm.

Pertinent facts

- Three to 5 days of sexual abstinence is necessary before collecting the sperm specimen. This is to ensure an adequate buildup of sperm. Prolonged abstinence before the collection should be discouraged, however, since the quality of the sperm cells and especially their motility may diminish.
- The sperm collection should be collected in a proper container given to the patient by the hospital laboratory.
- If the specimen will be obtained at home, the patient should be certain to bring the specimen to the laboratory for testing within 1 hour after the collection. The collection of sperm should be kept at room temperature. Exposure to heat or cold during the transportation may alter the sperm motility.
- When the specimen is delivered to the laboratory, the lab technician should write the exact date and time of the sperm collection on the lab slip.
- The customary cost of this study is approximately $25.

Uterotubal insufflation (Rubin's test)
Normal values

Patent (open) fallopian tubes.

Purpose

This study is used to determine the patency of the fallopian tubes by blowing carbon dioxide through the tubes. For this study, a flow meter and a pressure gauge are attached to a carbon dioxide source. A machine called a kymograph is used to record changes in pressure. With normal patency, as gas is insufflated into the uterus, there is a rise in pressure to about 80 to 100 mm of mercury, followed by a decrease to 40 to 80 mm of mercury as the gas passes through the tubes and into the abdominal cavity (Fig. 13-3). A pressure of 200 mm of mercury or more indicates tubal obstruction.

Spasm of the fallopian tubes can also be determined on this study. With tubal spasm, pressure rises to 160 to 200 mm of mercury and then falls rapidly as the

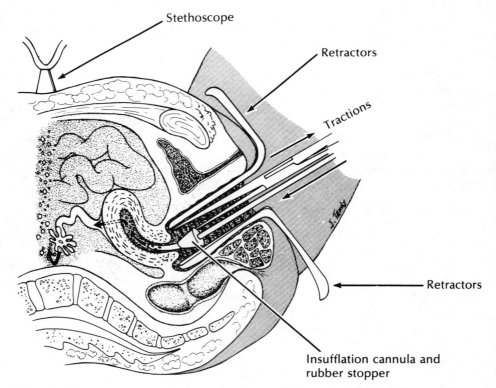

Fig. 13-3. Tubal insufflation, sagittal section. Note that gas flows through intrauterine cannula and escapes through the fallopian tubes. Cervix is closed by a rubber stopper. Resistance to flow is measured by back pressure on a mercury gauge. Attendant listens with a stethoscope on the abdomen.

From Jenson, M.D., Benson, R.C., and Bobak, I.M.: Maternity care: the nurse and the family, St. Louis, The C.V. Mosby Co.

tube opens. Because spasm can be caused by pain or emotional factors, a tranquilizer or analgesic (pain pill) may be given to the patient 1 hour before the test.

During the study, the physician listens with a stethoscope placed on the abdomen (Fig. 13-3). If the tubes are open, a swishing sound will be heard as the gas passes through the tubes into the abdominal cavity. Pain at the top of the shoulders may be felt. This is caused by the carbon dioxide within the abdomen.

Tubal obstruction cannot be diagnosed on the basis of a single study. The Rubin test should be repeated at the same sitting as well as at subsequent examinations. Repeated studies showing obstruction are necessary to prove tubal blockage. This is a safe procedure and can usually be performed on an outpatient basis. It is important that the Rubin test be performed 4 to 5 days after the last day of the menstrual period to avoid ovulation to ensure that a fertilized ovum is not displaced from the tube. Also at this time, mobilization of menstrual debris (which can transiently obstruct the tubes) is avoided. It is interesting to note that insufflation shortly before ovulation may aid in conception by interrupting thin adhesions that may have been blocking the tubes. The only conclusion that can be drawn from a normal Rubin test result is that *at least one fallopian tube* is patent. This test is not used as often today because of the availability of new and more accurate procedures.

Procedure

The Rubin test is usually performed on an outpatient basis in the physician's office. Usually the patient is instructed to take a laxative on the night before the study and an enema or suppository on the morning of the test.

After urinating, the patient is placed in a position as for a pelvic examination. The pelvic area is cleansed, and a vaginal speculum is introduced to expose the cervix. Then a special sterile cannula with a rubber tip is inserted into the cervical canal (Fig. 13-3). The rubber tip of the catheter is pressed tightly against the outer opening of the uterus to seal the opening.

A short rest period (2 minutes) is allowed to permit relaxation of any tubal spasm. A controlled amount of carbon dioxide is then insufflated (blown) into the uterus. Room air is never used.

The kymograph machine then records changes in the pressure. A stethoscope is placed over the abdomen to detect the gas flow into the abdomen (Fig. 13-3).

After this study, the patient will feel pain caused by irritation of the abdominal area by the carbon dioxide gas. If no pain occurs, occlusion of the tubes may be suspected, because the gas never passed through the tubes and into the abdominal cavity.

This study should not be performed in a patient with
1. Infections of the vagina and cervix or the fallopian tubes, because the infection may be spread by this procedure.
2. Blood clots.
3. Suspected pregnancy, because abortion may be induced by this procedure.

Pertinent facts

- This study is performed by a physician in approximately 30 minutes.
- During the test, the woman may have some discomfort when the cannula is in-

serted into the cervix. If the fallopian tubes are open (or patent), the patient will feel some pain in her shoulder area after the study. This pain therefore is a good sign, indicating that the fallopian tubes are open.
- After the study, the woman should rest for 2 to 3 hours. Pain, cramping, dizziness, nausea, and vomiting may be present and can be minimized by the patient reclining with the pelvis elevated so that gas will exit.
- The customary cost of this study is approximately $45.

Cervical mucus test (fern test)
Normal values
Ferning of cervical mucus during midcycle.

Purpose
The cervical mucus can be examined near midcycle and just before menstruation to detect ovulation. Ovulation requires a surge of estrogen during midcycle (see Fig. 12-3). Without this surge of estrogen, ovulation will not occur. Because pregnancy is impossible without ovulation, this study is used in the evaluation of fertility to predict the day of ovulation and to determine whether or not ovulation occurs.

The cervical mucus at ovulation is clear, abundant, watery, and elastic. If this mucus is spread on a clean glass slide and allowed to dry, the midcycle mucus creates a fern or palm leaf pattern. This pattern is correlated with estrogen activity and is therefore present in all ovulatory women at midcycle. When the cervical mucus is checked again immediately before menstruation, no ferning is found because progesterone is at is peak and inhibits ferning. Therefore during a normal menstrual cycle of an ovulatory female, the ferning of cervical mucus will occur at midcycle, and no ferning will occur before menstruation.

Procedure
This procedure is performed at the midcycle to detect estrogen-inducing ferning. It is then repeated approximately 7 days later to detect the progesterone inhibition of ferning. The patient is placed in a position with her legs in stirrups as for a Pap smear. An unlubricated speculum is inserted into the vagina to expose the cervix. A cotton-tip applicator is gently inserted into the cervical canal and rotated. The mucus that adheres to the cotton swab is spread on a clean glass slide and allowed to dry at room temperature. The dry spread of mucus is then examined for the presence of ferning under the lower power lens of the microscope.

Pertinent facts
- This procedure is performed by a physician in approximately 15 minutes.
- The only discomfort associated with this study is the insertion of the speculum (as for a Pap smear).
- The customary cost for this study is approximately $15.

Endometrial biopsy
Normal values

Uterine tissue prepared to receive and nourish a fertilized ovum 3 to 5 days before a normal period; no abnormal cells.

Purpose

One can determine whether ovulation has occurred by performing an endometrial biopsy. As discussed in the anatomy and physiology section of Chapter 12, ovulation is followed by the secretion of progesterone, which is responsible for building up the uterine tissue in preparation for implantation of a fertilized egg. A biopsy specimen taken 3 to 5 days before normal menses (days 21 to 25 of the cycle) should demonstrate uterine tissues ready to receive and nourish a fertilized ovum. If ovulation has not occurred, the uterine biopsy results will demonstrate uterine changes stimulated only by estrogen production (see Fig. 12-3).

Occasionally an endometrial biopsy is performed to indicate estrogen effect in patients with suspected ovarian dysfunction or absence. Likewise, adequate circulating progesterone levels can be determined by identifying uterine changes. Another major use of endometrial biopsy is to diagnose endometrial cancer. Complications of this study include perforation (making a hole) of the uterus, uterine bleeding, and interference with early pregnancy.

Procedure

This study is performed on the nonfasting and unsedated patient in the physician's office. No anesthesia is required. The patient is placed with her legs in stirrups (as for a Pap smear), and a pelvic examination is performed. Then the biopsy instrument is inserted into the uterus and specimens are obtained.

This procedure differs from a dilatation and curettage (D & C) in that no cervical dilatation is required. Also, the curettage (the cleansing of a diseased surface with a spoon-shaped instrument) is much less extensive for endometrial biopsy than for a D & C. In effect curettage involves the taking of biopsy specimens from the entire uterine wall. This latter procedure usually requires general anesthesia. When an endometrial biopsy alone is performed to rule out uterine cancern, it may easily miss the cancer. This is not true with a D & C. Polyps and other growths that cause uterine bleeding may be removed during a D & C.

Pertinent facts

- This study is performed by an obstetrician/gynecologist in approximately 10 to 30 minutes.
- Obtaining the biopsy tissue may cause the patient momentary discomfort (menstrual-type cramping).
- After the procedure, the patient should rest during the next 24 hours and avoid heavy lifting to prevent uterine bleeding.
- After the study, the patient should wear a vaginal pad because some vaginal bleeding is to be expected. If the patient's bleeding exceeds more than one pad per hour, the physician should be notified immediately.

- Douching and intercourse are not permitted for 72 hours after the biopsy specimen removal.
- Any temperature elevation should be reported to the physician because this may indicate infection.
- The customary cost for this procedure is approximately $70.

Basal body temperature measurement
Normal values

A slight drop in the basal body temperature followed by a sharp increase at the time of ovulation.

Purpose

The basal body temperature (BBT) measurement is a simple and inexpensive method of determining ovulation. Both the occurrence and the timing of ovulation can be determined by the taking of a daily rectal temperature reading throughout the menstrual cycle. The BBT remains at a relatively low level before ovulation. The onset of ovulation is marked by a slight drop in the BBT followed by a sharp increase of 0.5° to 0.7° Fahrenheit (Fig. 13-4). Ovulation is thought to occur 12 hours before this sharp increase in temperature. Patients who wish to become pregnant should have intercourse during this time of ovulation, while those who wish to avoid pregnancy, should abstain (the BBT method of birth control).

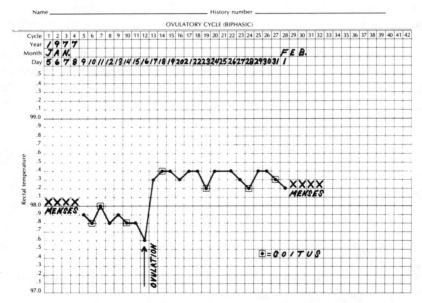

Fig. 13-4. Basal body temperature (BBT) record shows a drop and sharp rise at time of ovulation. Biphasic (two-phase) curve is indicative of ovulatory cycle.

From Jenson, M.D., Benson, R.C., and Bobak, I.M.: Maternity care: the nurse and the family, St. Louis, The C.V. Mosby Co.

The temperature rise is maintained with a slight variation until 1 or 2 days before menstruation. If both ovulation and fertilization have occurred, the temperature rise is maintained past the expected date of menses. A persistent elevation of the BBT for 7 to 10 days after a missed period is suggestive of early pregnancy. This temperature elevation will gradually fall after about 2 weeks of pregnancy.

Patients whose temperatures remain low during the complete menstrual cycle are considered to have a monophasic (one-phase) curve, which indicates that ovulation has not occurred. For proper evaluation, accurate temperature recordings should be kept over a period of at least three menstrual cycles. There are no complications to this study.

Procedure

The woman is instructed to keep a thermometer at the bedside and to take a daily rectal temperature reading before arising, smoking, drinking, eating, or moving about (that is, in a basal state). The temperature movement is taken with a special thermometer marked in tenths to enable the patient to read it more accurately. The temperature readings should be taken at approximately the same time each day and charted on a graph for several months. However, when BBT readings are obtained over long periods of time, the procedure may become a source of irritation to the patient and her husband.

Pertinent facts

- It is important that the patient practice reading a basal thermometer. She must also be shown how it is "shaken down" after each reading.
- The patient should be instructed in the proper method of recording the temperature on a chart.
- The patient should be aware that other sources of increased temperature, for example, an infection, may affect the chart and erroneously indicate ovulation.
- This procedure is performed by the patient and is therefore free of any charge.

Sims-Huhner test (postcoital test, postcoital cervical mucus test)
Normal values

Cervical mucus adequate for sperm transmission, survival, and penetration; 6 to 20 active sperm per high-power field.

Purpose

This study consists of a postcoital (after intercourse) examination of the cervical mucus to measure the ability of the sperm to penetrate the mucus and to maintain motility. It is also a measure of the quality of the cervical mucus. One can determine the effect of vaginal and cervical secretions on the activity of the sperm. Of course this test is only performed after a previously performed semen analysis (also discussed in this chapter) has been determined to be normal.

This study is performed in the middle of the ovulatory cycle because at this time, female secretion should be optimal for sperm penetration and survival. During ovulation, the quantity of cervical mucus is maximal, whereas the viscosity is minimal, thus facilitating sperm penetration. The cervical mucus sample is examined for color, viscosity, and tenacity. The fresh specimen is then spread on a clean glass microscopic slide and examined for the presence of sperm. Estimates of the total number of sperm and the number of motile sperm per high-power microscopic field are reported. Normally, 6 to 20 active sperm cells should be seen in each high-power field. If sperm cells are present but not active, this indicates that the cervical environment is unsuitable (for example, of abnormal acidity) for their survival. After the specimen has dried on a glass slide, the mucus is examined for ferning (see cervical mucus test in this chapter). This study is invaluable in fertility examinations.

This analysis is also helpful in documenting cases of rape by testing the vaginal and cervical secretions for the presence of sperm.

Procedure

During ovulation (as determined by BBT measurement, previous study), the patient is instructed to report to the physician for examination of her cervical mucus within 2 hours after sexual intercourse (coitus). Precoital lubrications and postcoital douching, bathing, or voiding are not permitted. This study should be performed after 3 days of sexual abstinence. After intercourse, the patient should rest in bed for 10 or 15 minutes to ensure cervical exposure to the semen. After resting, the patient should wear a vaginal pad until she is placed in stirrups in the physician's office. The cervix is then exposed by an unlubricated speculum. The specimen is aspirated from the cervical area and delivered to the laboratory for analysis.

Pertinent facts

- This test is performed by a physician in approximately 5 minutes.
- The specimen analysis is done in 15 minutes.
- The only discomfort associated with this study is the insertion of the speculum (as for a normal pelvic exam).
- Basal body temperature (BBT) recordings (see previous study) should be used to indicate the time of ovulation.
- No vaginal lubrication, douching, or bathing is permitted until after the vaginal cervical examination because these factors will alter the cervical mucus.
- After intercourse, the patient should rest in bed for 10 or 15 minutes and then wear a vaginal pad and report to her physician within 2 hours.
- The customary cost of this study is approximately $50.

Sample case report: infertility

After 1 year of unsuccessfully trying to conceive, Mrs. S and her husband, both age 28, were referred to an infertility specialist. The history and physical results were negative and a "five-step" diagnostic evaluation was scheduled and performed.

STUDIES	RESULTS
Step 1: Basic laboratory procedures	
Urinalysis	Husband: within normal limits (WNL)
	Wife: within normal limits (WNL)

Complete blood count (CBC)	Husband: WNL Wife: WNL
Serologic test for syphilis (STS)	Husband: negative Wife: negative
Blood type and Rh factor	Husband: B positive Wife: A positive
Thyroid function studies	Husband: WNL Wife: WNL

Step 2: Evaluation of semen (semen analysis)

Volume	5 ml (normal: 2 to 6 ml)
Sperm count	105 million/ml (normal: 20 to 200 million/ml)
Motility	62% actively motile (normal: 60% to 80% actively motile)
Sperm morphology	75% normally shaped (normal: 70% to 90% normally shaped)

Step 3: Evaluation of patency (openness) of the fallopian tubes

Uterotubal insufflation (Rubin's test)	Normal (patent fallopian tubes)
Hysterosalpingography	Normal passage of radioactive material through the tubes and into the abdominal area.

Step 4: Evaluation of ovulation

Cervical mucus test	Ovulation confirmed by "ferning"
Endometrial biopsy	Ovulation confirmed by appropriate changes in the uterine tissue
Basal body temperature (BBT) measurement	Normal two-phase (biphasic) curve
Twenty-four hour urine for pregnanediol	1.2 mg/24 hr (normal: greater than 1.0 mg for 24 hr)

Step 5: Evaluation of cervical factors

Sims-Huhner test	Normal (cervical mucus adequate for sperm survival, transmission, and penetration); 12 active sperm per high-power microscopic field
Laparoscopy	Normal appearing fallopian tubes

Because the results of all these studies were normal, laparoscopy was performed. The normal findings led the physician to suspect that the cause of infertility was probably the fact that the woman's immune system may have been recognizing the husband's sperm as foreign material and destroying the sperm.

Although the husband wore condoms during intercourse for several months to decrease his wife's level of antisperm antibodies (which destroy sperm and prevent conception), a pregnancy still did not occur within the last year. The physician then recommended they initiate adoption procedure. Surprisingly, however, 6 months later, Mrs. S. was pregnant, and a successful pregnancy and delivery followed.

14

Diagnostic studies used to evaluate the blood cells and clotting mechanism

ANATOMY, PHYSIOLOGY, AND COMMON PROBLEMS OF THE BLOOD CELLS AND CLOTTING PROCESS

The bone marrow is the site of blood cell production (hematopoiesis). The primary function of the red blood cells (RBCs) is to transport oxygen from the lungs to the tissues. White blood cells (WBCs) are primarily a defense against infection, foreign particles, and foreign tissue. Blood clotting (coagulation) is the primary function of the platelets. Each blood cell type will be discussed separately.

Red blood cells (RBCs)

Red blood cells (RBCs) are formed from cells within the bone marrow. As the RBCs are forming they are called *reticulocytes,* and they are deposited into the circulating blood vessels. They further differentiate into mature RBCs (erythrocytes). This process is stimulated by many factors (such as low oxygen and growth hormone); however, the major stimulating factor is erythropoietin, a hormone produced primarily by the kidney.

Packed within each RBC are molecules of hemoglobin that permit the transport and exchange of oxygen and carbon dioxide. Sickle cell disease and thalassemia result from genetically induced abnormal forms of hemoglobin.

Iron is the major component of hemoglobin and is essential for hemoglobin production. When the patient is deficient in iron, hemoglobin synthesis (production) will be markedly diminished.

The primary role of the RBC is the transportation of oxygen from the lungs to the tissues. Carbon dioxide is transported in the opposite direction, that is, from the tissues back to the lungs. Normally the RBCs exist in the blood for about 120 days. Toward the end of the RBC's life, the cell membrane becomes weakened, and the aged RBC is then broken down and extracted from the circulation by the spleen. With RBC destruction, the heme molecule of hemoglobin is broken down and metabolized into bilirubin (see Chapter 4). Bilirubin is then handled and excreted by the normal liver into bile. Liver disease, bile duct obstruction, or increased breakdown of RBCs all can result in hyperbilirubinemia (high levels of bilirubin in the blood) and jaundice. Increased RBC destruction occurs when hemoglobin is abnormal or when the spleen is enlarged.

White blood cells (WBCs)

The major function of the white blood cell (WBC) is to fight infection and to react against foreign bodies or tissues. There are five types of WBCs that can be identified on a routine blood smear. These cells include, in order of frequency, neutrophils, lymphocytes, monocytes, eosinophils, and basophils. All of these WBCs arise from cells within the bone marrow as do the RBCs. Beyond this origin, however, each cell line differentiates separately. The mature WBC is then deposited into the circulating bloodstream.

Neutrophils are produced in 7 to 14 days and exist in the circulation for only 6 hours. The primary function of the neutrophil is the killing and digestion of bacterial microorganisms. Acute bacterial infections and trauma stimulate neutrophil production, thereby increasing the WBC count. Often when neutrophil production is stimulated, early immature forms of neutrophils called "bands" or "stab" cells enter the circulation.

Lymphocytes are primarily formed to fight chronic (long-term) bacterial infections and acute viral infections.

Monocytes are capable of fighting bacteria in a way very similar to that of the neutrophils. However, they can be produced more rapidly and can spend a longer time in the circulation than the neutrophils.

Basophils and especially eosinophils are involved in the allergic reaction. Parasitic infestations can also stimulate production of these cell lines.

Platelets

Platelets are formed in the bone marrow, in the lungs, and to some extent in the spleen. Platelets play a major role in hemostasis (stopping blood flow) and blood clotting. Hemostasis is an ongoing response to injury of the blood vessel to avoid excessive loss of blood. The entire process involves platelet clumping around the site of the injury, thereby creating an early and temporary plug over the injury site. Several clotting factors result in the formation of fibrin (Fig. 14-1). Fibrin strengthens the platelet plug into a fibrin clot. After the vessel is repaired, the fibrin clot is then dissolved and the lysis (destruction) of the clot is accomplished by the fibrinolytic system. Fibrinolysis is necessary to appropriately police the clotting system by dissolving fibrin clots after the vessels are repaired.

Abnormalities in any part of this normal physiologic process can result in bleeding tendencies or in hypercoagulable states (abnormally increased clotting of the blood). The balance of hemostasis (stopping blood flow) and fibrinolysis (breaking up the fibrin clot) must be constantly intact, otherwise bleeding tendencies or hypercoagulation will result.

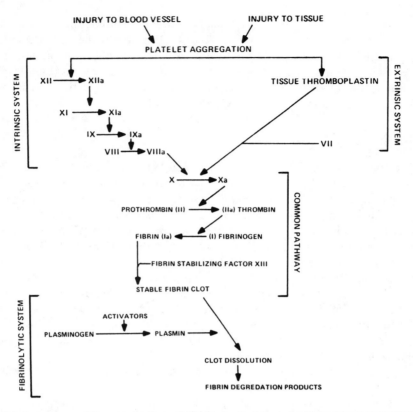

Fig. 14-1. Process of hemostasis and fibrinolysis. Injury to blood vessel surface or tissue initiates platelet aggregation. Intrinsic or extrinsic system is activated and then activates common pathway of fibrin formation. Finally, fibrin is physiologically dissolved by fibrinolytic system.

BLOOD TESTS
Complete blood count and differential count (CBC and diff, hemogram)
Normal values

Red blood cell (RBC) count
    Men: 4.7-6.1 million/cu mm
    Women: 4.2-5.4 million/cu mm
    Infants and children: 3.8-5.5 million/cu mm
    Newborns: 4.8-7.1 million/cu mm
Hemoglobin (Hgb) concentration
    Men: 14-18 g/dl
    Women: 12-16 g/dl
    Children: 11-16 g/dl
    Infants: 10-15 g/dl
    Newborns: 14-24 g/dl

Hematocrit (Hct) or packed red cell volume
  Men: 42%-52%
  Women: 37%-47%
  Children: 31%-43%
  Infants: 30%-40%
  Newborns: 44%-64%
Mean corpuscular volume (MCV)
  Adults and children: 80-95 cu μ
  Newborns: 96-108 cu μ
Mean corpuscular hemoglobin (MCH)
  Adults and children: 27-31 pg
  Newborns: 32-34 pg
Mean corpuscular hemoglobin concentration (MCHC)
  Adults and children: 32-36 g/dl (or 32%-36%)
  Newborns: 32-33 g/dl (or 32%-33%)
White blood cell (WBC) count
  Total WBCs
    Adults and children over 2 years old: 5000-10,000/cu mm
    Children 2 years old and younger: 6200-17,000/cu mm
    Newborns: 9000-30,000/cu mm
  Differential count
    Neutrophils: 55%-70%
    Lymphocytes: 20%-40%
    Monocytes: 2%-8%
    Eosinophils: 1%-4%
    Basophils: 0.5%-1%

Purpose

The CBC and differential is a series of tests of the blood that provides a tremendous amount of information about the blood-forming system and many other organ systems. It is cheaply, easily, and rapidly performed as a screening test on almost every patient that enters the hospital. Each test included in the series is discussed.

Red blood cell (RBC) count. RBC count is the count of the number of circulating RBCs in 1 cu mm of venous blood. Normal values vary according to sex and age. When the value is decreased by more than 10% of the normal value, the patient is said to be anemic. There are many causes for low RBC values. They include
  1. Hemorrhage (bleeding, as in stomach bleeding or trauma)
  2. Hemolysis (premature destruction of the red blood cells)
  3. Dietary deficiency (of iron or vitamin B_{12})
  4. Genetic problems (as in sickle cell anemia or thalassemia)
  5. Drug ingestion (as of quinidine)
  6. Bone marrow failure (as in leukemia or patients on cancer chemotherapy)
  7. Chronic illness (as in tumor)
  8. Other organ failure (as in kidney disease)
Greater than normal RBC counts can be physiologically induced as a result of

the body's requirement for greater oxygen-carrying capacity (such as high altitudes). Diseases that produce a chronic low oxygen level (such as congenital heart disease) also provoke this increase in RBCs. Polycythemia vera is a condition involving uncontrolled production of RBCs.

Hemoglobin (Hgb) concentration. Hemoglobin concentration is a measure of the total amount of hemoglobin in the blood. Hemoglobin serves as a vehicle for oxygen and carbon dioxide transport. As with RBC counts, normal values vary according to sex and age. The clinical implications of this test closely parallel the RBC count (see the previous discussion for implications of high and low values). In addition, however, changes in blood volume are more accurately reflected by hemoglobin concentrations. If the patient is overhydrated, the blood is diluted, thereby decreasing the concentration, whereas dehydration tends to artificially raise the Hgb because of the greater concentration.

Hematocrit (Hct), or packed RBC volume. Hematocrit is a measure of the percentage of the volume of RBCs when compared to blood volume. Therefore it closely reflects the hemoglobin and RBC values. The hematocrit, measured in percentage points, is usually about three times the hemoglobin concentration. Normal values also vary according to sex and age. Abnormal values indicate the same disease conditions as do abnormal RBC counts and hemoglobin concentrations (see previous discussion). The value also is affected by the state of hydration.

Mean corpuscular volume (MCV). MCV is a measure of the average volume, or size, of a single RBC and is therefore useful in classifying anemia. Normal values vary according to sex and age. When the MCV value is increased, the RBC is said to be abnormally large. This is most frequently seen in megaloblastic anemias (such as vitamin B_{12} or folic acid deficiency). When the MCV value is decreased, the RBC is said to be abnormally small. This is associated with iron deficiency anemia or thalassemia.

Mean corpuscular hemoglobin (MCH). MCH is a measure of the average amount of hemoglobin within an RBC. Because abnormally large cells generally have more hemoglobin and because abnormally small RBCs have less hemoglobin, the causes for these values closely resemble those for the MCV value.

Mean corpuscular hemoglobin concentration (MCHC). The MCHC is a measure of the average concentration of the percentage of hemoglobin within a single RBC. When the MCHC values are decreased, the cell has a deficiency of hemoglobin. This is frequently seen in iron deficiency anemia and thalassemia. Because the RBCs cannot contain more hemoglobin than is physiologically possible, increased MCHC values cannot occur even when the MCV level increases.

When one investigates the cause of an anemia, it is helpful to categorize the anemia according to the results of the MCV, MCH, and MCHC values. These values are called *RBC indexes*.

White blood cell (WBC) count. The WBC count has two components. One is a count of the total number of WBCs (leukocytes) in 1 cu mm of venous blood. The other component, the differential count, measures the percentage of each type of WBC present in the same specimen. These leukocyte types can be identified easily by their structure on a peripheral blood smear. The total WBC count enjoys a wide range of normal values, but many diseases can induce abnormal values. An increased total WBC count (leukocytosis) usually indicates infection, and a markedly increased level indicates leukemia. Trauma or stress, either emotional or physical, can increase the WBC count. Leukopenia (that is, a decreased WBC count) occurs in many forms of bone marrow failure (such as with cancer chemotherapy), overwhelming infections, dietary deficiencies, and other conditions.

In the body's defense against bacterial invasion, the neutrophils are the most important leukocytes. These cells are called "stab" or "band" cells in their immature stage of development (see Anatomy and physiology). Elevation of any one type of leukocyte may indicate a specific disease. Therefore the differential categorization can be very valuable in the diagnosis and the treatment of disease processes. An increasing WBC count may indicate a worsening of an ongoing process (such as appendicitis).

Procedure

A needle stick is made and approximately 2 to 3 teaspoons of blood are obtained in a Vacutainer tube. Capillary needle sticks of the finger may be performed for some of these individual tests.

Most modern clinical hospital laboratories have a machine capable of automatically measuring the RBC, hemoglobin, hematocrit, MCV, MCH, MCHC, and WBC values. The differential count is performed by a technician who examines a cubic millimeter of a blood smear under a microscope. Each type of WBC is counted and the percentages are recorded.

Pertinent facts

- The only discomfort associated with this test is the needle stick.
- Blood is drawn by a laboratory technician or by a nurse.
- Pressure is applied to the puncture site after the blood is drawn.
- The customary cost of the study is approximately $12.

Reticulocyte count
Normal values

Adults and children: 0.5%-2% total RBCs
Infants: 0.5%-3.1% total RBCs
Newborns: 2.5%-6.5% total RBCs

Purpose

This is a test for determining bone marrow function. A reticulocyte is an immature RBC (red blood cell) that can be readily identified under the microscope. The reticulocyte count represents a direct measurement of RBC production by the bone marrow. Increased RBC counts are expected as a normal response to patients who are anemic. A low or normal reticulocyte count in an anemic patient indicates that the bone marrow production of RBCs is inadequate and is perhaps the cause of the anemia (as in iron deficiency or in a vitamin B_{12} deficiency).

An elevated reticulocyte count found in patients with a normal hemoglobin indicates abnormal RBC overproduction (polycythemia vera). One would expect the reticulocyte count to be increased in the patient who is anemic. A reticulocyte index can be performed to determine if the increased reticulocyte count is reflective of adequate red blood cell production in these patients.

Procedure

Blood is obtained as for a CBC (see previous study). Young RBCs (reticulocytes) are counted, and their percentage of the total RBCs is determined.

Pertinent facts

- See preceding study.
- The customary cost of this study is approximately $6.50

Iron level and total iron-binding capacity test (Fe and TIBC)
Normal values

Iron: 60-190 μg/dl.
TIBC: 250-420 μg/dl.

Purpose

Abnormal levels of iron and total iron-binding capacity are characteristic of many diseases, including iron deficiency anemia. Most of the iron in the body is bound in the hemoglobin of the red blood cells (see Anatomy and physiology). Iron supplied by the diet is absorbed in the small intestine and transported into the bloodstream. There the iron is bound to a protein called *transferrin* and carried to the bone marrow for incorporation into hemoglobin. The serum (blood) iron determination is a measurement of the quantity of iron bound to transferrin. The TIBC is a direct quantitative measurement of transferrin. The percentage of saturation is calculated by dividing the serum iron level by the TIBC. The normal value for transferrin saturation is between 30% and 40%. Calculation of transferrin saturation is helpful in determining the cause of abnormal iron and TIBC levels.

Iron deficiency anemia has many causes including
1. Insufficient iron intake in the diet
2. Inadequate absorption of iron from the intestines
3. Increased requirements of iron (as in growing children)
4. Loss of blood (as in excessive menstruation, bleeding peptic ulcer, or colon cancer)

Iron deficiency results in a decreased production of hemoglobin, which in turn results in small, pale red blood cells.

Because serum iron levels may vary significantly during the day, specimens for them should be drawn in the morning, especially when the results are used to monitor iron replacement theory. Blood transfusions may markedly raise the iron level, although only transiently, and should be avoided before serum iron determination. TIBC, on the other hand, varies minimally according to intake. The TIBC is more of a reflection of liver function and nutrition than of iron metabolism. Often the TIBC values are used to monitor the course of patients receiving hyperalimentation (a form of nutritional feeding whereby the patient receives a complete diet by means of the intravenous [IV] route or by means of a small feeding tube passed through the nose and into the stomach).

Procedure

The patient should refrain from eating for about 12 hours to avoid artificially high iron measurements caused by eating food high in iron content. One test tube of blood is drawn from a vein in the arm. Some laboratories require the use of iron-free needles and iron-free plastic containers for the blood collection.

Pertinent facts

- The patient should be kept fasting for at least 12 hours before the test to avoid artificially elevating the iron level by eating a meal. However, water is permitted.
- Before the blood is drawn, the patient is assessed for a history of having received blood transfusions, because this will artificially raise the iron level.
- The only discomfort associated with this study is the needle stick.
- The customary cost of iron and iron-binding capacity is approximately $28.

Hemoglobin electrophoresis
Normal values

Hemoglobin A_1: 95%-98%
Hemoglobin A_2: 2%-3%
Hemoglobin F: 0.8%-2%
Hemoglobin S: 0
Hemoglobin C: 0

Purpose

This is a test that enables one to detect abnormal forms of hemoglobin (see Anatomy and physiology). Although many different hemoglobin variations have been described, the more common types are A_1, A_2, F, S, and C. Each major hemoglobin type is magnetically charged to varying degrees. When placed in an electromagnetic field, the hemoglobin variants migrate at different rates and therefore spread apart from each other. One is able to measure each type as a percentage of the total hemoglobin.

Hemoglobin A_1 constitutes the major component of hemoglobin in a normal RBC. Hemoglobin A_2 is only a minor component (2% to 3%) of the normal hemoglobin total. Hemoglobin F is the major hemoglobin in the fetus yet exists in only minimal quantities in the normal adult. Levels of hemoglobin greater than 2% in patients over the age of 3 years are considered abnormal. Patients who are incapable of transporting adequate amounts of oxygen (as in thalassemia) may show an increased level of hemoglobin F.

Hemoglobin S is an abnormal form of hemoglobin and is associated with sickle cell anemia, which occurs in American blacks. When little oxygen is available, hemoglobin S assumes a crescent (sickle-type) shape that greatly distorts the structure of the RBC. Blood vessel occlusion results from the sickling and may lead to organ destruction.

Hemoglobin C is another hemoglobin variant that exists in American blacks. RBCs containing hemoglobin C have a decreased life span and are more readily lysed (destroyed) than normal RBCs. An anemia may result. There are no complications associated with hemoglobin electrophoresis.

Procedure

A needle stick is performed and 2 or 3 teaspoons of blood drawn from a vein in the arm is sent to the blood laboratory. Because not all clinical laboratories are equipped to perform this test, frequently the blood must be sent to a commercial laboratory, often requiring days for the results to be received. The test itself takes only between 2 and 36 hours to be performed, depending on the method used. Patients who have received a blood transfusion within the previous 12 weeks should not have hemoglobin electrophoresis. If the donor's blood is normal, it can mask and dilute any abnormal hemoglobin variations that may exist in the recipient's blood.

Pertinent facts

- This test is no more uncomfortable than a routine needle stick.
- If the patient has received a blood transfusion within the previous 12 weeks, the test results could be altered.
- After the blood is drawn, pressure is applied to the needle stick site.
- The customary cost of the study is approximately $25.

Peripheral blood smear
Normal values

Normal quantity of red blood cells, white blood cells, and platelets; normal size, shape, and color of red blood cells; normal white cell differential count.

Purpose

When adequately prepared and examined microscopically by an experienced physician, a smear of blood is the most informative of all blood studies. All three cell lines (red blood cells, white blood cells, and platelets) can be thoroughly examined.

Microscopic examination of the red blood cells (RBCs) can reveal variations in RBC size, shape, color, or intracellular content. The classification of RBCs according to these variables is most helpful in defining the cause of anemia.

The white blood cells (WBCs) are examined for total quantity, for differential count (see CBC study), and for their degree of maturity. An increased number of immature WBCs may indicate leukemia. A decreased WBC count may indicate bone marrow failure caused by drugs, chronic disease, or cancer.

Finally, an experienced cell examiner can estimate platelet number (see p. 237-238) and function on a blood smear.

Procedure

A small needle stick in the finger is usually performed after the finger has been cleansed with an alcohol swab. A drop of blood is spread on a slide, and a second slide is used to smear the drop across the first slide. The slide is usually stained. The stained slide is then examined under the microscope. The slide is prepared by a technician and best examined by an experienced physician.

Pertinent facts

- The only discomfort associated with this study is a needle stick in the finger.
- The needle stick is usually done in the laboratory.
- The smear takes only a few minutes to prepare for examination.
- The customary cost of this study is approximately $25.

Sickle cell test (sickle cell preparation, Sickledex, and hemoglobin S test)
Normal values

No sickle cell.

Purpose

Sickle cell anemia is caused by hemoglobin S, which is an abnormal form of hemoglobin. Both sickle cell disease (the patient has received abnormal hemoglobin genes from both patients) and sickle cell trait (the patient has received the hemoglobin S gene from one parent) can be detected by this study. When hemoglobin S becomes deoxygenated (loses oxygen), it tends to band in a way that causes the RBC to assume a sickle shape. These sickled RBCs cannot pass freely through the small blood vessels and therefore plug the tiny blood vessels. This may compromise the blood supply to various organs of the body. Hemoglobin S is found in 8% to 10% of the black population.

The routine peripheral blood smear of a patient with sickle cell disease does not contain any sickled RBCs unless oxygen is not present. In the sickle cell test, an agent to remove oxygen is added to the patient's blood. If 25% or more of the patient's hemoglobin is of the S variation, the cells will assume a crescent (sickle) shape, and the test is positive. If there is no sickling, the test is negative. A negative test indicates that the patient has no or very little hemoglobin S.

This test is only a screening test, and its sensitivity varies according to the method used by the laboratory. The definitive diagnosis is made by hemoglobin electrophoresis (also discussed in this chapter), where hemoglobin S can be identified and quantitated.

Any blood transfusion within 3 months before the sickle cell test can cause false negative results, because the donor's normal hemoglobin may dilute out the recipient's abnormal hemoglobin S. Some drugs may also cause false negative results.

There are no complications associated with this study.

Procedure

Approximately one tube of blood is drawn from a vein in the arm. In the laboratory, a technician mixes a small quantity of blood with a special solution and then examines the blood smear for crescent-shaped RBCs. The sickling procedure takes less than 30 minutes.

Pertinent facts

- The only discomfort associated with this study is the needle stick.
- Before the test, the patient should be assessed for recent blood transfusions, which could alter the test results.
- If the test is positive, the patient should be offered genetic counseling. A patient with one recessive gene (from one parent) is said to have sickle cell *trait*. A patient with two recessive genes (from both parents) has sickle cell *anemia*.
- Patients with sickle cell anemia should avoid situations in which a low blood oxygen may occur (such as strenuous exercise, air travel in unpressured aircraft, and travel to high-altitude regions).
- The customary cost of the study is approximately $25.

Blood typing
Purpose

Human blood is grouped according to the presence or absence of ABO and Rh antigens. The two major antigens, A and B, form the base of the ABO system. (Group A RBCs contain A antigen, group B RBCs contain B antigens, group AB RBCs contain both A and B antigens, and group O RBCs contain neither A nor B antigens.) The presence or absence of Rh antigens on the RBC determines the classification of Rh + (positive) or Rh − (negative).

Blood transfusions are actually transplantations of tissue (blood) from one person to another. It is important that the recipient (the one who receives the blood) does not have the antibodies (cells that destroy the antigens) to the RBCs of the donor (the one who gives the blood) and that the donor does not have antibodies to the recipient's RBCs. If either of these conditions exists, there will be a reaction that can vary in severity from a mild fever to severe shock. Although typing for the major ABO and Rh antigens does not guarantee that a reaction will not occur, it does greatly reduce the possibility of such a reaction. There are many potential minor antigens not routinely detected during blood typing. If allowed to go unrecognized, these minor antigens can also initiate a blood transfusion reaction. Therefore blood not only is typed but also is *cross matched* to identify a mismatch of blood caused by these minor antigens. Cross matching consists of the mixing of the recipient's blood with the donor's blood in saline (salt water) followed by the addition of Coombs' serum (see indirect Coombs' test, next study).

Procedure

Blood is drawn from a vein in the arm. Usually two tubes of blood are filled and sent to the blood bank. The blood is first typed and then cross matched. The type and cross match are done in the blood bank in approximately 45 minutes.

Cross matching is not performed when the patient requires immediate transfusion and the risk of a blood reaction is outweighed by the urgent need of a blood transfusion (such as in acute bleeding). In these situations, type-specific (ABO and Rh) matched blood can be given by only performing blood typing. In those very rare situations when the transfusion cannot be delayed even for the few minutes required for blood typing, type O-negative blood is given. Type O-negative blood contains no major antigens, and therefore the chances of blood reaction are fewer when it is given to the patient with unknown blood type. Type O blood is often referred to as the "universal donor."

Pertinent facts

- The only discomfort associated with this study is a needle stick.
- If someone is to receive blood, a history should be done to determine if he or she has ever had a blood transfusion before and if he or she had a reaction to that transfusion.
- Blood can only be administered by a physician or by a nurse. Before the blood is administered, the blood bag is checked carefully to verify the blood typing and compatibility. Two professional nurses must verify this information and sign a blood transfusion sheet, indicating that the proper blood was given to the proper patient.
- Before a blood transfusion is administered, an intravenous (IV) line is begun with a saline solution. Vital signs (temperature, pulse, respirations, and blood pressure) are taken before the blood is administered. During the blood administration, the patient is carefully evaluated for signs of any reaction such as fever, back pain, hives, increased heart rate, or wheezing.
- If the patient will need further transfusions, more blood samples must be drawn to type and cross match the new blood.
- The customary cost of typing and cross matching is approximately $40.

Indirect Coombs' test (blood antibody screening)
Normal values

Negative.

Purpose

This study detects the presence of circulating antibodies (agents that attack foreign tissue) against red blood cells (RBCs). The major purpose of this test is to determine if the patient has blood antibodies to RBCs that he or she is about to receive by a blood transfusion. If the patient does have such antibodies, a blood reaction will occur with the transfusion.

In this test, a small amount of the recipient's blood is mixed with some of the donor's blood. Then Coombs' serum is added to the mixture. Visible agglutination (clumping) indicates that the recipient has antibodies to the donor's RBCs. This patient should not receive blood from that perspective donor, because a blood transfusion reaction would occur. If the recipient has no antibodies against the donor's RBCs, no clumping will occur. Transfusion should then proceed safely and without any cross reaction. Circulating antibodies against RBCs may also occur in a pregnant woman who is Rh negative and is carrying an Rh-positive fetus.

Procedure

One tube of blood is drawn from a vein in the patient's arm. The proposed recipient's blood is mixed with the donor's RBCs, and Coombs' serum is added. Clumping indicates a positive test. No clumping indicates a negative, or normal, test.

Pertinent facts

• The only discomfort associated with this study is the needle stick.
• The customary cost of the study is approximately $18.

Direct Coombs' test (direct antiglobulin test)
Normal values

Negative.

Purpose

This is a test used to detect autoantibodies against red blood cells (RBCs). This means antibodies that will destroy the patient's own RBCs. Many diseases (such as lupus erythematosus, lymphomas, and certain infections) along with drugs (such as penicillin) are associated with the production of these antibodies. These antibodies will destroy the RBCs and result in anemia.

When a transfusion with incompatible blood is given, the Coombs' test can detect the antibodies coating the transfused RBCs. The Coombs' test is therefore very helpful in evaluating a suspected transfusion reaction. No complications are associated with this study.

Procedure

Blood is drawn from a vein in the arm. The patient's blood is collected in one red-top tube and transported to the blood bank. In the blood bank, the patient's RBCs are mixed with Coombs' serum. Agglutination (clumping) indicates a positive test, and the patient is said to produce antibodies against RBCs that will cause RBC hemolysis (destruction). No agglutination indicates a negative study.

Pertinent facts

• The only discomfort associated with this study is a needle stick.
• The customary cost of this study is approximately $13.

Prothrombin time test (pro-time, PT test)
Normal values

11-12.5 seconds; 85%-100%.

Purpose

This study is used to evaluate the blood clotting mechanism. When certain clotting factors exist in deficient quantities, the prothrombin time is prolonged. Many diseases and drugs are associated with decreased levels of these factors. These include

1. Liver disease (such as cirrhosis, hepatitis, and cancer).
2. Obstruction of the bile duct (caused by a tumor or a stone). Bile is necessary for intestinal absorption of fat and fat-soluble vitamins. Vitamin K, a fat-soluble vitamin, is required for the formation of many clotting factors. Therefore when the bile duct is blocked, no bile enters the intestine, and ab-

sorption of vitamin K does not occur. Many important clotting factors are not made. The result is an abnormal prothrombin time.

3. Warfarin (Coumadin) ingestion. The coumarin derivatives (dicumarol and warfarin [Coumadin, Panwarfin]) are used to prevent coagulation (clotting) in patients with thromboembolic disease (such as pulmonary embolism, thrombophlebitis, and arterial embolism). These drugs interfere with the production of vitamin K–dependent clotting factors, which will result in a prolongation of the prothrombin time value. The adequacy of coumarin therapy can be monitored by following the patient's PT results. Appropriate coumarin therapy should prolong PT by 1½ to 2 times the control value (or 20% to 30% of the normal value if percentages are used).

Coumarin derivatives are slow acting, but their action may persist for 7 to 14 days after discontinuation of the drug. The action of coumarin drugs can be reversed by an injection of vitamin K.

The action of the coumarin drugs can be potentiated by drugs such as aspirin. Barbiturates and oral contraceptives may diminish the effects of coumarin drugs.

PT results are usually given in seconds along with a control value. The control value usually varies somewhat from day to day because of the different chemicals used to assess this study. Normal patients who are not on coumarin drugs should have a PT about equal to the control value. Some laboratories report PT results as percentages of normal activity, as the patient's results are compared with a curve representing normal clotting time. Normally the patient's PT is 85% to 100%. A patient receiving drugs to prevent blood coagulation should be within a therapeutic range of 20% to 30%.

Procedure

Usually one or two blue-top tubes of blood are drawn from a vein in the arm. The tubes must be filled to capacity; otherwise the PT results may be artificially prolonged because of the solution within the blue-top tube. The blood sample should be taken to the laboratory as soon as possible and analyzed. The time required for clotting is then noted.

Pertinent facts

- There is no discomfort associated with this study other than the needle stick.
- The study is done to assess how quickly the blood clots. If the patient is receiving coumarin-type drugs, the PT specimen should be drawn *before* the patient is given the daily dose of that medication. The daily dose may then be increased, decreased, or kept the same, depending on the PT results.
- After the blood is drawn, the site will be checked for bleeding. It should be remembered that the bleeding time will be prolonged if the patient is taking any anticoagulation drugs or if the patient has any bleeding problem.
- If the PT is markedly prolonged, the patient should be carefully evaluated for any bleeding tendencies (that is, the patient is instructed to check for blood in the urine and in the stool). The patient should also report bruising or abdominal or back pain to the physician.

- If severe bleeding would occur, the anticoagulant effect of warfarin (Coumadin) can be reversed by an injection of vitamin K and transfusion of plasma-containing vitamin K–dependent clotting factors.
- Because of drug interactions, the patient should not take any medication unless it is specifically ordered by the physician. This especially includes common medications such as aspirin or sleeping pills.
- When a patient on warfarin (Coumadin) has been discharged from the hospital, the patient will be required to come to the hospital laboratory for routine blood evaluation. Generally in the beginning, this is done once a week to regulate the PT value.
- The customary cost of this study is approximately $11.

Partial thromboplastin time (PTT, activated partial thromboplastin time [APTT] test)
Normal values

30-40 seconds.

Purpose

The partial thromboplastin time (PTT) test is used to assess certain clotting factors involved in the blood clotting system. When any of these factors exist in inadequate quantities (as in hemophilia), the PTT is prolonged. Because certain of these factors are vitamin K–dependent factors produced in the liver, liver disease or bile duct obstruction can reduce their concentration and thus prolong the PTT.

Heparin has been found to inactivate prothrombin in addition to preventing the formation of the thromboplastin (Fig. 14-1). These actions prolong this clotting pathway for about 4 to 6 hours after each dose of heparin. Therefore heparin is capable of providing therapeutic anticoagulation. The appropriate dose of heparin can be monitored by the PTT. PTT test results are given in seconds along with a control value. The control value may vary slightly from day to day because of different chemicals used in the testing. Recently activators have been added to the PTT test chemicals to shorten the normal clotting time and to provide a narrow range of normal. This shortened time is called the activated partial thromboplastin time (APTT). The normal APTT is 30 to 40 seconds. The desired ranges for the therapeutic anticoagulation are 1½- to 2½-times normal (for example, 70 seconds). The APTT specimen should be drawn 30 to 60 minutes *before* the patient's next heparin dose is given. If the APTT is less than 60 seconds, the patient is not receiving therapeutic anticoagulation and needs more heparin. An APTT of greater than 100 seconds indicates that too much heparin is being given. A significant risk of spontaneous bleeding exists when the APTT is this high. The effects of heparin can be reversed immediately by the administration of protamine sulfate.

Heparin's effects, unlike those of warfarin (Coumadin) (see previous study), are immediate. This drug is often given during cardiac and blood vessel surgery to prevent clotting within the vessels. When a thromboembolic episode (such as pulmonary embolism or thrombophlebitis) occurs, immediate and complete anticoagulation is achieved by heparin administration. Often small doses of heparin are given to prevent blood clots in patients who are at risk for clotting. This would include patients on temporary bed rest.

Procedure

One or two blue-top tubes of blood are drawn from the vein in the arm. The blue-top tubes must be filled to capacity, otherwise the PTT may be incorrect because of the anticoagulant solution within the blue-top tube. The blood is usually transported immediately to the laboratory.

Pertinent facts

- The PTT is drawn to assess how quickly the blood clots.
- Usually the PTT specimen is drawn daily, 30 minutes to 1 hour before the heparin administration. Usually heparin is given intravenously (IV) or subcutaneously (into the skin) four or six times a day. The heparin dosage must be altered, depending on the PTT results. A flowchart indicating PTT results, control values, and the dosage of heparin is maintained.
- The only discomfort associated with this study is the needle stick.
- After the blood is drawn, the site will be checked for bleeding.
- The customary cost of this study is approximately $16.

Platelet count
Normal values

150,000-400,000/cu mm.

Purpose

This is an actual count of the number of platelets (see Anatomy and physiology) per cubic millimeter (cu mm) of blood. Platelet activity is essential to blood clotting. Because platelets can clump together, automated counting is subject to at least a 10% to 15% error. Counts between 150,000 and 400,000/cu mm are considered normal. Counts below 100,000/cu mm are considered low, and counts above 400,000/cu mm are high.

Spontaneous bleeding is a serious danger when the platelet count falls below 15,000/cu mm. With counts above 40,000/cu mm, spontaneous bleeding rarely occurs; however, prolonged bleeding from trauma or surgery may occur at this level. Causes of thrombocytopenia (decreased number of platelets) include

1. Reduced production of platelets (caused by bone marrow failure)
2. Destruction of platelets
3. Platelet loss from hemorrhage or bleeding

Thrombocytosis (increased number of platelets) may occur as a response to severe hemorrhage. Other conditions associated with the thrombocytosis include polycythemia vera, leukemia, and various types of cancer.

Procedure

One tube of blood is drawn from the vein in the arm. A quantity of blood is then analyzed by a machine simultaneously with the CBC.

Pertinent facts

- The only discomfort associated with the study is the needle stick.
- Pressure is applied to the puncture site after the blood is drawn. Patients with thrombocytopenia will bleed longer than those with a normal platelet count.
- The customary cost of the study is approximately $12.

Bleeding time test (Ivy bleeding time)
Normal values

1-9 minutes.

Purpose

This test is used to evaluate the vessels and the platelet factors associated with hemostasis (stopping bleeding). When injury occurs, the first response of the body is spastic contraction of any lacerated vessels. Next, platelets adhere to the wall of the vessel at the area of the laceration in an attempt to plug the hole. Failure of either of these processes results in a prolonged bleeding time.

For this study, a small incision is made in the forearm, and the time required for the bleeding to stop is recorded. This is called a bleeding time. Normal values vary according to the method used. The method most commonly used today is the *Ivy bleeding test*. Prolonged values occur in the following:

1. Decreased platelet count caused by bone marrow failure (such as after chemotherapy)
2. Infiltration of the bone marrow by cancer
3. Destruction of platelets
4. Inadequate platelet function
5. Increased blood vessel fragility (that is, weak blood vessel walls)
6. Ingestion of anti-inflammatory drugs (such as aspirin)

Because this test requires only a small incision, it is rare to have a complication such as laceration of a nerve, tendon, artery, or vein. Infections do not occur if the skin is cleansed properly before the test.

Procedure

The bleeding time test is usually performed at the patient's bedside or on an outpatient basis. The skin of the inner part of the forearm is cleansed carefully. A blood pressure cuff (tourniquet) is placed on the arm above the elbow, inflated to 40 mm of mercury, and maintained at this pressure during the study. A small laceration (cut) is made 3 mm deep into the skin and the time is recorded. Bleeding ensues and the blood is blotted clean at 30-second intervals. When no new bleeding occurs, the time is again recorded. The time intervals from the beginning to the end of the bleeding is calculated and called the *bleeding time*. The blood pressure cuff is then removed, and a bandage is applied to the patient's forearm.

If the bleeding persists for more than 10 minutes, the test is stopped, and a pressure dressing is applied. If the patient has a clotting factor deficiency, the bleeding time may be normal, but subsequent oozing of blood from the test site may be seen within 20 minutes after the original bleeding has stopped. Pressure should be applied to the wound.

Pertinent facts

- The only discomfort associated with this study is a small cut in the forearm.
- Before this test, the patient should be assessed for taking aspirin during the week preceding the test. Aspirin ingestion may prolong the bleeding time.
- After the study, a small dressing is applied to the patient's arm. The site should be carefully observed for bleeding for at least ½ hour after the test.
- The customary cost of this study is approximately $11.

Coagulating factors concentration test
Normal values

50%-200% of normal.

Purpose

This is a measure of the concentration of specific coagulating factors in the blood. When these factors exist in concentrations below their normal value, the clotting time will be prolonged. Liver disease, hemophilia, and disseminated intravascular coagulation (DIC) are examples of medical conditions associated with decreased factor concentrations. It is important to identify the exact factor or factors involved in the coagulating defect so that appropriate blood component replacement can be administered. The necessary factors can be supplied by blood components such as fresh frozen plasma, fresh whole blood, unfrozen plasma, and cryoprecipitate.

Procedure

Blood is drawn from a vein in the arm and placed in a blue-top tube. The blood is then sent to the blood bank, and the coagulating factors are assessed. In most hospitals, the specimen is sent to a commercial laboratory for analysis. The test results usually require 1 to 7 days to be reported, depending on whether the specimen has been sent to a commercial laboratory or can be done in the hospital.

Pertinent facts

- The only discomfort associated with the study is a needle stick.
- After the blood is drawn, the site is checked for bleeding in case the clotting time is prolonged because of a coagulation factor deficiency.
- The customary cost of this study is approximately $21.

SPECIAL STUDIES
Bone marrow examination (bone marrow biopsy, bone marrow aspiration)
Normal values

Normal number, size, and shape of the RBCs, WBCs, and platelets.

Purpose

By examination of a bone marrow specimen, the physician can fully evaluate blood cell production. Examination of the bone marrow reveals the number, size, and shape of the RBCs, WBCs, and platelets (see Anatomy and physiology) as these cells evolve through various stages of development in the bone marrow. Samples of the bone marrow can be obtained with a needle and syringe or by surgical removal. Bone marrow examination is often required to detect suspected metastatic tumor involving the bone marrow. Examination also is very helpful in determining the cause of marrow failure in patients with a decrease in the number of one or more types of blood cells. Patients receiving anticancer treatment often require bone marrow examination to assess their marrow reserve before more treatment is given.

Rare complications of bone marrow biopsy or aspiration include severe bleeding, infection, or puncture of a blood vessel when the test is performed.

This study is contraindicated in

1. Patients with a bleeding disorder (such as hemophilia), because severe bleeding can occur
2. Uncooperative patients

Procedure

Bone marrow aspiration is performed on the sternum (breast bone), the ilium (hip bone), or the tibia (leg bone). Bone marrow aspiration (removal of a specimen of bone marrow using a needle and syringe) is usually performed in the patient's room. Biopsy specimen removal requires some anesthesia because the specimen is surgically removed.

For bone marrow aspiration, the patient is positioned on his or her back or side according to the specific site selected. The area overlying the bone is cleansed and draped in a sterile manner. The skin and soft tissue are locally anesthetized with lidocaine. If aspiration is done, a large needle is inserted through the soft tissue and into the bone. Once the needle is inside the bone marrow, a syringe is attached. A little less than 1 teaspoon of bone marrow is aspirated, smeared on slides, and allowed to dry. The slides are then sprayed with a preservative and taken to the pathology laboratory.

If bone marrow biopsy is to be performed, the skin and soft tissue overlying the bone are incised (cut), and a biopsy instrument is screwed into the bone. A specimen is obtained and sent to the pathology laboratory.

Pertinent facts

- Signed consent for this procedure is obtained before this study.
- A nurse or technician usually assists the physician in obtaining the specimen. During the study, the patient must remain very still.
- Before the study is performed, tests are done to make sure that the patient's blood clotting ability is intact.
- The patient usually feels pain during the injection of the local anesthetic into the tissue and also pressure when the syringe plunger is pulled back to aspirate (draw up) the bone marrow specimen. The patient may also be frightened by the pressure applied to the bone during the biopsy specimen removal or aspiration.
- After the study, the site is assessed for bleeding. Ice packs may be used.

- After the study, the patient's vital signs are again checked for any sign of bleeding. (Usually the pulse will increase and the blood pressure will decrease with bleeding.) Normally, the patient is asked to rest for 30 to 60 minutes after the study. After that time, the patient can resume normal activities.
- Some patients complain of tenderness at the puncture site for several days after the study. Mild pain pills may be given as needed.
- The study is performed in approximately 10 to 20 minutes.
- The customary cost of this study is approximately $80 to $200.

Sample case report: hemophilia

Kenny D., a 10-year-old boy, fell and lacerated (cut) his lower leg while climbing a fence. In the emergency department, no signs of nerve or major vessel damage were detected, and the wound was closed. One hour later, the dressing was saturated with blood. The patient was taken to the operating room where the wound was further explored. No major blood vessel lacerations were seen. In a review of the patient's bleeding history, it was found that he seemed to have a tendency to bleed larger quantities and for a greater duration than would seem normal.

STUDIES	RESULTS
Routine laboratory studies	Within normal limits (WNL)
Prothrombin time (PT)	Patient/control: 11 sec/12 sec, or 85% (normal: 11-12.5 sec, or 85%-100%)
Activated partial thromboplastin time (APTT)	62 sec (normal: 30-40 sec)
Platelet count	200,000/cu mm (normal: 150,000-400,000/cu mm)
Ivy bleeding time	8.5 min (normal: 1-9 min)
Coagulation factor concentration (factor VIII)	10% of normal

The abnormal APTT result indicated a defect in the clot formation system. The normal bleeding time and platelet count eliminated insufficient platelet quantity or function as a cause of this bleeding problem. The factor VIII concentration was well below normal and was found to be the cause of the failure to clot. Hemophilia was diagnosed, and the patient was given factor VIII concentration. All obvious bleeding ceased, and the leg wound healed.

After discharge, the patient returned to the hospital at regular intervals for factor VIII concentration (such as cryoprecipitate). He had no further bleeding difficulties.

15

Routine and miscellaneous testing

ROUTINE LABORATORY TESTING

Although a complete and thorough history and a physical examination are essential to an adequate patient evaluation, serious illnesses may go undetected. Today with the availability of multiphasic laboratory testing machines, the patient can be more completely and cheaply screened for the presence of disease. With multiphasic laboratory testing machines, a number of tests (from 6 to 40) can be performed at the same time. The most common screening test is the SMA (sequential multiple analyzer), which can simultaneously perform 6 or 12 studies. The cost varies between $6 and $15. The *SMA 12* includes measurement of the following:

Calcium (see Chapter 10)
Phosphorus (Chapter 15)
Triglycerides (see Chapter 1)
Uric acid (see Chapter 7)
Creatinine (see Chapter 8)
BUN (see Chapter 8)
Total bilirubin (see Chapter 4)
Alkaline phosphatase (see Chapter 4)
SGOT (see Chapters 1 and 4)
LDH (see Chapters 1 and 4)
Total protein (see Chapter 4)
Albumin (see Chapter 4)

The *SMA 6* refers to the sequential multiple analysis of a six-item test that includes measurement of the following:

Sodium (Chapter 15)
Potassium (Chapter 15)
Chloride (Chapter 15)
Total CO_2 (Chapter 15)
Glucose (see Chapter 11)
BUN (see Chapter 8)

Various other terms can be used instead of SMA for comprehensive multiple-test screening. Another common term is *Astra*. An Astra 6 is the same as an SMA 6. An Astra 7 includes analysis for the above six items plus creatinine.

The complete blood count (CBC) also can be performed easily with the help of automation. Because many unsuspected diseases can be detected by the use of chest x-ray (see Chapter 5) and electrocardiography (EKG) (see Chapter 1), the performance of these tests also have been standardized so that they too can be performed rapidly and easily. These studies are all part of the complete medical evaluation of most patients.

Because multiple simultaneous testing techniques permit an easily performed and inexpensive evaluation of numerous patient samples at the same time, coagulation studies (see Chapter 14) have become part of routine testing. Furthermore, the development of the multiple dipstick testing (as with multistick, see Chapter 8) has greatly increased the ease and availability of routine urine evaluation.

Routine testing, coupled with a thorough history and physical examination, allows one to detect a large number of diseases that might otherwise go undetected until symptoms developed and the chance of cure was reduced. The cost of routine testing is relatively small in comparison to its effectiveness.

When blood evaluations are performed singly, they are both costly and time consuming, and as a result they cannot be performed frequently (such as for monitoring therapy). However, multiphasic automation has made a single blood test easily and cheaply available as part of the multiphasic test. A cheap and practical method for effectively monitoring electrolyte abnormalities and diseases such as gout and diabetes is thus available.

Most of these studies that are included in routine testing have been discussed in previous chapters. The discussion in this chapter will only include studies that have not been discussed previously and other miscellaneous studies.

X-RAYS AND SCANS
Lymphangiography (lymphangiogram)
Normal values
Normal nodes without evidence of tumor.

Purpose
Lymphangiography is an x-ray examination of the lymphatic system after the injection of a contrast medium into a lymphatic vessel in each foot or in each hand. The lymphatic system consists of lymph vessels and lymph nodes. Lymph is a transparent fatty fluid that goes from fatty tissues back into the bloodstream. Cancer tends to spread via the lymphatic system. When lymph vessels become obstructed, edema (water retention) usually results. Lymphangiography is indicated in patients who have swollen extremities (caused by edema) or signs of tumor (such as unexplained fever, weight loss, and large lymph nodes) or to evaluate the spread of cancer within the body. Lymphangiography is helpful in determining the appropriate therapy for cancer and in evaluating the results of chemotherapy or radiation therapy.

Procedure

No fasting or sedation is required for this study. This procedure is performed in the x-ray department with the patient lying on his or her back. A blue dye is injected between each of the first three toes of each foot to outline the lymphatic vessels. This blue dye may give the skin and vision a bluish tinge and discolor the urine and stool for 2 days. Then a local anesthetic is injected before a small incision is made in each foot. A lymphatic vessel is identified and a cannula (small tube) is inserted to infuse the iodine contrast agent. The patient must lie very still during the injection of the dye. The flow of the iodine dye throughout the body is followed by a fluoroscopy (moving x-ray pictures on a television monitor). When the injection reaches a certain level of the lumbar vertebrae, the dye is discontinued. Films are then taken of the stomach, pelvis, and upper body to demonstrate the filling of the lymphatic vessels. The patient must return in 24 hours to have repeat x-rays taken. When the injection is made into the hand, the axillary (arm) and supraclavicular (neck) lymph nodes are evaluated.

Pertinent facts

- Before this study, the patient must sign a consent form.
- Before the study is performed, the patient should be assessed for any allergies to iodine, seafood, or any of the dyes used in diagnostic studies such as intravenous pyelography (IVP).
- The injection of dye between the toes causes transient discomfort. Discomfort will also be felt when the toes are locally anesthetized (numbed).
- After the lymphatic vessels are cannulated, dye is infused into the vessels for approximately 1½ hours. The infusion is usually done using an infusion pump to inject the dye at a slow continuous rate.
- This test takes approximately 3 hours to perform. Note that additional x-ray films must be taken again at 24 hours, but these take only about 30 minutes to perform.
- When the injection is completed, needles are removed and the incision is sutured closed.
- After the study, the patient is checked for any signs of shortness of breath, chest pain, fever, or hypotension (low blood pressure).
- Usually after this test, the patient is placed on bed rest for about 24 hours.
- After this test, the patient's feet may be elevated to help reduce swelling.
- Ice packs may be applied to the incision site to relieve discomfort.
- The incision site may be sore for several days after the study.
- The sutures placed in the wound will be removed in approximately 1 week. Until this time, the incision site should be kept clean and dry.
- This study is performed by a radiologist.
- The customary cost of this study is approximately $100.

BLOOD TESTS
Serum electrolyte concentration test
Normal values

Sodium (Na): 136-145 mEq/L.
Potassium (K): 3.5-5 mEq/L.
Chloride (Cl): 90-110 mEq/L.
Carbon dioxide (CO_2): 23-30 mEq/L.

Purpose

Sodium. The sodium content of blood is the result of a balance between sodium (salt) intake and kidney excretion. Many factors assist in sodium balance. The adrenal hormone called aldosterone causes retention of sodium by decreasing kidney losses. Water and sodium are physiologically very closely interrelated. As free body water is increased, the blood sodium is diluted, and the concentration may decrease. The kidney compensates by conserving sodium and excreting water. If free body water were to decrease, the serum sodium concentration would rise. The kidney would then respond by conserving free water.

Some of the causes of *hypernatremia* (increased levels of sodium in the blood) include excessive dietary intake, excessive sodium in intravenous (IV) fluids, Cushing's syndrome (see Chapter 10), excessive free water loss (sweating), extensive burns, diabetes insipidus, and diuretics. Symptoms of hypernatremia may include dry mucous membranes, thirst, agitation, restlessness, hyperflexia, mania, and convulsions. *Hyponatremia* (low levels of sodium in the blood) may be caused by deficient dietary intake of sodium, deficient sodium in intravenous (IV) fluids, Addison's disease (see Chapter 10), diarrhea, vomiting, diuretics, and kidney disease. Symptoms of hyponatremia include weakness, confusion, lethargy, stupor, or coma.

Potassium. Potassium is a major ion within the cell. Because the blood concentration of potassium is so small, minor changes in its concentration have significant consequences.

Blood potassium concentration depends on many factors, including

1. Aldosterone (This hormone tends to increase the kidney losses of potassium.)
2. Sodium reabsorption (As sodium is reabsorbed, potassium is lost.)
3. Acid-base balance (Acidotic states tend to raise the blood potassium levels, and basic states tend to lower the blood potassium levels by causing a shift of the potassium out of or into cells, respectively.)

Some of the causes of *hyperkalemia* (increased potassium levels in the blood) include excessive dietary intake, kidney failure, Addison's disease, and infection. Symptoms of hyperkalemia include irritability, nausea, vomiting, and diarrhea. Increased potassium levels may be detected on an EKG reading. The causes of *hypokalemia* (decreased blood potassium levels) include decreased dietary intake, diarrhea, vomiting, diuretic drugs, Cushing's syndrome, licorice ingestion, and insulin, glucose, or calcium administration. Signs of hypokalemia include weakness, paralysis, decreased reflex response, increased heart sensitivity to digoxin, and cardiac arrhythmias.

Chloride. The major purpose of chloride is to maintain electrical neutrality mostly in combination with sodium to follow sodium losses and accompany sodium excesses. Chloride also serves as a buffer to assist in acid-base imbalance.

Carbon dioxide (CO_2). As discussed in Chapter 5 (see p. 88-89), CO_2 content is a measure of the bicarbonate ion (HCO_3) that exists in the blood. This anion is of secondary importance in electrical neutrality of cellular fluid. Its major role is in acid-base balance as discussed in Chapter 5. Increases occur with alkalosis, and decreases occur with acidosis.

Procedure

One red-top tube of blood is drawn from a vein in the arm. If the patient has an intravenous (IV) line, the venipuncture (needle stick) should be performed in the opposite arm to avoid artificial results caused by the fluid infusion.

Pertinent facts

- The only discomfort associated with this study is a needle stick.
- Because this study is usually performed with a glucose (sugar) level (see p. 174-176) determination in an SMA 6, the time of day should be recorded on the lab slip to avoid confusion in the sugar readings.
- If the results are abnormal, the test will be repeated because the chance of laboratory error is very great in this test, since many specimens are tested at the same time. The machine that performs the determinations can malfunction.
- The customary cost of the serum electrolyte study is approximately $53.

Rheumatoid factor (RF)
Normal values

Negative.

Purpose

Rheumatoid arthritis is a disease accompanied by an antibody known as the rheumatoid factor (RF). Demonstration of this factor in the blood is a very useful laboratory test for confirming the diagnosis when rheumatoid arthritis is suspected. Rheumatoid arthritis is an inflammatory disease of the joints characterized by joint swelling, pain, and inflammation.

Positive RF titers (levels) are found in 80% of the patients with rheumatoid arthritis. Titers ranging above 1:80 are usually diagnostic for rheumatoid arthritis. Lower titers may occur in healthy individuals over 60 years of age or in individuals with other inflammatory disease processes such as syphilis, cirrhosis, hepatitis, leprosy, or viral infections. Also a negative RF titer does not negate the possibility of rheumatoid arthritis. The rheumatoid factor is not reactive sometimes until 6 months after the onset of active disease. Repeating this test at a later date will be useful in detecting the RF.

Procedure

No fasting of food or fluids is required. One red-top tube of blood is drawn from a vein in the arm.

Pertinent facts

- The only discomfort associated with this test is a needle stick.
- Since patients with rheumatoid arthritis may not be able to effectively fight infections either because of the disease or because of disease treatment, these patients may easily acquire infections. Therefore the venipuncture site should be checked for signs of infection.
- The customary cost of the study is approximately $20.

Lupus erythematosus (LE) cell preparation (LE PREP)
Normal values

No LE cells present.

Purpose

The lupus erythematosus (LE) cell preparation is a study used to diagnose systemic lupus erythematosus (SLE) by the detection of LE cells. SLE is a chronic disease of the connective tissues that produces changes in the skin, joints, and muscles of the body. Other organs are usually involved in SLE, and death will usually result from failure of vital organ functions. There is no specific treatment for SLE, though corticosteroids may be used to control the bothersome symptoms. The LE prep may be repeated occasionally to monitor the response of steroid treatment. If treatment is effective, LE cells will disappear after several weeks of therapy.

Although LE cells occur primarily with SLE, they may also be found in other diseases such as hepatitis, rheumatoid arthritis, and scleroderma and in certain drug reactions. Some patients with SLE will not even demonstrate LE cells. Therefore this test cannot be used to definitely diagnose SLE. Confirmation of the diagnosis may be done by performing an ANA (antinuclear antibody test, see next study).

Procedure

One red-top tube of blood is drawn from a vein in the arm. No fasting is required for this study.

Pertinent facts

- The only discomfort associated with this study is a needle stick.
- Since many patients who have SLE have a compromised immune system, they cannot effectively fight infection. Therefore these patients should have the venipuncture site checked for the presence of infection.
- If the test results are positive for SLE, the patient should be informed that repeated studies may be needed to monitor therapy.
- The customary cost of the LE prep is approximately $20.

Antinuclear antibodies (ANA) (anti-DNA antibody test)
Normal values

Less than 1:10.

Purpose

Antinuclear antibodies (ANA) are a group of antibodies that the body produces against its own tissue. These antibodies react with the body's tissues and cause connective tissue damage (as in systemic lupus erythematosus, SLE). SLE is an inflammatory disease that causes deterioration of the connective tissues in various part of the body. About 99% of patients with SLE exhibit ANA. If ANA are not detected, SLE cannot be confirmed. The ANA test can also be used to monitor the effectiveness of therapy for SLE.

ANA are also found in other disease conditions such as rheumatoid arthritis, rheumatic fever, juvenile arthritis, and lupoid hepatitis. Therefore positive test results are found in many other organ involvements. The test results cannot confirm one particular disease; they can only partially confirm what clinical evidence has already determined. Also the appearance of antinuclear antibodies does not necessarily indicate a disease process, because ANA are present in some normal individuals.

Procedure

No fasting for food or fluids is required. The test requires only a blood sample. One red-top tube of blood is drawn from a vein in the arm.

Pertinent facts

- The only discomfort associated with this test is a needle stick.
- The site where blood was drawn should be checked for infection, because patients who have certain immune diseases cannot effectively fight infection.
- The customary cost of the ANA test is approximately $20.

Mono spot test (monoscreening test, heterophile antibody titer test, heterophile agglutination test)
Normal values

Negative, or a titer (level) of less than 1:56.

Purpose

The mono spot and heterophile antibody test are routinely used to diagnose infectious mononucleosis. Infectious mononucleosis is an infectious disease process that primarily affects children and young adults. Symptoms of mononucleosis include headache, sore throat, mental and physical fatigue, weakness, and flu-like symptoms.

Heterophile antibodies are present in the blood of approximately 80% of people with infectious mononucleosis. A gradual increase in the titer during weeks 3 and 4 followed by a gradual decline during weeks 4 to 8 is most conclusive for mononucleosis. A negative titer does not preclude the diagnosis of mononucleosis, because the titer may not yet have become reactive. If symptoms persist, the test should be repeated in 2 weeks.

High titers (above 1:56) cannot confirm the diagnosis of mononucleosis. Other disease processes (such as syphilis and systemic lupus erythematosus) can cause elevated titers.

Procedure

No fasting is required. One tube of blood is drawn from a vein in the arm.

Pertinent facts

- The only discomfort associated with this test is a needle stick.
- The customary cost of this study is approximately $6.

Venereal disease testing (serologic test for syphilis)
Normal values

Negative.

Purpose

The serologic test for syphilis (STS) is a test used to detect antibodies to *Treponema pallidum,* the causative agent of syphilis. There are two groups of antibodies. The first is an antibody directed against a substance produced by the *Treponema pallidum* infection. The second is an antibody directed against the *Treponema* organism itself. The first is relatively nonspecific and is most commonly detected by the Wassermann test or the Venereal Disease Research Laboratory (VDRL) test. The second is much more specific and is usually measured by the fluorescent treponemal antibody (FTA) test.

The VDRL test, by virtue of its testing for a nonspecific antibody, has a high false positive rate. Nearly 20% of all positive VDRL test results are incorrectly positive. Conditions such as pneumonia, malaria, bacterial and viral infections, and pregnancy may cause false positive results. VDRL tests become positive about 2 weeks after the patient is innoculated with *Treponema* and returns to normal shortly after adequate treatment. The test is positive in nearly all of the early stages of syphilis and in most patients with later stage syphilis.

The FTA test, which tests for a more specific antibody, is more accurate than the VDRL test. False positive and false negative results are rare in all stages of the disease. The FTA test is required before the diagnosis of syphilis can be made with certainty.

Procedure

Both the VDRL test and the FTA test can be performed on a specimen of blood collected in one red-top tube. The blood is drawn from a vein in the arm.

Pertinent facts

- This test is performed by a technician and is not associated with any patient discomfort except for the needle stick.

- If the test result is positive, a history of the patient's recent sexual contacts will be obtained so that these persons can be evaluated for syphilis also.
- If the test is positive, the patient will receive the appropriate antibiotic therapy.
- The customary cost of the study is approximately $7.

Erythrocyte sedimentation rate (ESR) test (sed rate test)
Normal values (Westergren method)

Men: Up to 15 mm/hr.
Women: Up to 20 mm/hr.
Children: Up to 10 mm/hr.

Purpose

The erythrocyte sedimentation rate (ESR) test is a nonspecific test used to detect inflammatory, infectious, and cancer processes. Since the ESR test is a nonspecific test, it is not diagnostic for any specific organ, disease, or injury. The test is performed by measuring the distance (in millimeters) that red blood cells (RBCs) descend (or settle) in blood in 1 hour. Because the conditions just mentioned increase the protein content of plasma, RBCs have a tendency to stack up on one another, thus increasing their weight, which causes them to descend faster. Therefore the ESR will be increased in disease processes.

This test can be used to detect disease that is otherwise not suspected. Many physicians use this test in this way for routine patient evaluation. Other physicians regard this test as so nonspecific that it is useless as a routine study. The ESR test can occasionally be helpful in differentiating disease entities or complaints (for example, in a patient with chest pain, the ESR will be increased with heart attack but normal with just angina or chest pain).

ESR is a fairly reliable indicator of the course of disease and can therefore be used to evaluate or monitor disease therapy. In general as the disease worsens, the ESR increases, and as the disease improves, the ESR decreases.

Procedure

Blood is drawn from a vein in the arm. The blood is immediately taken to the laboratory where the ESR is measured. If the specimen is allowed to stand around before the test is done, the ESR may be retarded, thereby causing artificially low levels. Therefore the study should be performed within 3 hours after the specimen has been obtained.

Pertinent facts

- The only discomfort associated with this test is the needle stick.
- The customary cost of the study is approximately $7.

Antistreptolysin O titer (ASO titer)
Normal values
Adults: 160 Todd units/ml or less.
Children:
   Newborn: Similar to mother's value.
   6 mo-2 yr: 50 Todd units/ml or less.
   2-4 yr: 160 Todd units/ml or less.
   5-12 yr: 200 Todd units/ml or less.

Purpose
The antistreptolysin O (ASO) titer is a blood study that demonstrates the reaction of the body to infection caused by group A streptococci bacteria. It is used primarily in the differential diagnosis of poststreptococcal diseases such as glomerulonephritis, rheumatic fever, bacterial endocarditis, and scarlet fever.

The streptococcus organism produces an enzyme called streptolysin O, which has the ability to destroy (lyse) red blood cells. The body reacts to streptolysin O by producing antistreptolysin O (ASO), a neutralizing antibody. ASO appears in the blood 1 week to 1 month after the onset of streptococcal infection. A high titer (level) is not specific for a certain type of poststreptococcal disease but is merely an indication that a streptococcal infection is or has been present. When the ASO elevation is seen in a patient with glomerulonephritis or endocarditis, one can safely assume that the disease was caused by the streptococcal infection.

Procedure
One red-top tube of blood is collected from a vein in the arm. No fasting is required.

Pertinent facts
- The only discomfort associated with the study is the needle stick.
- The customary cost of the study is approximately $15.

Phosphate (phosphorous) concentration test
Normal values
Adults: 2.5-4.5 mg/dl.
Children: 3.5-5.8 mg/dl.

Purpose
Most of the body's phosphorus exists within the skeleton. However, approximately 15% exists in the blood as a phosphate salt. Dietary phosphorus is absorbed in the small intestines. The absorption is very efficient, and only rarely is hypophosphatemia (low blood levels of phosphorus) caused by intestinal malabsorption. However, antacids can bind phosphorus and decrease its intestinal absorption.

Phosphorus levels are determined by calcium metabolism (see p. 152), by parathormone (PTH, p. 152), and to a lesser degree by intestinal absorption. Because an inverse relationship exists between calcium and phosphorus, a decrease in one mineral results in an increase in the other. Serum phosphorus levels therefore depend on calcium metabolism and vice versa.

Hyperphosphatemia (high levels of phosphorus in the blood) can be caused by hypoparathyroidism, kidney failure, or increased dietary or intravenous (IV) intake. Symptoms are few; however, calcium phosphate deposits in soft tissue may occur with chronic and persistent elevations of phosphate levels.

Hypophosphatemia (low levels of phosphorus in the blood) may occur with inadequate dietary ingestion of phosphorus, chronic antacid ingestion, hyperparathyroidism, and hypercalcemia (high levels of calcium in the blood) resulting from other causes. Symptoms of hypophosphatemia may include retarded skeletal growth in children, anorexia, dizziness, muscle weakness, waddling gait, skeletal and cardiac muscle diseases, decreased red blood cell oxygen transport, and red blood cell destruction.

Procedure

This test is usually indicated in an SMA 12 or any other multiphasic automated systems analysis of serum (see p. 242). Some hospitals require that the patient be fasting. Usually for these multiphasic analyses, two red-top tubes of blood are filled from a vein in the arm.

Pertinent facts

- The only discomfort associated with this test is a needle stick.
- The time that the blood was obtained should be indicated on the laboratory slip, because often a blood glucose (sugar) determination is performed simultaneously in a multiphasic test.
- The customary cost of this study is approximately $6.

Serum osmolality test
Normal values

275-300 mOsm/kg.

Purpose

This is a measure of the number of particles per kilogram of the patient's blood. When the number of particles within the blood increases, serum osmolality is elevated. In diabetic patients, the number of glucose particles in the blood increases markedly, thus raising serum osmolalities to levels as high as 400 mOsm/kg. Patients whose blood osmolality values reach this level are usually in a coma. Hypernatremia (high levels of sodium in the blood), dehydration, and diabetes insipidus can also cause increased blood osmolality. Low serum (blood) osmolality usually results from fluid overload and inappropriate secretion of the antidiuretic hormone. There are no complications associated with this study.

Procedure

One red-top tube of blood is drawn from a vein in the arm. No fasting is required for this test.

Pertinent facts

- The only discomfort associated with this study is a needle stick.
- The customary cost of the serum osmolality test is approximately $20.

SPECIAL STUDIES
Culture and sensitivity testing (C & S of the throat, sputum, urine, blood, or wound)
Normal values

Normal value for all cultures: negative.

Purpose

When a patient develops a fever of unknown origin (FUO), all of the major potential causes of that infection must be investigated. This investigation includes a thorough history and physical examination along with the obtaining of appropriate specimens for culture and sensitivity (C & S) testing. When the patient has an obvious site of infection, this too should be cultured to identify the infecting agent. Knowledge about the organism's *sensitivity* to the commonly used antibiotics allows the physician to accurately determine the appropriate antibiotic therapy. If the organisms are not sensitive to the antibiotic being administered, no improvement in the disease will occur. In addition, when more than one organism is causing the infection, the sensitivity report assists the physician in choosing one drug to which all of the involved organisms will be sensitive.

All cultures should be performed *before* antibiotic therapy is initiated. Otherwise the antibiotic may interrupt the growth of the organism in the laboratory. More often than not, however, the physician will want to institute antibiotic therapy after the culture has been taken but before the culture results are reported. In these instances, a Gram stain of the specimen smeared on a slide is most helpful and can be reported in less than 10 minutes. All forms of bacteria are grossly classified as gram positive or gram negative. Knowledge of the shape of the organism can also be very helpful in the tentative identification of the infecting organism. With knowledge of the Gram stain results, the physician can institute a reasonable antibiotic regimen based on past experience as to what the organism might be. Most organisms take about 24 hours to grow in the laboratory, and a preliminary report can be given at that time. Occasionally 48 to 72 hours are required for growth and identification of the organism. Cultures may be repeated after appropriate antibiotic therapy to assess for complete resolution of the infection (especially in urinary tract infection).

Procedure

In general all culture specimens should be delivered to the microbiology (bacteriology) laboratory and cultured as soon as they are obtained. Otherwise, overgrowth of the bacteria will occur while the specimen is "sitting around." If the specimen is obtained at night or on weekends, and the bacteriology laboratory is closed, the specimen should be refrigerated until it can be placed in a culture medium.

Throat culture. Because the throat is normally colonized by many organisms, culture technique of this area serves only to isolate and identify a few particular pathogens (such as streptococci and meningococci). Recognition of these organisms requires treatment. Streptococci are most commonly looked for because a beta-hemolytic streptococcal pharyngitis (strep throat) may be followed by rheumatic fever or glomerulonephritis. This type of streptococcal infection most commonly affects children between the ages of 3 and 15 years. Therefore all children who have a sore throat and fever should have a throat culture done to identify streptococcal infection. In adults, however, fewer than 5% of patients with pharyngitis have a streptococcal infection. Therefore throat cultures in adults are only indicated when the patient has a severe sore throat, fever, and palpable lymph nodes. All other adults with a severe sore throat usually do not receive throat cultures.

One can best obtain a throat culture specimen by depressing the tongue with a wooden tongue blade and touching the back wall of the throat with a sterile cotton swab. One must avoid touching any other part of the mouth. The swab is placed in a sterile container and sent to the microbiology laboratory.

Sputum culture. Sputum cultures aid in the identification of organisms caused by a pulmonary (lung) infection. However, because the specimen is usually obtained through the mouth cavity, which is normally heavily colonized with bacteria, sputum culture results are frequently inaccurate.

When there is an overabundance of one type of bacterial organism mixed in with microscopic evidence of white blood cells (WBCs), one can be relatively certain that the bacteria is the cause of the infection. Deep pulmonary secretions are routinely obtained by having the patient cough when he or she awakens (see Chapter 5, p. 89-91). The cough may be induced by aspiration, nebulizers, or pulmonary physical therapy.

Urine culture. The urine culture specimen must be a clean catch, midstream collection. This method of collection is described in Chapter 8 (p. 143). Frequently it is beneficial to culture the urine of a patient who has an indwelling Foley catheter immediately before removal of the catheter. This procedure is called a "terminal urine for C & S." It is usually more accurate than is culturing the tip of the catheter.

Blood culture. Bacteremia (bacteria in the blood) is usually intermittent and transient except in endocarditis or suppurative thrombophlebitis. Bacteremia is usually marked by chills and fever. For this reason, blood for blood cultures should be drawn at the time the patient manifests the chills and fever. A culture specimen should be obtained from two different sites. The two culture specimens are important because if one produces a bacterium and the other does not, it is safe to assume that the bacterium in the first culture is a contaminant and not the infecting agent. When both cultures produce the infecting agent, bacteremia exists. If the patient is receiving antibiotics, the laboratory should be notified, and the blood culture specimen should be drawn shortly before the next dose of the antibiotic is administered. This is because the blood level of the antibiotic should be at its lowest at this point.

In the taking of the blood specimens, two different venous sites are carefully cleansed usually with a Betadine solution. The tops of the blood culture bottles are cleaned and allowed to dry. The blood is drawn and then immediately sent in the culture bottles to the laboratory. Culture specimens drawn through an intravenous (IV) catheter are frequently contaminated, and tests using them should not be performed unless catheter sepsis (infection) is suspected. In these situations, blood culture specimens drawn through the catheter more accurately indicate the causative agent than does the culture specimen from the catheter tip.

Wound culture. Wound infections are most commonly caused by pus-forming organisms. One can best obtain the specimen for a wound culture by placing a sterile cotton swab into the pus and then placing the swab into a sterile, covered test tube. The specimen is transported to the laboratory as soon as possible. A culture of specimens taken from the skin edge is much less accurate than a culture of the puslike material.

Pertinent facts

- All specimens should be handled carefully as though they were capable of transmitting disease. Specimens should be transported to the laboratory immediately (at least within 30 minutes).
- Culture specimens should be taken *before* antibiotic therapy is begun. Antibiotics will alter the growth of the organisms in culture media.
- All cultures should be carefully labeled as to what kind of specimen was collected. Also any medication that the patient is taking should be indicated on the laboratory slip.
- The customary cost of most culture studies is about $25. The sensitivity testing is approximately $30.

Sample case report: routine admission workup

Mrs. A., a 51-year-old woman, developed an umbilical hernia after her last pregnancy at age 41. She had no other medical problems, and the results of her physical examination were normal. She was admitted to the hospital for repair of the hernia.

STUDIES	RESULTS
Complete blood count (CBC) (see Chapter 14)	
Hemoglobin (Hgb) concentration	14 g/dl (normal: 12-16 g/dl)
Hematocrit (Hct)	43% (normal: 37%-47%)
White blood cells (WBC)	5300 (normal: 5000-10,000)
Differential count	
Neutrophils	60% (normal: 55%-70%)
Lymphocytes	30% (normal: 20%-40%)
Monocytes	7% (normal: 2%-8%)
Eosinophils	3% (normal: 1%-4%)
Basophils	1% (normal: 0.5%-1%)
Red blood cells (RBC)	4.8 million/cu mm (normal: 4.2-5.4 million/cu mm)
Mean corpuscular volume (MCV)	88 cu u (normal: 80-95 cu u)
Mean corpuscular hemoglobin concentration (MCHC)	34 g/dl (normal: 33-36 g/dl)

STUDIES	RESULTS
Mean corpuscular hemoglobin (MCH)	30 pg (normal: 27-31 pg)
Platelet count	350,000/cu mm (normal: 150,000-400,000 cu mm)
SMA 12 (sequential multiple analyzer, 12-item test)	
Calcium (see Chapter 9)	9.9 mg/dl (normal: 9-10.5 mg/dl)
Phosphorus (Chapter 15)	3.2 mg/dl (normal: 2.5-4.5 mg/dl)
Triglycerides (see Chapter 1)	100 mg/dl (normal: 40-150 mg/dl)
Uric acid (see Chapter 7)	6.1 mg/dl (normal: 2.5-8.5 mg/dl)
Creatinine (see Chapter 8)	1 mg/dl (normal: 0.7-1.5 mg/dl)
BUN (see Chapter 8)	9 mg/dl (normal: 5-20 mg/dl)
Total bilirubin (see Chapter 4)	0.8 mg/dl (normal: 0.1-1 mg/dl)
Alkaline phosphatase (see Chapter 4)	45 ImU/ml (normal: 30-85 ImU/ml)
SGOT (see Chapters 1 and 4)	25 IU/L (normal: 5-40 IU/L)
LDH (see Chapters 1 and 4)	125 ImU/ml (normal: 90-200 ImU/ml)
Total protein (see Chapter 4)	7.2 g/dl (normal: 6-8 g/dl)
Albumin (see Chapter 4)	3.8 g/dl (normal: 3.2-4.5 g/dl)
Serologic test for syphilis (VDRL)	Negative, nonreactive (normal: negative, nonreactive)
SMA 6 (sequential multiple analyzer, six-item test)	
Sodium	138 mEq/L (normal: 136-145 mEq/L)
Potassium	4.1 mEq/L (normal: 3.5-5 mEq/L)
Chloride	103 mEq/L (normal: 90-110 mEq/L)
Carbon dioxide	24 mEq/L (normal: 23-30 mEq/L)
Glucose (see Chapter 11)	90 mg/dl (normal: 60-120 mg/dl)
BUN (see Chapter 8)	9 mg/dl (normal: 5-20 mg/dl)
Erythrocyte sedimentation rate (ESR)	14 mm/hr (normal: up to 20 mm/hr)
Urinalysis (see Chapter 8)	
pH	6.2 (normal: 4.6 to 8.0)
Specific gravity	1.020 (normal: 1.010-1.025)
Color	Yellow (normal: amber, yellow)
Glucose	0 (normal: negative)
Protein	0 (normal: negative)
Blood	0 (normal: up to 2 RBCs)
Casts	
RBCs	0 to 1 (normal: negative)
WBCs	0 to 1 (normal: negative)
Crystals	0 (normal: negative)
Coagulation profile (see Chapter 14)	
Prothrombin time (PT)	90% (normal: 11-12.5 sec or 85%-100%)
Activated partial thromboplastin time (APTT)	32 sec (normal: 30-40 sec)
EKG (see Chapter 1)	Normal heart rhythm
Chest x-ray study (see Chapter 5)	No disease seen
Tuberculin skin test	Negative

In light of the completely normal laboratory evaluation, the patient underwent hernia repair surgery. The patient had no complications and was discharged from the hospital in 2 days.

Appendix 1

Abbreviations and symbols

cc	Cubic centimeter	min	Minute
cg	Centigram	ml	Milliliter
cm	Centimeter	mm	Millimeter
cm H_2O	Centimeter of water	mM	Millimole
cu	Cubic	mm Hg	Millimeter of mercury
cuμ	Cubic micron	mm H_2O	Millimeter of water
cu mm	Cubic millimeter	mOsm	Milliosmole
dl	Deciliter (100 ml)	mμ	Millimicron
g	Gram	mU	Milliunit
hr	Hour	mV	Millivolt
ImU	International milliunit	μ	Micron
IU	International unit	μg	Microgram
IμU	International microunit	μm	Micrometer
kg	Kilogram	μU	Microunit
L	Liter	ng	Nanogram
m	Meter	pg	Picogram
m^2	Square meter		(or micromicrogram)
m^3	Cubic meter	pl	Picoliter
mEq	Milliequivalent	sec	Second
mEq/L	Milliequivalent per liter	U	Unit
mg	Milligram	yr	Year

Appendix 2

Blood, plasma, or serum values

TEST	NORMAL VALUES
Acetoacetate plus acetone	0.3-2 mg/dl
Acetone	Negative
Acid phosphatase	0.10-0.63 U/ml (Bessey-Lowry)
	0.5-2.0 U/ml (Bodansky)
	1.0-4.0 U/ml (King-Armstrong)
ACTH (adrenocorticotropic hormone	15-100 pg/ml
Activated partial thromboplastin time (APTT)	30-40 sec
Albumin	3.2-4.5 g/dl
Alcohol	Negative
Aldolase	Adults: 3-8.2 Sibley-Lehninger units/dl
	Children: approximately 2 X adult values
	Newborns: approximately 4 X adult values
Aldosterone	Peripheral blood
	Supine: 3-10 ng/dl
	Upright: 5-30 ng/dl
	Adrenal vein: 200-800 ng/dl
Alkaline phosphatase	Adults: 30-85 ImU/ml
	Children and adolescents
	Less than 2 yr: 85-235 ImU/ml
	2-8 yr: 65-210 ImU/ml
	9-15 yr: 60-300 ImU/ml (active bone growth)
	16-21 yr: 30-200 ImU/ml
Alpha-aminonitrogen	3-6 mg/dl
Alpha-fetoprotein (AFP)	Less than 30 ng/ml
Ammonia	15-110 μg/100 ml
Amylase	56-190 IU/L
	80-150 Somogyi units/ml
Antinuclear antibodies (ANA)	Less than 1:10
Antistreptolysin O (ASO)	Less than 160 Todd units

Ascorbic acid (vitamin C)	0.6-1.6 mg/dl
Australian antigen (hepatitis-associated antigen, HAA)	Negative
Barbiturates	Negative
Base excess	Men: -3.3 to $+1.2$
	Women: -2.4 to $+2.3$
Bicarbonate (HCO_3^-)	22-26 mEq/L
Bilirubin	
Direct (conjugated)	0.1-0.3 mg/dl
Indirect (unconjugated)	0.2-0.8 mg/dl
Total	0.1-1 mg/dl
In newborns	1-12 mg/dl
Bleeding time (Ivy method)	1-9 min
Blood count	See CBC (complete blood count)
Blood gases	
pH	7.35-7.45
P_{CO_2}	35-45 mm Hg
HCO_3	22-26 mEq/L
P_{O_2}	80-100 mm Hg
O_2 saturation	95%-100%
Bromide	Up to 5 mg/dl
Bromsulfalein (BSP)	Less than 5% retention after 45 min
BUN (blood urea nitrogen)	5-20 mg/dl
C reactive protein	Negative
Calcium (Ca)	9-10.5 mg/dl (total)
Carbon dioxide (CO_2)	23-30 mEq/L
Carotene	50-200 μg/dl
CBC (complete blood count)	
RBC (red blood cell) count	Men: 4.7-6.1 million/cu mm
	Women: 4.2-5.4 million/cu mm
	Infants and children:
	3.8-5.5 million/cu mm
	Newborns: 4.8-7.1 million/cu mm
Hemoglobin (Hgb)	Men: 14-18 g/dl
	Women: 12-16 g/dl
	Children: 11-16 g/dl
	Infants: 10-15 g/dl
	Newborns: 14-24 g/dl
Hematocrit (Hct)	Men: 42%-52%
	Women: 37%-47%
	Children: 31%-43%
	Infants: 30%-40%
	Newborns: 44%-64%
Mean corpuscular volume (MCV)	Adults and children: 80-95 cu μ
	Newborns: 96-108 cu μ
Mean corpuscular hemoglobin (MCH)	Adults and children: 27-31 pg
	Newborns: 32-34 pg

Mean corpuscular hemoglobin concentration (MCHC)	Adults and children: 32-36 g/dl Newborns: 32-33 g/dl

WBC (white blood cell) count	Adults and children older than 2 yr:
	  5000-10,000/cu mm
	Children 2 yr or less:
	  6200-17,000/cu mm
	Newborns: 9000-30,000/cu mm

Differential count	
Neutrophils	55%-70%
Lymphocytes	20%-40%
Monocytes	2%-8%
Eosinophils	1%-4%
Basophils	0.5%-1%
Platelet count	150,000-400,000/cu mm
CEA (carcinoembryonic antigen)	Up to 2 ng/ml
Cholesterol	150-250 mg/dl
Chloride (Cl)	90-110 mEq/L
CO_2 (carbon dioxide)	23-30 mEq/L
Complement	C3: 70-176 mg/dl C4: 16-45 mg/dl
Complete blood count	See CBC
Coombs' test	
Direct	Negative
Indirect	Negative
Copper (Cu)	70-140 μg/dl
Cortisol	6-28 μg/dl (AM) 2-12 μg/dl (PM)
CPK (creatinine phosphokinase)	5-75 mU/ml
Creatinine	0.7-1.5 mg/dl
Creatinine phosphokinase	5-75 mU/ml
Cryoglobulin	Negative
Cu (Copper)	70-140 μg/dl
Differential (WBC) count	
Neutrophils	55%-70%
Lymphocytes	20%-40%
Monocytes	2%-8%
Eosinophils	1%-4%
Basophils	0.5%-1%
Digoxin	
Therapeutic level	0.8-2 ng/ml
Toxic level	Greater than 2.5 ng/dl
Erythrocyte count	See RBC
Erythrocyte sedimentation rate (ESR)	Men: up to 15 mm/hr Women: up to 20 mm/hr Children: up to 10 mm/hr
Ethanol	Marked intoxication: 0.3%-0.4% Alcoholic stupor: 0.4%-0.5% Alcoholic coma: 0.5% or more

Fats	Up to 200 mg/dl
FDP (fibrin degradation products)	Less than 10 µg/ml
Fe (iron)	60-190 µg/dl
Ferritin	Men: 30-200 ng/ml
	Women: 20-120 ng/ml
Fibrin degradation products	Less than 10 µg/ml
Fibrinogen (factor I)	200-400 mg/dl
Fluoride	Less than 0.05 mg/dl
Folate (serum)	2.2-18.7 ng/ml
Follicle-stimulating hormone (FSH)	Men: 0.1-15 ImU/ml
	Women: 6-30 ImU/ml
	Children: 0.1-12 ImU/ml
	Castrate and postmenopausal:
	30-200 ImU/ml
FTA (fluorescent treponemal antibody)	Negative
G 6-PD (glucose 6-phosphate dehydrogenase)	8.6-18.6 IU/g of hemoglobin
Gamma globulin	0.5-1.6 g/dl
Gamma-glutamyl transpeptidase (GGTP)	Up to 65 IU/L
Gastrin	40-150 pg/ml
GGTP (gamma-glutamyl transpeptidase)	Up to 65 IU/L
Glucose, fasting (FBS)	60-120 mg/dl
Glucose, 2 hr postprandial (2 hr PPG)	60-120 mg/dl
Glucose 6-phosphate dehydrogenase (G 6-PD)	8.6-18.6 IU/g of hemoglobin
Glucose tolerance test (GTT)	30 min: 145 mg/dl
	1 hr: 135 mg/dl
	2 hr: 100 mg/dl
	3 hr: 80 mg/dl
	4 hr: 80 mg/dl
Gonadotropins (human chorionic gonadotropin)	See Chapter 12
Growth hormone	Less than 10 ng/ml
Haptoglobin	100-150 mg/dl
HB,Ag (hepatitis B surface antigen)	Nonreactive
HCG (human chorionic gonadotropin)	See Chapter 12
Hematocrit (Hct)	Men: 42%-52%
	Women: 37%-47%
	Children: 31%-43%
	Infants: 30%-40%
	Newborns: 44%-64%

Hemoglobin	Men: 14-18 g/dl
	Women: 12-16 g/dl
	Children: 11-16 g/dl
	Infants: 10-15 g/dl
	Newborn: 14-24 g/dl
Hemoglobin electrophoresis	Hgb A$_1$: 95%-98%
	Hgb A$_2$: 2%-3%
	Hgb F: 0.8%-2%
	Hgb S: 0
	Hgb C: 0
Hepatitis B surface antigen	Nonreactive
Heterophile antibody	Negative
5-Hydroxyindole acetic acid (5-HIAA)	2.8-8 mg/24 hr
Immunoglobulin quantification	IgG: 565-1765 mg/dl
	IgA: 85-385 mg/dl
	IgM: 55-375 mg/dl
Insulin	4-24 μU/ml
Iron (Fe)	60-190 μg/dl
Iron-binding capacity, total (TIBC)	250-420 μg/dl
Iron (transferrin) saturation	30%-40%
K (potassium)	3.5-5 mEq/L
Ketone bodies	Negative
Lactic acid	0.6-1.8 mEq/L
Lactic dehydrogenase (LDH)	90-200 ImU/ml
LDH isoenzymes	LDH-1: 17%-27%
	LDH-2: 28%-38%
	LDH-3: 19%-27%
	LDH-4: 5%-16%
	LDH-5: 6%-16%
Lead	50 μg/dl or less
Leukocyte count (WBC)	See WBC
Lipase	Up to 1.5 units/ml
Lipids	
Total	400-1000 mg/dl
Cholesterol	150-250 mg/dl
Triglycerides	40-150 mg/dl
Phospholipids	150-380 mg/dl
Magnesium (Mg)	1.6-3 mEq/L
MCH, MCHC, MCV	See RBC indexes
Methanol	Negative
Microsomal antibody	Negative
Na (sodium)	136-145 mEq/L
Nuclear antibody (ANA)	Less than 1:10
5′-Nucleotidase	Up to 1.6 units
Osmolality	275-300 mOsm/kg

Oxygen saturation	95%-100%
P (phosphorus, PO₄)	Adults: 2.5-4.5 mg/dl
	Children: 3.5-5.8 mg/dl
Parathormone (PTH)	Less than 2000 pg/ml
Partial thromboplastin time, activated (APTT)	30-40 sec
P_{CO_2}	35-45 mm Hg
pH	7.35-7.45
Phenylalanine	Up to 2 mg/dl
Phenytoin (Dilantin)	Therapeutic level: 5-20 μg/ml
Phosphatase (acid)	0.10-0.63 U/ml (Bessey-Lowry)
	0.5-2.0 U/ml (Bodansky)
	1.0-4.0 U/ml (King-Armstrong)
Phosphatase (alkaline)	Adults: 30-85 ImU/ml
	Children and adolescents
	Less than 2 yr: 85-235 ImU/ml
	2-8 yr: 65-210 ImU/ml
	9-15 yr: 60-300 ImU/ml (active bone growth)
	16-21 yr: 30-200 ImU/ml
Phosphorus	Adults: 2.5-4.5 mg/dl
	Children: 3.5-5.8 mg/dl
Platelet count	150,000-400,000/cu mm
P_{O_2}	80-100 mm Hg
Primidone (Mysoline)	Therapeutic level: 4-12 μg/ml
Protein (total)	6-8 g/dl
Albumin	3.2-4.5 g/dl
Globulin	2.3-3.5 g/dl
Prothrombin time (PT)	11-12.5 sec
PTH (parathormone)	Less than 2000 pg/ml
Pyruvate	0.3-0.9 mg/dl
RBC (red blood cell) count	Men: 4.7-6.1 million/cu mm
	Women: 4.2-5.4 million/cu mm
	Infants and children:
	3.8-5.5 million/cu mm
	Newborns: 4.8-7.1 million/cu mm
RBC indexes	
Mean corpuscular volume (MCV)	Adults and children: 80-95 cuμ
	Newborns: 96-108 cuμ
Mean corpuscular hemoglobin (MCH)	Adults and children: 27-31 pg
	Newborns: 32-34 pg
Mean corpuscular hemoglobin concentration (MCHC)	Adults and children: 32-36 g/dl
	Newborns: 32-33 g/dl
Reticulocyte count	Adults: 0.5%-2.0%
	Infants: 0.5%-3.1%
	Newborns: 2.5%-6.5%

Salicylates	Negative
	Therapeutic: 20-25 mg/dl
	(to age 10: 25-30 mg/dl)
	Toxic: greater than 30 mg/dl
	(after age 60: greater than 20 mg/dl)
SGOT (serum glutamic oxaloacetic transaminase)	12-36 U/ml or 5-40 IU/L
SGPT (serum glutamic pyruvic transaminase)	5-35 IU/L
Sickle cell	Negative
Sodium (Na$^+$)	136-145 mEq/L
STS (serologic test for syphilis)	Negative (nonreactive)
Sugar	See glucose
Syphilis	See STS, VDRL, FTA
T$_3$ (Triiodothyronine)	110-130 ng/dl
T$_4$ (Thyroxine)	4-11 μg/dl (Murphy-Pattee)
	5-10 μg/dl (radioimmunoassay)
Thymol flocculation	Up to 5 units
Thyroglobulin antibody	Negative
Thyroid-stimulating hormone (TSH)	1-4 μU/ml
Thyroxine (T$_4$)	See T$_4$
Thyroxine-binding globulin (TBG)	2.7-5.1 mg/dl
TIBC (total iron-binding capacity)	250-420 μg/dl
Transaminase	See SGOT, SGPT
Triglycerides	40-150 mg/dl
Triiodothyronine (T$_3$)	100-130 ng/dl
TSH (thyroid-stimulating hormone)	1-4 μU/ml
Urea nitrogen (BUN)	5-20 mg/dl
Uric acid	Men: 2.5-8.5 mg/dl
	Women: 2-6.6 mg/dl
VDRL (Veneral Disease Research Laboratory)	Negative
Vitamin A	0.15-0.6 μg/ml
Vitamin B$_{12}$	290-1270 pg/ml
Vitamin C	0.6-1.6 mg/dl
WBC (white blood cell) count	Adults and children greater than 2 yr: 5000-10,000/cu mm
	Children 2 yr or less: 6200-17,000/cu mm
	Newborns: 9000-30,000/cu mm
Zinc	50-150 μg/dl

Appendix 3

Urine values

TEST	NORMAL VALUES
Acetone plus acetoacetate (ketone bodies)	Negative
Addis count (12 hr)	Adults
	WBCs and epithelial cells:
	1.8 million/12 hr
	RBCs: 500,000/12 hr
	Hyaline casts: Up to 5000/12 hr
	Children
	WBCs: less than 1 million/12 hr
	RBCs: less than 250,000/12 hr
	Casts: less than 5000/12 hr
	Protein: less than 20 mg/12 hr
Amino acid	50-200 mg/24 hr
Albumin	Random: negative
	24 hr: 10-100 mg/24 hr
Aldosterone	2-26 μg/24 hr
Ammonia nitrogen (24 hr)	20-70 mEq/24 hr
	500-1200 mg/24 hr
Amylase	5000 Somogyi units/or less 24 hr
	35-260 Somogyi units/hr
Arsenic (24 hr)	Less than 50 μg/L
Ascorbic acid (vitamin C)	Random: 1-7 ng/dl
	24 hr: greater than 50 mg/24 hr
Bence Jones protein	Negative
Bilirubin	Negative
Blood or hemoglobin	Negative
Borate (24 hr)	Less than 2 mg/L
Calcium	Random: 1+ turbidity
	24 hr: 1-300 mg (diet dependent)
Catecholamines (24 hr)	
Epinephrine	5-40 μg/24 hr
Norepinephrine	10-80 μg/24 hr
Metanephrine	24-96 μg/24 hr
Normetanephrine	75-375 μg/24 hr
Chloride (24 hr)	110-250 mEq/24 hr
Chorionic gonadotropin (HCG)	Negative

Color	Amber-yellow
Concentration test (Fishberg test)	Specific gravity: greater than 1.025
	Osmolality: greater than 850 mOsm/L
Copper (24 hr)	Up to 100 μg/24 hr
Coproporphyrin (24 hr)	50-250 μg/24 hr
Creatine	Adults: Less than 100 mg/24 hr or less than 6% of creatinine
	Pregnant women: 12% or less
	Children less than 1 yr: equal to creatinine
	Older children: 30% or less of creatinine
Creatinine (24 hr)	15-25 mg/kg body wt/24 hr
Creatinine clearance (24 hr)	Men: 90-140 ml/min
	Women: 85-125 ml/min
Cystine or cysteine	Negative
Epithelial cells and casts	Occasional
Epinephrine (24 hr)	5-40 μg/24 hr
Estriol (24 hr)	Greater than 12 mg/24 hr
Fat	Negative
Follicle-stimulating hormone (FSH) (24 hr)	Men: 2-12 IU/24 hr
	Women
	During menses: 8-60 IU/24 hr
	During ovulation: 30-60 IU/24 hr
	During menopause: greater than 50 IU/24 hr
Glucose	Negative
Granular casts	Occasional
Hemoglobin and myoglobin	Negative
Homogentistic acid	Negative
Hyaline casts	Occasional
17-Hydroxycorticosteroids (17-OCHS) (24 hr)	Men: 5.5-15 mg/24 hr
	Women: 5-13.5 mg/24 hr
	Children: lower than adult values
5-Hydroxyindole acetic acid (5-HIAA, serotonin) (24 hr)	2-9 mg/24 hr (women lower than men)
Ketones (acetone)	Negative
17-Ketosteroids (17-KS) (24 hr)	Men: 8-15 mg/24 hr
	Women: 6-12 mg/24 hr
	Children
	12-15 yr: 5-12 mg/24 hr
	Less than 12 yr: less than 5 mg/24 hr
Lead	0.08 μg/ml or 120 μg/24 hr
Odor	Aromatic

Osmolality	500-800 mOsm/L
pH	4.6-8.0
Phenolsulfonphthalein (PSP)	15 min: at least 25%
	30 min: at least 40%
	120 min: at least 60%
Phenylketonuria (PKU)	Negative
Phenylpyruvic acid	Negative
Phosphorus (24 hr)	0.9-1.3 g/24 hr
Porphobilinogen	Random: negative
	24 hr: up to 2 mg/24 hr
Potassium (K+) (24 hr)	40-80 mEq/24 hr
Pregnancy test	Negative
Pregnanediol	After ovulation: greater than
	1 mg/24 hr
Protein (albumin)	Negative
	10-100 mg/24 hr
Sodium (Na+) (24 hr)	80-180 mEq/24 hr
Specific gravity	1.010-1.025
Steroids	See 17-Hydroxycorticosteroids and
	17-Ketosteroids
Sugar (glucose)	Negative
Titratable acidity (24 hr)	20-150 mEq/24 hr
Turbidity	Clear
Urea nitrogen (24 hr)	6-17 g/24 hr
Uric acid (24 hr)	250-750 mg/24 hr
Urobilinogen	0.1-1 Ehrlich units/dl
Uroporphyrin	Negative
Vanillylmandelic acid (VMA) (24 hr)	1-9 mg/24 hr
Zinc (24 hr)	0.20-0.75 mg/24 hr

Index

Neva Baburan